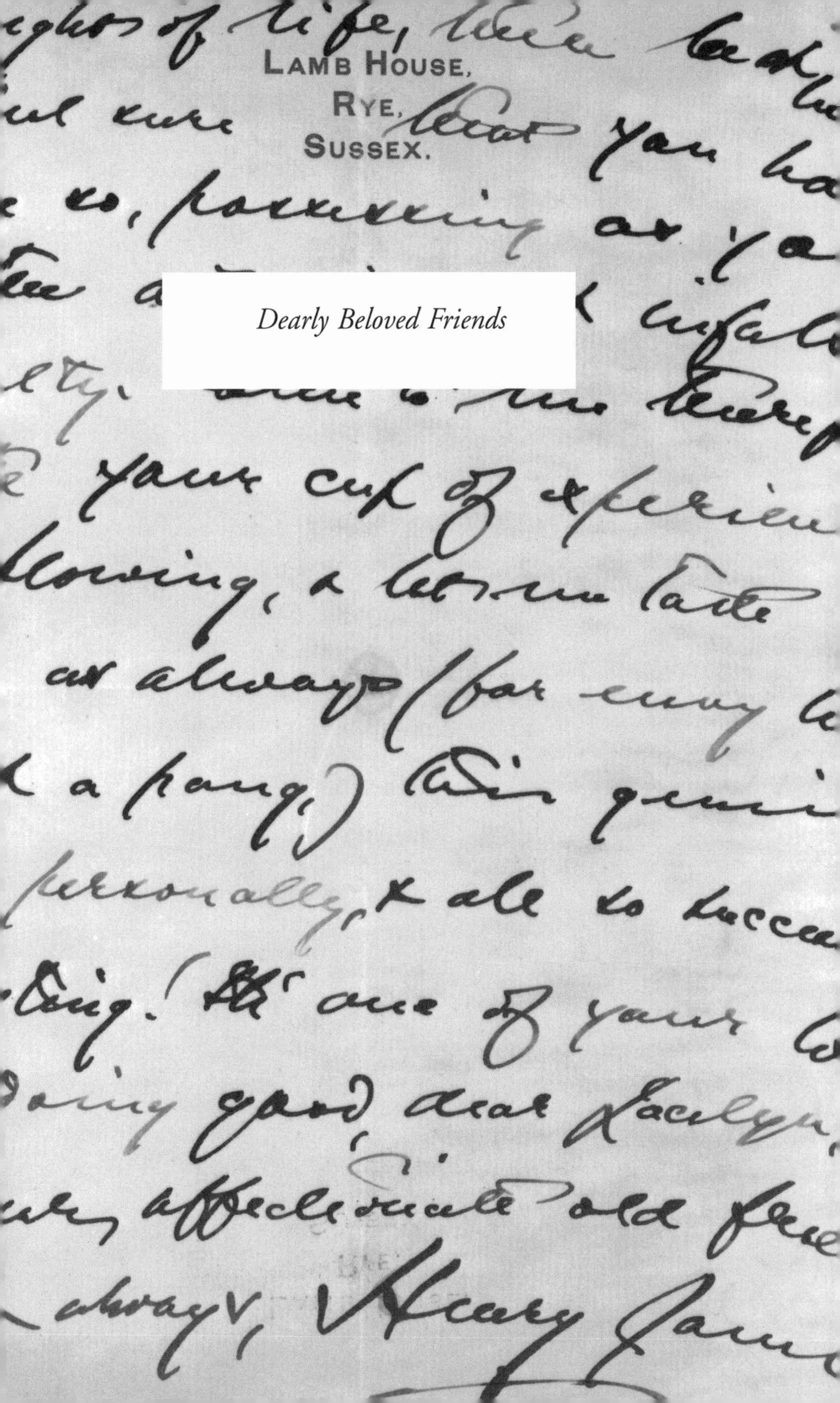

Dearly Beloved Friends

Dearly Beloved Friends

Henry James's Letters to Younger Men

Susan E. Gunter
Steven H. Jobe, Editors

Ann Arbor

THE UNIVERSITY OF MICHIGAN PRESS

Copyright © by Susan E. Gunter and Steven H. Jobe 2001
All rights reserved
Published in the United States of America by
The University of Michigan Press
Manufactured in the United States of America
∞ Printed on acid-free paper

2004   2003   2002   2001   4   3   2   1

A CIP catalog record for this book is available from the British Library.

Library of Congress Cataloging-in-Publication Data

James, Henry, 1843–1916.
    Dearly beloved friends : Henry James's letters to younger men / Susan E. Gunter,
Steven H. Jobe, editors.
        p. cm.
    Includes index.
    ISBN 0-472-11009-8 (cloth : alk. paper)
    1. James, Henry, 1843–1916—Correspondence. 2. James, Henry, 1843–1916—
Relations with men. 3. James, Henry, 1843–1916—Friends and associates. 4. Authors,
American—19th century—Correspondence. 5. Authors, American—20th century—
Correspondence. I. Gunter, Susan E., 1947– II. Jobe, Steven H. 1956– III. Title.

PS2123 .A4 2002
813'.4—dc21
[B]
                                                                            2001048036

Page i: Sample from a letter from Henry James to Dudley Jocelyn Persse,
Houghton bMS 1094.1 (1905). Courtesy of the Houghton Library,
Harvard University, and Bay James.

Acknowledgments

This volume has been made possible by Bay James, literary executor of the Henry James estate, who graciously granted unrestricted permission for publication of the letters and generously shared with us her knowledge of the James family. Our thanks for publication permission go as well to the several libraries housing the letters: to the Clifton Waller Barrett Library, Special Collections Department, University of Virginia Library for use of James's letters to Hendrik C. Andersen; to the Houghton Library, Harvard University for use of James's letters to both Dudley Jocelyn Persse and Howard O. Sturgis; and to the Harry Ransom Humanities Research Center, University of Texas at Austin, for use of James's letters to Hugh Walpole. The late Sir Rupert Hart-Davis permitted us to quote from Hugh Walpole's diaries, now at the Humanities Research Center, in our annotations to the letters. Various other permissions for the use of archival material are acknowledged in the notes and in the illustration credits.

The idea for what are in some ways companion volumes of James's letters—this edition of selected letters to younger men and an earlier volume, *Dear Munificent Friends: Henry James's Letters to Four Women* (University of Michigan Press, 1999)—grew out of conversations in Cambridge in 1994 between Susan Gunter and David Lehman, who provided excellent advice and encouragement. Work on this volume has since benefited enormously from the unstinting advice or the prior work of friends, of James scholars, and of friends who are James scholars: John Kimmey of the University of South Carolina; Philip Horne of University College, London; Sheldon Novick of Vermont Law School; Robert Gale, Professor Emeritus at the University of Pittsburgh; Roberta A. Sheehan, of the Boston Athenaeum; Rayburn Moore, Professor Emeritus of the University of Georgia, and Margaret Moore; Adeline Tintner of New York City; and the late Leon Edel. While they bear no responsibility for the weaknesses of this edition, they deserve much credit for whatever virtue may be found herein.

We are indebted as well to our home institutions for crucial research support in the form of both time and funding. Grants from the Gore Faculty Development Fund at Westminster College of Salt Lake City sustained the research of Susan Gunter, while the Faculty Development Committee of Hanover College generously supported the work of Steve Jobe. At Westminster, necessary support and encouragement, including a merit leave, were always forthcoming from Dr. Stephen Baar, Academic Vice-President, and Dr. Ray Ownbey, Dean of Arts and Sciences. At Hanover, the Faculty Development Committee was instrumental in approving and proposing to the Vice-President for Academic Affairs, to the President, and to the Board of Trustees both a sabbatical and a Spring Term leave for Steve Jobe. In an age of declining public commitment to research in the humanities, such support of scholarship by private colleges and their donors deserves particular recognition.

Librarians, curators, and archivists from numerous institutions facilitated our work at every stage: at Westminster College's Giovale Library (Dick Wunder, Oresta Esquibel, Tanya Stasny, David Hales, Hildy Benham, Diane Raines), at Hanover College's Duggan Library (Lori Ferguson, Laurel Carter, Heather Bennett), at the Houghton Library (Leslie Morris, Melanie Wisner, Susan Halpert, Jennie Rathbun, Denison Beach, and others), at the Harry Ransom Humanities Research Center at the University of Texas at Austin (Cathy Henderson, Tara Wegner), in the Special Collections Department of the University of Virginia Library (Michael Plunkett, Greg Johnson, Sharon Defibaugh, Margaret Hrabe, Virginia Smyers), at the Cambridge University Library (Kathleen Cann), at Oxford University's Bodleian Library (Steven Tomlinson), at Yale University's Beinecke Library (Alfred Mueller), in the Rare Book and Manuscript Department of McGill University's McLennan Library (Richard Virr), and at the Redwood Library and Athenaeum in Newport, Rhode Island (Maris Humphreys). Patricia Teter of the Getty Museum provided timely assistance in identifying some of James's more esoteric reading.

Throughout this project able research assistants—Jennifer McLing and Natalie Martinez at Westminster; Miranda Bailey, Mandy Blythe, John Connell, and Drew Eisenhut at Hanover—searched out obscure individuals, labored over transcripts, compiled calendars, and patiently rode herd over piles of paper on our office floors. Helen Hodgson's students Janice Eberhardt, Deborah Pearson, and Elizabeth Sweeten from Westminster College's Professional Communications graduate program edited our introduction for style and flow.

Special thanks are due to Elizabeth Kaplan and Marissa Walsh of the Ellen Levine Agency for finding a home for this project at the University of Michigan Press. There, LeAnn Fields and her editing team deserve praise for their expertise in shepherding this manuscript through the publication process.

Finally, our gratitude continues to flow to two families—to Terry and Phillip Jobe; to Bill, Colin, Jennifer, Ben, and Dan Gunter—for unending patience, encouragement, and tolerance.

Contents

Editors' Note

This volume presents 166 letters from Henry James to four men—Hendrik Andersen, Jocelyn Persse, Howard Sturgis, and Hugh Walpole—that were selected from 391 extant letters to these men. Of these letters, 95 have never before been published; until the appearance in 2000 of Rosella Zorzi's *Amato Ragazzo,* an edition of the James-Andersen letters, 133 of them had remained unpublished in the eighty-five years since James's death. Although we have benefited in several ways from Professor Zorzi's work, her volume differs significantly enough from ours—in conception, in audience, in editorial practices, in transcriptions, and occasionally in assignment of reckoned dates and provenances—to warrant our reprinting of so many of the Andersen letters.

Our selection of letters affords an ample and fresh perspective on, if not an exhaustive account of, James's late-life relationships with younger men. In eschewing the encyclopedic approach, we take our consolation, such as it is, from James's own observation, "The *whole* of anything is never told; you can only take what groups together." What groups together, we believe, are those budgets of letters from relationships that either began or flourished after 1897; that display James's epistolary style as it rises from the affectionate to the markedly intimate, physical, and even erotic; and that, excepting the Andersen letters, have been least "ventilated," to use James's word, by previous editors.

The prevailing tenor of each group of letters is warmly adhesive, to resurrect by way of Whitman a phrenological term sufficiently broad to encompass the varieties of James's same-sex affections and attractions. But that is not to say that the letters are uniformly or unvaryingly passionate or erotic in tone or content. Seemingly quotidian or pedestrian letters are occasionally necessary to limn the breadth and depth of each relationship. Moreover, James's language of attraction and desire, of commitment and convergence, is always contending with divergent forces that were anything but subtle or erotic: his final decades of alternating bouts of good and ill health, circumstances of proximity and distance, clashing tastes and wills and temperaments, and the inevitably disparate needs of relative youth and age. In short, the reader who seeks herein the single sustained note of ardor will be disappointed. But the reader appreciative of the nuanced complexity of relations—appreciative, that is, of the essential Jamesian subject—will find satisfaction in the variegated contours of these several relationships.

The letters herein have been transcribed from the original holographs or typescripts and are arranged chronologically within each section of the book. Following each letter we indicate the provenance of the copy-text, identifying both the location and, whenever possible, the cataloging information for the holograph or typescript.

Although the transcriptions are not facsimile reproductions of the originals, they do preserve more than words alone. We retain James's occasional misspellings and repetitions, his oftentimes erratic punctuation (especially the highly variable punctuation of inside addresses, dates, salutations, and closings), his abbreviations and numerals, and the occasional typographical errors of his amanuenses. Lest James's apparent errata be confused with our own, we note the few such occurrences with *sic* or insert missing letters within brackets. We have kept as well other distinctive orthographical features: the free use of dashes, parentheses, and his habitual avoidance in midsentence of the conjunctive *and* (his use of a sign that looks to be a cross between the arithmetical plus sign and the ampersand is represented here by an ampersand). James seldom reparagraphed by twentieth-century conventions, making a typical letter a long note, with dashes of various lengths and vigor indicating pauses of equally various durations. He placed short dashes within sentences (which we have indicated with em dashes) and longer dashes between sentences (which we have rather arbitrarily represented with two-em dashes). But occasionally James used an exceptionally long dash between sentences that seems to indicate a pause or a shift in his train of thought, and we have attempted to preserve this feature through the use of a line that approximates James's original dash length. All of these features contribute to simultaneous impressions of both haste and immediacy in James's letter writing.

Typographical constraints, house styling, and book design have led us to adopt several silent but consistent editorial conventions that should be noted. Words, phrases, and numbers that James underlined are here italicized, with no discrimination—unless remarked upon in a note— between James's single, double, and sometimes triple underlinings. Super- scripted letters of ordinals are demoted (e.g., *1st*). In addition, we have not attempted to reproduce the original placement of inside addresses, dates, and signatures. Instead, we have standardized and relineated the placement of these elements: inside addresses and dates are aligned on the right margin at the top of each letter, with the full address on a single line (excepting only occasional telephone numbers, which follow on separate lines), with double spacing between elements originally written on separate lines; James's signature is placed to the right of center on a separate line after the last line of text. Letterhead imprints and embossings are distinguished from manuscript by the use of small capitals.

Editorial insertions have been kept to a minimum and are always marked by square brackets. For ease of reference, provenances and dates that James placed at the ends of letters are repeated, within brackets, at the beginnings of letters. Provenances and dates omitted by James but reck- oned on the basis of internal or external evidence are supplied at the outset as well, again within brackets, with accompanying rationales in the notes. Bracketed translations follow James's foreign words and phrases (italicized only if James underlined them). On rare occasions when James seemingly omitted a word or words essential to the clarity of his sentence, we have inserted bracketed words. Initials for individuals and places are frequently expanded within brackets for clarity or to avoid festooning the letters with additional note numbers.

James's distinctive handwriting is usually legible, given time, but it is not without its challenges. When a word or series of words defies con- fident deciphering, we place inside angled brackets what we think are James's words and indicate our uncertainty with a question mark (e.g., ⟨break?⟩).

The edition is intended to provide all readers with a highly accessible and legible page, with texts accurate within the limits of clear-text editing. While a plain-text edition might well have better served the needs of some scholars, we suspect that specialists interested in textual variants would, in any case, still feel compelled to consult the original letters. We therefore do not distinguish text that has been inserted into a letter, nor do we attempt to indicate and restore cancellations. We rely upon admittedly selective notes to highlight those instances when, in our opinion, the act of inser- tion or cancellation seems to affect markedly one's grasp of James's tone, meaning, or emphasis.

Personal, topical, and literary references are identified in the notes whenever possible. If we have erred in our annotations, we have erred on the side of excess, preferring that readers bypass in the notes what is already familiar rather than stall in the texts over what is unexplained.

Biographical Register

Andersen, Andreas
(c. 1870–1902)

Brother of Hendrik Andersen, he was also an artist, and, for one month prior to his death from tuberculosis, husband of Olivia Cushing Andersen.

Beerbohm, Sir Henry Maximilian
(Max)
(1872–1956)

British writer, drama critic, and caricaturist; his cartoons satirizing HJ were famous. James enjoyed his wit. His books include *The Happy Hypocrite* (1897), *More* (1899), *Zuleika Dobson: Or, an Oxford Love Story* (1911), *And Even Now* (1920), *A Variety of Things* (1928), and *Lytton Strachey* (1943).

Benson, Arthur Christopher
(1862–1925)

Writer and educator, Benson was president and then master of Magdalene College at Cambridge. He published more than a hundred volumes, including biographies, novels, poetry, essays, and autobiography. Parts of his 180-volume diary have been published. He and HJ were close friends, and he was also a friend to Sturgis and Walpole. His books include *Babylonica* (1895), *The Life of Edward Benson* (1899), *The Upton Letters* (1905), *From a College Window* (1906), *Beside Still Waters* (1907), *The House of Quiet: An Autobiography* (1907), and *The Leaves of the Trees* (1911).

Broughton, Rhoda
(1840–1920)

British novelist, she wrote prolifically and successfully for decades. She was educated in languages and literature at home, beginning her career by writing three-volume sentimental novels tinged with irony and rebellion. HJ denigrated them in an 1876 review, but the two became good friends nonetheless, visiting each other often and corresponding. She knew both Sturgis and Walpole. Her books include *Not Wisely but Too Well* (1867), *Joan* (1876), *Mrs. Blight* (1892), *Lavinia* (1902), and *Concerning a Vow* (1914).

Clifford, Sophia Lucy Lane (Mrs. William Kingdon) (c. 1853–1929)

Popular English novelist and playwright, she and HJ were friends for decades, sharing many acquaintances, including Walpole. She was born in Barbados and married a mathematician and philosopher cited by William James. He died when Clifford was twenty-four, leaving her with two small children. She and HJ socialized often, and he left her a small legacy in his will. A writer of short stories, novels, and plays, she was best known for her novels *Keith's Crime* (1885) and *Aunt Anne* (1893) and her play *The Likeness of the Night* (1900).

Elliott, John (1858–1925)

Scottish-born artist Jack Elliott emigrated to Newport and married Maud Howe, daughter of Julia Ward Howe. He painted murals and portraits, and he helped found the Newport Art Association. It was in the Elliotts' Roman palazzo that HJ first met sculptor Hendrik Andersen.

Elliott, Maud Howe (Mrs. John) (1854–1948)

American novelist, journalist, lecturer, art critic, and suffragist, she was the daughter of Julia Ward Howe. Her books include *A Newport Aquarelle* (1883), *Phillida* (1891), *Two in Italy* (1905), *Uncle Sam Ward and His Circle* (1938), and *This Was My Newport* (1944).

Emmet, Ellen Gertrude (Bay) (1876–1941)

American painter, she was the daughter of HJ's first cousin, Ellen James Temple Emmet Hunter. HJ considered Bay a talented painter and predicted great success for her. She painted HJ's portrait at Lamb House in 1900. She married William Blanchard Rand in the early 1900s.

Forbes-Robertson, Sir Johnston (1853–1937)

London-born actor, he was also an important manager and producer. HJ knew both Forbes-Robertson and his wife, American actress Gertrude Elliott. In 1907 he

Fullerton, William Morton
(1865–1952)

asked HJ to revise "Covering End" as a play. It became *The High Bid,* a three-act play. American man of letters and one of HJ's intimate friends, he was on the staff of the London *Times* from 1890 to 1911 and met HJ during this time. He had various homosexual and heterosexual affairs, including one with Edith Wharton. When he was blackmailed for his bisexual activities, HJ helped him escape his blackmailer's clutches. He knew Sturgis, as well. He wrote a number of books, in English and in French, including *In Cairo* (1891), *Problems of Power* (1913), and *The American Crisis and the War* (1916).

Gardner, Isabella Stewart
(Mrs. John L.)
(1849–1924)

Boston art collector and social leader, Mrs. Gardner amassed a great art collection during her travels abroad, a collection now housed at the Fenway Museum in Boston. She studied art history with Charles Eliot Norton and painted watercolors. She and HJ were close friends and frequent correspondents.

Gosse, Sir Edmund William
(1849–1928)

British man of letters, British Museum staff member, translator for the Board of Trade, professor at Cambridge, and librarian of the House of Lords, Gosse met HJ in 1879 at a luncheon in London with Andrew Lang and Robert Louis Stevenson, and the two subsequently became close friends. Gosse was one of HJ's sponsors when he applied for British citizenship in 1915. HJ wrote him almost four hundred intimate letters, many of which are reproduced in Rayburn Moore's *Selected Letters of Henry James to Sir Edmund Gosse, 1882–1915.* His many books include *Seventeenth-Century Studies* (1883), *A Short History of Modern English Literature* (1898), *French Profiles* (1905), and *The Collected Poems of Edmund Gosse* (1911).

Gregory, Lady Isabella Augusta
Persse (Mrs. William)
(1852–1932)

Irish playwright, theatrical producer, and critic, Lady Gregory founded the Irish National Theatre Society with W. B. Yeats.

HJ knew her socially for many years. Her nephew, Jocelyn Persse, became HJ's close friend. Her books include *Seven Short Plays* (1910), *Our Irish Theatre* (1913), *The Dragon* (1920), and *Last Plays* (1928).

James, Alice Howe Gibbens (Mrs. William) (1849–1922)

Mother of five, she was a strong and responsible woman. After William's death in 1910, HJ spent several months in America with Alice and her children. When he became ill in 1915, Alice went to England and cared for him until his death in 1916, smuggling his ashes home for burial.

James, William (1842–1910)

Famous American philosopher and psychologist, William James was HJ's older brother. For years a Harvard professor and international lecturer, WJ had great influence on subsequent work in philosophy, psychology, and education. His most important works include *The Principles of Psychology* (1890), *The Will to Believe and Other Essays* (1897), *The Varieties of Religious Experience* (1902), *Pragmatism* (1907), *A Pluralistic Universe* (1909), and *Essays in Radical Empiricism* (1912).

Jones, Mary Cadwalader Rawle (Minnie) (Mrs. Frederick) (1850–1935)

Wife of Edith Wharton's brother, she was a socialite and one of HJ's intimate friends. He met her in 1883 and later saw her in late summer when she acted as hostess at her cousin John Cadwalader's hunting camp in Scotland. He stayed with her in New York when he visited America in 1904–5 and again in 1910–11. Her works include *Lantern Slides* (1937).

Lapsley, Gaillard Thomas (1871–1949)

Constitutional historian, he met HJ in 1897 through a letter of introduction from Isabella Stewart Gardner. The two socialized frequently. According to a notebook entry, Lapsley gave HJ the idea for "Fordham Castle." Lapsley, Robert Norton, and Edith Wharton compiled *Eternal Passion in English Poetry* (1939). Lapsley's books include *The Origin of*

	Property in Land (1903) and *Crown, Community, and Parliament in the Later Middle Ages* (1951).
Lascelles, Helen (Mrs. Eric Maclagan) (1879–1942)	A British writer, she was connected with the British art world. She was a friend to Walpole and James; HJ attended her wedding on 8 July 1913. Her father was Commander Frederick Lascelles, and her husband was a prominent figure in the art world who directed the Victoria and Albert Museum for a time.
Lubbock, Percy (1879–1965)	British historian, biographer, and librarian, he met HJ at Lamb House in 1901. In 1909 Lubbock wrote a laudatory essay on James for the *Times Literary Supplement,* and after HJ's death Lubbock was chosen to edit a two-volume selection of his letters. In addition, he assembled three books HJ left in fragmentary form and a thirty-five-volume set of his novels and stories. The two had many mutual acquaintances. Lubbock's books include *The Craft of Fiction* (1921), *The Region Cloud* (1925), *Shades of Eton* (1929), and *Portrait of Edith Wharton* (1947).
Smith, William Haynes ("The Babe")	A distant cousin to Howard Sturgis, he was an active outdoorsman who enjoyed hunting and sports. He became Sturgis's live-in companion at Queen's Acre, staying with Howard until his death in 1920.
Story, Maud Broadwood (Mrs. Thomas Waldo) (c. 1860–1932)	Daughter of Mary and Thomas C. Broadwood, she married the sculptor Story and lived with him in the Barberini Palace in Rome. They separated in 1898 and later divorced. James wrote a biography of her father-in-law, *William Wetmore Story and His Friends* (1903).
Sturgis, Julian Russell (1848–1904)	British writer, he was the son of Russell Sturgis, an expatriate American banker in London, and the older brother of Howard Sturgis. HJ met him socially in 1877 and was a frequent dinner guest in his home. He wrote *Stephen Calinari* (1901).

Sturgis, Mary Maud Beresford (Mrs. Julian Russell)	She was the daughter of Irishman Col. Marcus de la Poer Beresford and the sister-in-law of Howard Sturgis.
Sturgis, Russell (1805–1887)	Expatriate American banker in London, he became friends with HJ in 1877, entertaining him at his home. His son, Howard Sturgis, was one of HJ's closest friends.
Symonds, John Addington (1840–1893)	Victorian literary historian, poet, biographer, essayist, translator, and known homosexual, he met HJ in 1877 through writer Andrew Lang. HJ and Symonds praised one another's work, and they shared many common friends. His most enduring work is *Renaissance in Italy* (7 vols., 1875–86). His other books include *A Problem in Greek Ethics* (1883) and *A Problem in Modern Ethics* (1891), two controversial books that discussed homosexuality.
Wharton, Edith Newbold Jones (Mrs. Edward Robbins) (1862–1937)	Major American writer, she long admired HJ's works. The two met in Paris around 1887 but did not become friends until later. She sent HJ her work to critique and appreciated his advice. He cherished Wharton but sometimes deplored her energy and her commercial success, calling her a "Devastating Angel." In 1910 she unsuccessfully nominated him for the Nobel Prize. She and HJ socialized often with Howard Sturgis, visiting him at Queen's Acre. Her books include *The Greater Inclination* (1899), *The Valley of Decision* (1902), *The House of Mirth* (1905), *The Fruit of the Tree* (1907), *Ethan Frome* (1911), *The Custom of the Country* (1913), *The Age of Innocence* (1920), *Old New York* (1924), *The Children* (1928), *A Backward Glance* (1934), and *The Buccaneers* (1938).

Chronology

1843	Henry James is born on April 15 to Mary Walsh James and Henry James Sr., religious thinker and writer, in New York City.
1848–55	Young HJ attends day schools, has tutors, sees theaters and museums and plays with his three brothers and one sister but receives no systematic education.
1855–60	Adolescent HJ travels with family and attends school in Switzerland, England, France, and Newport, Rhode Island. His studies include languages, science, and art.
1862–65	The James family moves to Boston, and HJ briefly attends Harvard Law School.
1864	James's story "A Tragedy of Errors" appears in *Continental Monthly.* The same year he writes reviews for *North American Review,* launching a brilliant writing career that will last half a century.
1869–70	The adult HJ travels to Europe. His first novel, *Watch and Ward,* appears as a serial in *Atlantic Monthly.*
1870–74	James makes his first efforts to establish himself in Europe. He settles in Rome and Florence and writes *Roderick Hudson* (published 1875) but then returns to New York at his family's insistence.
1874–76	James lives and writes in New York but finds it too provincial. He tries Paris next but does not find a home there. In Paris he meets the attractive Russian Paul Jukovsky; they become close companions, temporarily.
1876–77	He moves to London, where he finds his own life. He eventually becomes a much-sought-after and loved figure in English society, and England becomes his permanent home. A number of prominent English befriend him, among them the Russell Sturgis family, whose son Howard Sturgis later becomes a close friend.
1878–80	In a period of just three years, James has an incredible outpouring of books and stories: "Daisy Miller: A Study" (1878), *The Europeans* (1878), *French Poets and Novelists* (1878), *Confidence* (1879), *Hawthorne* (1879), *Washington Square* (1880), and a new volume of stories.

1880–81	*Portrait of a Lady,* one of the great books of his career, appears first in serial form.
1882–83	James visits America twice. He returns to London after his mother dies, but then sails back when his father dies.
1883–86	James writes *The Bostonians* and then *The Princess Casamassima.* In late 1884 sister Alice James moves to England with Katharine Loring; Alice and HJ are close friends until her death in 1892.
1887	James begins the next of his novels, *The Tragic Muse,* this time selecting the worlds of theater, politics, and art as a setting.
1890	In an attempt to find a more lucrative form of writing, James begins to write plays, first adapting his early novel *The American* for the stage. While he never achieves success in the theater, the lessons he learns enrich his later work. By this time he knows Irish playwright Lady Augusta Gregory, aunt to Jocelyn Persse, who will become one of his closest friends.
1892	Alice James, Henry's loved younger sister, dies of breast cancer in England.
1896	Abandoning the theater, James writes another novella, *The Spoils of Poynton,* which draws on both his empathy for women and his fascination with the outward trappings of the wealthy English: their great estates and their complicated social relationships.
1897	*What Maisie Knew,* another novella, also reveals James's extensive acquaintance with the amorality and self-centeredness of upper-class British society.
1898	James moves from London to rural Rye, where he leases (and later buys) Lamb House. Here he can write in peace as well as entertain friends and a series of loved younger men, including Hendrik Andersen, Morton Fullerton, Jocelyn Persse, Jonathan Sturges, Howard Sturgis, and Hugh Walpole.
1899	James visits Rome this year, meeting sculptor Hendrik Christian Andersen at the home of Maud Howe and John Elliott.
1900	James makes an initial payment on Lamb House and writes *The Sacred Fount,* a satiric novel that draws heavily on the innumerable country weekends he spent observing British manners and morals.
1902	With the publication of *Wings of the Dove* James inaugurates his major phase, a brief but glorious period when he writes the greatest of his novels and tales. His relationships with Andersen, Persse, and Sturgis all blossom during the time he composes his three major novels.
1903	James publishes *The Ambassadors,* telling Jocelyn Persse that its hero, Lambert Strether, bore "a vague resemblance (though not facial)" to himself. James meets Persse in July of this year at the home of the Sir Sidney Colvins. He critiques Howard Sturgis's novel in progress, *Belchamber,* most severely.

1904	*The Golden Bowl,* the last and one of the greatest of James's novels, appears first in America, followed by British publication early the next year.
1905	After an absence of more than two decades, James revisits America and writes *The American Scene,* an incisive commentary on American commercial life.
1906	Back at Lamb House, James begins his extensive revisions of all his written work for a twenty-four-volume definitive edition, the *New York Edition of the Novels and Tales of Henry James.* He continues to welcome his friends in his home, as long as his health allows.
1906–15	James writes his autobiographies: *A Small Boy and Others* (1913), *Notes of a Son and Brother* (1914), and the unfinished *Middle Years* (1917). He continues his lifelong habit of letter writing. Letters, in fact, become his last artistic triumph, as he composes long and moving epistles to his myriad friends of both sexes. Plagued by depression and ill health in 1910, he burns most of the letters written to him, yet many of the letters he writes survive to proclaim him one of the greatest correspondents in all history.
1907	HJ visits Andersen in Rome in May and June.
1909	Hugh Walpole dines with James in London in February, launching a friendship that lasts until the end of HJ's life.
1910	HJ sails to America with Alice James and the ailing William James, who dies at Chocorua on 26 August 1910.
1911	HJ returns to England.
1913	In January HJ resumes residence in London at 21, Carlyle Mansions and hereafter uses Lamb House only in the summers.
1914	Walpole travels to Russia as a war correspondent. Although their correspondence continues, Walpole will never see James again.
1915	HJ is naturalized as a British subject on 26 July. In December a stroke and then pneumonia mark the beginning of his final illness.
1916	Alice James comes to Rye to nurse her beloved brother-in-law during his final illness. Just before his death, James receives the Order of Merit from King George V. After he dies, on February 28, Alice has him cremated and smuggles his ashes back to Cambridge for burial in the James family plot. In his will, James leaves Jocelyn Persse and Hugh Walpole each one hundred pounds.

Introduction

Excepting the social notes that he himself dismissed as "the mere twaddle of graciousness,"[1] the letters of Henry James are invariably noteworthy, whether for their inimitable style, for their range of reference, for their contextualization of key points in his relationships, or for their illumination of an unparalleled literary consciousness that was cast over Anglo-American culture for more than half a century. Yet the publication to date of less than one-third of James's extant letters has left significant gaps in the epistolary record of his life as both a man of letters and a man of feelings. This volume fills one of those gaps by publishing an ample selection of what can only be called love letters from an aging James to four younger men: the Norwegian-born sculptor Hendrik Andersen (1872–1940), the eminently companionable Jocelyn Persse (1873–1943), the American expatriate Howard Sturgis (1855–1920), and the British writer Hugh Walpole (1884–1941). At once witty and poignant, the letters are most remarkable for an intensity of emotion and a physicality that frequently verge on the amorous and the erotic and that counterpoint James's persistent loneliness in his later years.

The four men represented in this edition, with whom James deliberately and self-consciously created his epistolary love life, were all younger men from different walks of life. They nonetheless shared a respect, almost an adoration, for the aging giant of Lamb House who, after 1898, was the master of both his profession and his home. And he made room for all of them: room in his life and room in his Rye home. James's resettlement from London to Rye in early 1899 allowed him to entertain more freely and

---

1. HJ to Sarah Orne Jewett, 5 October 1901, in *Henry James Letters,* ed. Leon Edel, 4 vols. (Cambridge: Belknap Press of Harvard University Press, 1974–84), 4:208.

lavishly. He had always treated those he loved well, but he could now invite his friends to spend weekends with him, guaranteeing them a degree of privacy hitherto lacking in his crowded London world. Ever the generous and expansive host, he offered studio space and rural respites to sculptor Hendrik Andersen, a sense of history to Howard Sturgis in the 1723 brick home visited by George I, and to all of his friends a lovely walled garden with an orchard and a centuries-old mulberry tree.

What use did James himself make of these friends? Like another nineteenth-century American writer, Walt Whitman, James had many younger male friends, friends he seemed to move among with ease.[2] Indeed, the readiness with which he cultivated male companions reflects the increasingly homosocial complexion of the fin de siècle and Edwardian literary world in which he lived. While he may have regretted failing to establish intimacy with a single companion, the human variety afforded him by these younger men must have nourished both his life and his writing. And the homoerotic elements evident in this correspondence, the loving relationships he maintained, surely contributed to the eroticism of his last novels. Without himself loving, he could not have portrayed passion with such masterstrokes.

But James's rustication to Rye was something other than a quasi-pastoral remove to enable and facilitate forbidden amours. To see it as such is to confuse cause and effect. The isolation of Rye made passionate friendships all the more salient to James as loneliness increasingly became the tenor of his life. As death drew smaller the circle of his contemporaries, his work of a lifetime seemed increasingly fated to oblivion, and his failing physical and emotional health rendered him less and less secure. Hugh Walpole was never more correct about James than in his opinion that "in spite of his friends, his art, the love that he won from others, he *was* lonely. Not, perhaps, more than any of us, but he saw more deeply *into* that loneliness."[3]

---

2. James's connections with Whitman, albeit indirect ones, and his appreciation of the poetry increased as he aged: one of his correspondents in 1898, Dr. John Johnston, was a Whitman devotee who had visited the poet in Camden, New Jersey, during the last years of his life; another correspondent and occasional Rye visitor, Herbert H. Gilchrist (1857–1914), was allegedly one of Whitman's younger lovers (see *Calamus Lovers: Walt Whitman's Working Class Camerados,* ed. Charley Shively [San Francisco: Gay Sunshine Press, 1987], 146); and James declaimed Whitman's poetry at Edith Wharton's Lenox home, The Mount, during his 1904–5 American tour.

3. Hugh Walpole, *The Apple Trees: Four Reminiscences* (Waltham Saint Lawrence, Berkshire: Golden Cockerel, 1932), 61.

That is not to say that the letters herein are the sentimental maunder-
ings of a senescent, lonely writer. Rather, they are seminal documents for
any serious consideration of Jamesian sexuality in the carefully nuanced
definition of that term that David Kirby offers: "the forces of attraction
and denial that operate among loving human beings, forces that make it
possible for people to achieve what they want biologically and, in the case
of Henry, artistically as well."[4] They illuminate the depth and the eroticism with which an aging James loved four younger men. But they will not
resolve for most readers which, if any, of the commonly heard labels should
be applied to James: homosocial male, homoerotic male, homosexual,
repressed homosexual, gay-inflected author, exemplar of "male homosexual panic," nonheterosexual. On the one hand, the letters are compelling
personal evidence in support of Adeline Tintner's literary observation that
"once the frontier of the new century had been crossed, James allowed
himself to write certain things that he had not dared to write before."[5] Yet
at the same time the letters would seem to confirm Ross Posnock's apt
assessment of James's bachelorhood as a "mode of perennial vagueness or
deferral of sexual identity that would be simplified if labeled 'homosexual'
or anything other than indeterminate."[6] James himself was aware of the
inadequacy of language to convey the full weight and nature of his devotion to men who were in many ways his disciples. Writing to Jocelyn
Persse, he claimed that "these things are beyond words—words almost
vulgarize them."[7]

As testaments to James's abiding attachments and even dependencies in
late life, however, the letters further erase the conventional image of a
reserved, austere, awesome, and slightly inhuman "Master" whose intercourse with the world was exclusively aesthetic and intellectual.[8] Readers
unfamiliar with the most recent biographical and critical work on James
will be surprised to meet herein a far more emotionally complex figure.
While one critic's description of the elder James as a "vulnerable, sexually
anxious, and lonely writer" may seem too insistent in its catalog of human

---

4. "The Sex Lives of the James Family," *Virginia Quarterly Review* 64 (1988): 56–57.

5. "A Gay *Sacred Fount*: The Reader as Detective," *Twentieth-Century Literature* 41
(1995): 227.

6. *The Trial of Curiosity: Henry James, William James, and the Challenge of Modernity*
(New York: Oxford University Press, 1991), 204.

7. See HJ to Jocelyn Persse, 23 October 1903.

8. The "Master" image was in many ways first encouraged by James's own criticism
and fictions of the artistic life, later perpetuated in formalist criticism, and enshrined in
Leon Edel's *Henry James*, 5 vols. (Philadelphia: J. B. Lippincott, 1953–72).

frailties, the frailties are at least recognizably human ones.[9] This transfiguration of James is but a new version of Edith Wharton's altered perception in the spring of 1910. She left the London bedside of a physically stricken and emotionally distraught James with an entirely new sense of his emotional state and needs. She wrote to Morton Fullerton that heretofore she had always "seen him so serene, so completely the master of his wonderful emotional instrument—who thought of him . . . as so sensitive to human contacts & yet so *secure* from them." But security and mastery were no longer tenable terms: "How little I believe in Howard Sturgis's theory, that he [James] is self-sufficient, & just lets us love him out of godlike benevolence! I never saw anyone who needed *warmth* more than he does—he's dying for want of it."[10] What was agitating for Wharton, however, can be humanizing for later generations of readers.

Wharton's idea of dying for want of emotional fulfillment would not have struck James as either an original or an excessively melodramatic idea. In his notebook entry for 5 February 1895 James mused, "What is there in the idea of *Too late*—of some friendship or passion or bond—some affection long desired and waited for, that is formed too late?—I mean too late in life altogether."[11] The question arose again in a variety of fictions— "The Beast in the Jungle" (1903), *The Ambassadors* (1903), and "The Jolly Corner" (1908), to name only a few. Though his own friendships, passions, and affections may have been long in coming to a man expatriated from his natal land before he was thirty, bereft of his parents before he was forty, deprived of all but occasional contact with his siblings before he was fifty, and rusticated to the south of England before he was sixty, they nonetheless arrived for him before it was, indeed, too late. In the last decades of his life, at a time when many of us relinquish amorous attachments, his relationships with younger men became more pronounced and intense. His emotions were sure even if our language, like that of the notebooks, has to be tenuous: "It's love, it's friendship, it's mutual comprehension—it's whatever one will."[12] However indeterminate—to echo Posnock—the precise

9. John Carlos Rowe juxtaposes the traditionally "awesome" with the more recent "anxious" James in his foreword to *Henry James's New York Edition: The Construction of Authorship*, ed. David McWhirter (Stanford: Stanford University Press, 1995), xxiv.

10. Edith Wharton to W. Morton Fullerton, 19 March [1910] and [18 March 1910], in *The Letters of Edith Wharton*, ed. R. W. B. Lewis and Nancy Lewis (New York: Charles Scribner's Sons, 1988), 202, 200.

11. *The Complete Notebooks of Henry James*, ed. Leon Edel and Lyall Powers (New York: Oxford University Press, 1987), 112.

12. *Complete Notebooks of Henry James*, 112.

nature of those attachments, they were passionate, they were rewarding, they were mutual, and they were warm.

Despite the pervasive image of the "secure" Master, the suspicion has always been with us that James nonetheless enjoyed a rich sensual life, that he was not one of those upon whom sexuality was wholly lost. The possibility has lurked beyond the margins of the documented life in persistent literary gossip, in recollections published after his death, and in selective quotations from the many unpublished letters. But only recently has the probability of a sexually self-aware—and, for some, a sexually active—James been acknowledged by his biographers.[13] At least one contemporary novelist has gone so far as to fantasize a sensual life for a more "modern" James.[14] Yet, while new readings of his life and work explore the personal and fictive varieties of Jamesian sexual experience, these critical and biographical excursions have tended to roam freely, unaccompanied by those primary sources that might more convincingly document the full range of James's sensual and emotional life.

Almost all of the letters published here clearly reveal same-sex emotional attachments. And no small number of them can only be described as passionate love letters from James to men he obviously adored. Yet the letters nonetheless vary widely in the range and intensity of feelings they express.[15] Just as heterosexual relationships tolerate a range of expression, so these letters demonstrate James's capacity to feel a continuum of emotions amid a diversity of roles. James is alternately the fervent admirer, the paternal adviser, the fraternal comrade, the consoling spirit, the modest patron, the severe mentor, the faithful champion, the genial host, the ready confidant, the enamored soul, the ardent suitor, the plaintive lover, and the passionate devotee. Elsewhere, with one eye fixed on the energy and spontaneity of youth and the other on his own increasingly apparent mortality,

---

13. See Lyndall Gordon, *A Private Life of Henry James: Two Women and His Art* (New York: Norton, 1999); Wendy Graham, *Henry James's Thwarted Love* (Stanford: Stanford University Press, 1999); Fred Kaplan, *Henry James: The Imagination of Genius* (New York: Morrow, 1992); and Sheldon Novick, *Henry James: The Young Master* (New York: Random House, 1996).

14. See David Plante, *The Ghost of Henry James* (Boston: Gambit, 1970).

15. In *Gay New York: Gender, Urban Culture, and the Making of the Gay Male World, 1890–1940* (New York: Basic Books, 1994), George Chauncey explores in other nineteenth-century men the range of feeling and behavior exhibited in same-sex relationships. Noting that in this era young men often slept in the same bed and expressed passionate love for one another, Chauncey claims that only late in the century did such relationships become suspect.

James would seem to be the Platonic or "Uranian" lover that J. A. Symonds sought to define in *A Problem in Modern Ethics* (1891), a privately printed work that James is known to have borrowed from Edmund Gosse.[16] Similarly, before the Queen's Bench in April and May 1895, Oscar Wilde tried to defend his associations by asserting the purity, beauty, nobility, perfection, and naturalness of the "Love that dare not speak its name."[17] In this distinctly intellectualized form of masculine passion, founded on a Socratic eros derived from the *Symposium* and emphasizing spiritual over sexual procreancy, "an older man, moved to love by the visible beauty of a younger man, and desirous of winning immortality through that love, undertakes the younger man's education in virtue and wisdom."[18]

Jacques Barzun long ago cautioned readers against "the love of exaggeration" and the "magnification of feeling" in James's speech. "With the exquisiteness of a Lilliputian, his sensorium yields Brobdingnagian images," Barzun so neatly expressed his point.[19] These letters would be prime exhibits of such rhetorical exaggeration were it true that from these men "what James most desired was someone with whom he might talk, walk, bicycle, garden, and, perhaps, above all *work*."[20] But the language of the letters expresses the desire for something more than companionship. Admonitions about exaggeration are something of a canard when the rhetorical difference that so distinctly marks these letters is one of kind, not degree. If, as at least one scholar contends, "the gendered body is performative,"[21] then James had a clear sense of performativity in his correspondence, creating and re-creating himself as a sexual being who wanted to communicate with other sexual beings who might return his emotions. The letters thus become a series of fictions at least as creative as the novels,

---

16. See HJ's letter to Edmund Gosse of 7 January [1893], in Edel, *Henry James Letters,* 3: 398, 398n.

17. Wilde's (temporarily) stirring defense can be found in Richard Ellmann's *Oscar Wilde* (New York: Knopf, 1988), 463.

18. The characterization of Uranian love is from Linda Dowling's *Hellenism and Homosexuality in Victorian Oxford* (Ithaca: Cornell University Press, 1994), 81, an insightful tracing of the erotic consequences of the Pateresque "liberty of the heart" that were "so unintentionally yet unmistakably posited" by Victorian liberalism's embrace of Hellenism (92).

19. "James the Melodramatist," *Kenyon Review* 5 (1943): 518, 519.

20. The quotation is from John Carlos Rowe's *The Other Henry James* (Durham: Duke University Press, 1998), 179, as he summarizes, approvingly, Fred Kaplan's understanding of HJ's "passionate friendships."

21. Judith Butler, *Gender Trouble: Feminism and the Subversion of Identity* (New York: Routledge, 1990), 136.

plays, and tales. Hugh Stevens suggests that James used language as a means of agency to construct identities within the context of a given text:

> If we consider that "identity" might be up for grabs, might be worked out (rather than expressed) within a text, then James's writing itself can be thought of as the scene of erotic exploration: it is not necessary to conceive of a Jamesian body prior to the scene of writing. Freed from the burden of biographical priority, James's fictions emerge as dynamic in their erotic adventurousness.[22]

The overall effect of James's rhetoric is to invite these younger men into his world in an almost physical way. In his letters to women with whom he maintained especially close and abiding friendships James constructed intimacy in very different ways, emphasizing the familial and the daily rather than the physical and the erotic.[23] But references to the body, to holding, to touching, to caressing, and to gazing permeate his letters to younger men. It is impossible to read them and not recognize that James yearned to touch these men through language if in no other way.[24] He wished to "invoke" Persse through the act of writing.[25] He ended a dictated letter to Walpole with a note in his own hand, saying, "Only addressing you by that impersonal medium [the typewriter] is scarce better than making love to you through the telephone would be."[26] Writing to Persse

---

22. "Queer Henry *In the Cage*," in *The Cambridge Companion to Henry James*, ed. Jonathan Freedman (Cambridge: Cambridge University Press, 1998), 122.

23. See *Dear Munificent Friends: Henry James's Letters to Four Women*, ed. Susan Gunter (Ann Arbor: University of Michigan Press, 1999) for a fuller view of HJ's relationships—epistolary and otherwise—with close female friends. While James frequently uses terms of affection, such as *embrace* or *hug*, in his correspondence with women, only in his letters to Lady Louisa Wolseley does his rhetoric ever become flirtatious or erotic.

24. Exactly what emphasis should be placed on James's habitually tactile nature is, of course, debatable:

> Certain of his friendships, leanings, gestures, could, I know [said Mengin], make one think he was capable of submitting himself . . . but those gestures were in themselves a signal, and I'd say a proof, that he wasn't capable of this kind of surrender. His affectionate manner of grasping your arm, or of patting you on the shoulder, or giving you a hug—he would never have done this if these gestures had, for him, the slightest suggestion of a pursuit of physical love.

See Robert Mengin, *Monsieur Urbain* (Paris, 1984), qtd. in Leon Edel, *Henry James: A Life* (New York: Harper and Row, 1985), 724–25n. We are indebted to Philip Horne of University College, London for calling to our attention this passage.

25. See HJ to Jocelyn Persse, 4 May 1907.

26. See HJ to Hugh Walpole, 25 December 1912.

in Rome, James clearly assigned to language the power to arouse: "Irresistible to me always any tug on your part at the fine & firm silver cord that stretches between us—as I think I never fail to show you: at any twitch of it by your hand, the machine, within me, enters into vibration & I respond ever so eagerly & amply!"[27]

Because he feared that language alone was not always sufficient, James frequently enclosed photographs with these letters (something he did much less frequently with his intimate female correspondents). The images obviously evoked his physical presence, but, consciously or subconsciously, James may also have intended them as reminders to these younger men of his powerful presence in their lives. For his erotic entanglements with them were always a mixture not merely of love and loneliness but of love and power as well. In 1899, when his correspondence with Andersen and Sturgis began, he had survived the debacle of his experiments in playwriting and was poised to write three of his greatest novels: *The Wings of the Dove* (1902), *The Ambassadors* (1903), and *The Golden Bowl* (1904). In the first decade of the twentieth century, when both his literary labors and his romantic pangs were strongest, he apparently felt confident enough to direct his correspondents' careers—excepting only Jocelyn Persse, who had no public aspirations. To Sturgis he dispatched a series of bitingly critical letters that wounded the aspiring writer and nearly aborted his third novel, *Belchamber* (1904). Yet, apparently unaware of the influence he wielded over a struggling novelist, he professed only amazement when Sturgis proposed to withdraw the novel from publication: "If you think of anything so insane you will break my heart & bring my grey hairs, the few left me, in sorrow & shame to the grave. Why would you have an inspiration so perverse & so criminal?"[28] While not a sculptor himself, James also felt free to advise Andersen in his career, pointedly urging him, in violently physical rhetoric, to abandon his obsession with monumental public statuary in favor of sculpting more lucrative small portrait busts: "With your talent you easily can—& if I were but near you now I should take you by the throat & squeeze it till you howled & make you do my Bust!"[29] And, finally, Hugh Walpole received copious criticism from James regarding the form and "center" of his many novels. Of Walpole's *Maradick at Forty* (1910) James wrote that

---

27. See HJ to Jocelyn Persse, 22 January 1907.
28. See HJ to Howard Sturgis, 2 December 1903.
29. See HJ to Hendrik Andersen, 25 November 1906.

the whole thing is a monument to the abuse of voluminous dialogue, the absence of a plan of composition, alternation, distribution[,] structure, & other phases of presentation than the dialogue—so that line (the only thing I value in a fiction &c,) is replaced by a vast formless featherbediness—on which one sinks & is lost.[30]

In short, James's insistence in one of his letters to Walpole that the younger man address him as " 'Très-cher Maitre,' or 'my very dear Master' " is telling.[31] Forgetting the disastrous examples of so many of his well-intentioned but meddling characters, he readily conflated his roles as lover (whether epistolary or real) and mentor in a manner that licensed him to intervene, sometimes harshly, in the lives and careers of those friends whose affection and devotion he simultaneously sought. If not disastrous, the consequences were assuredly dampening.

This sense of power may have become pervasive for James, for the act of writing such loving letters was perhaps bolder (and potentially disastrous) than actually loving his friends. James surely sensed an erotic attraction to other men early in his life, while recognizing that he would never desire a physically intimate heterosexual relationship. And although he would have known that his sexual preferences differed from those of the "average" Victorian, he would not necessarily have considered himself deviant. Before the Criminal Law Amendment Act of 1885, the Cleveland Street scandal of September 1889, the Wilde trials in April and May 1895, and the growing interest in so-termed sexual deviation as defined by prominent sexologists in England and abroad, a variety of consenting human sexual behaviors were imaginable, at least legally if not socially, along a continuum of possibilities.[32]

In *One Hundred Years of Homosexuality and Other Essays in Greek Love*, David Halperin notes, "Homosexuality and heterosexuality, as we currently understand them, are modern, Western, bourgeois productions.

---

30. See HJ to Hugh Walpole, 13 May 1910.
31. See HJ to Hugh Walpole, 27 April 1909.
32. The revelation of a London brothel where young postal workers were available to upper-class male customers, perhaps including even Prince Albert Victor, led to a sensational prosecution under the 1885 Criminal Law Amendment Act, Section 11 of which created a new legal category, the vaguely defined "acts of gross indecency." Psychologists, sexologists, and physicians were meanwhile creating a new but equally vague category, that of the "homosexual." See Ed Cohen's *Talk on the Wilde Side: Toward a Genealogy of a Discourse on Male Sexualities* (New York: Routledge, 1993), 121–23, 9.

Nothing resembling them can be found in classical antiquity."[33] And Thomas Laqueur tells us that even conceptions of sexual differences are a relatively recent invention: "The notion, so powerful after the eighteenth century, that there had to be something outside, inside, and throughout the body, which defines male as opposed to female and which provides the foundation for an attraction of opposites is entirely absent from classical or Renaisance medicine."[34] Or, according to Jeffrey Weeks,

> To put it another way, the various possibilities of . . . homosexual desire, or what more neutrally might be termed homosexual behaviors, which seem from historical evidence to be a permanent and ineradicable aspect of human sexual possibilities, are variously constructed in different cultures as an aspect of wider gender and sexual regulation.[35]

Indeed, while gender roles may have been more fluid throughout history, by the end of the nineteenth century more rigid expectations for masculinity and femininity were in place, as exemplified by none other than William James and his cohorts at Harvard University.[36] Along with this binary division of sex roles as masculine/feminine came the concomitant designation of deviant sexualities, particularly the homosexual:

> Coined in 1869 by the Austro-Hungarian translator and litterateur Karl Maria Kertbeny and popularized in the writing of the German sexologists, the word 'homosexual'—the now ubiquitous, quasi-scientific denotation both for sexual intimacies between men and for the men who engaged in them—made its first widespread British appearance in Charles Chaddock's 1892 translation of Kraft-Ebbing's seminal *Psychopathia Sexualis*.[37]

The sociological became political as the events culminating in the conviction and imprisonment of Wilde made it clear to everyone in England and

---

33. *One Hundred Years of Homosexuality and Other Essays in Greek Love* (New York: Routledge, 1988), 8.

34. *Making Sex: Body and Gender from the Greeks to Freud* (Cambridge: Harvard University Press, 1990), 22.

35. "Discourse, Desire, and Sexual Deviance: Some Problems in a History of Homosexuality," in *The Making of the Modern Homosexual*, ed. Kenneth Plummer (London: Hutchinson, 1981), 81.

36. For a fuller discussion of the rise of the "manly man," see Kim Townsend's *Manhood at Harvard: William James and Others* (Cambridge: Harvard University Press, 1996). In chapter 8 of *The Trial of Curiosity*, Posnock also comments on these same constructions of masculinity among William James and his Harvard colleagues.

37. Cohen, *Talk on the Wilde Side*, 9.

abroad that the outward expression of same-sex feelings would incur severe social and legal punishment.[38] Surely James must have realized that he did not want to be identified by such a confining and potentially dangerous role specification.[39]

Richard Ellmann has noted that passage in 1885 of the Criminal Law Amendment Act changed the status of private correspondence and ushered in the age of the blackmailer.[40] The Wilde trials subsequently confirmed and increased the new dangers inherent in the language of passion and desire, be it private or public language, fact or fiction. This consequence of the Wilde trials could hardly have been lost on James—or any fellow writer—who followed the proceedings carefully, albeit at a safe distance. In Wilde's initial libel suit against Lord Queensberry, the failure of his counsel's efforts to minimize the evidentiary impact of certain letters to Alfred Douglas by differentiating between the pedestrian prose of "ordinary" letters and the exceptional language of "literary" letters was portentous.[41] In the ensuing criminal trials against Wilde, the prosecutorial strategy of relying heavily on Wilde's own language—on his poems, his letters, and *The Picture of Dorian Gray*—for "evidence" of his "perverse"

---

38. See Alan Sinfield, *The Wilde Century: Effeminacy, Oscar Wilde, and the Queer Movement* (New York: Columbia University Press, 1994), 118: "The Wilde trials exploded in the midst of all this urgent ideological work [of the sexologists who were creating a binary opposition between heterosexual and homosexual]. As a consequence, the insouciance, decadence and aestheticism, which Wilde was perceived as initiating, was transformed into a brilliantly precise image."

39. In this sense James seems to reject the essentialist view that sexuality is a fixed attribute like eye or hair color. Posnock notes James's refusal to be fixed within a binary gender orientation:

> The alleged passivity and weakness of Henry James and [George] Santayana (when judged by the standards of William's muscular pragmatism) are more accurately regarded as expressing their effort to diffuse traditional gender polarities that define the masculine as the repudiation of the feminine and the embracing (indeed, the fetishizing) of a rigid autonomy. (*The Trial of Curiosity*, 200)

For further discussion of essentialist versus constructionist theories of sexuality, see Kenneth Plummer, "Homosexual Categories: Some Research Problems in the Labelling Perspective of Homosexuality," in *The Making of the Modern Homosexual*, ed. Kenneth Plummer (London: Hutchinson, 1981), 53–75.

40. Ellmann, *Oscar Wilde*, 409.

41. See Michael Foldy, *The Trials of Oscar Wilde: Deviance, Morality, and Late-Victorian Society* (New Haven: Yale University Press, 1997), 3.

inclinations was both inevitable and damning.[42] It is accordingly easy to understand how Hugh Stevens can claim, "In homophobic turn-of-the-century Britain verbal expressions of affection and erotic endearment between men required more courage than acts of physical gratification." He does so, though, in order to emphasize that a "preoccupation with James's sexual behavior leads us away from a much more important and remarkable fact about James: within his own circle, James was increasingly daring in the way he constituted himself as a sexual and desiring subject, and acknowledged freely—indeed, with pleasure—that his desires were for (young and attractive) men."[43]

---

42. The connection between law and language was not lost on Michel Foucault, whose *History of Sexuality: An Introduction* (New York: Vintage, 1990) traces at length the imbrication of power and sexuality in eighteenth- and nineteenth-century England, demonstrating how the culture elicited sexual discourse and then defined and punished any deviant sexualities found within such discourse.

43. Stevens, *Henry James and Sexuality* (Cambridge: Cambridge University Press, 1998), 167. At the same time, though, Stevens would seem to ignore the very social, legal, and cultural context that he acknowledges, and thereby to diminish the risks involved in HJ's rhetoric, by reading the published late love letters as "camp epistolary outpourings" to individuals who were ultimately unattainable (167–69).

The Letters

Hendrik Andersen

Henry James first met the young sculptor Hendrik Andersen in the spring of 1899 in the Rome drawing room of Maud Howe Elliott, the novelist, journalist, lecturer, art critic, and suffragist from Newport. She and her Scottish-born husband, the artist John Elliott, occupied the top-floor apartment of the so-called Palazzo Rusticucci, on the piazza of the same name, in the Trastevere district of Rome. While Jack Elliott labored on a commission for the Boston Public Library, Maud Elliott maintained a salon where she entertained writers and artists and handsome young men. The Norwegian-born but Newport-raised Andersen fit the last two categories. After three years spent studying art and architecture, first in Paris and then in Naples, he had come to Rome in 1897 to set up his studio. According to Olivia Cushing Andersen, Hendrik's sister-in-law, Maud Elliott was quick to embrace "a talented fellow townsman"; she "quickly spread out her wing, easily included him [*sic*] a special pet and charge whose golden haired and graceful figure, could while she mothered him add a picture[s]que note to her salon."[1]

In 1896–97 Andersen was, again in the words of Olivia, "very charming, tall, slender, broad shouldered. Every line of his face and body denoted activity and his aquiline profile and the corners of his mouth decision. There was no [h]esitation in his glance nor in his manner, but a clear frankness in both that quickly attracted people to him."[2] And such was the

---

1. See Olivia Cushing Andersen's sixteen-page typescript "(H[endrik]—Rome '96–97)" in Hendrik Christian Andersen Papers (hereafter, HCA Papers), Manuscript Department, Library of Congress: Box 40, Folder 1, p. 4.
2. "(H[endrik]—Rome '96–97)," p. 1.

effect of this the "touchingly innocent youth" of twenty-seven on the fifty-six-year-old James.[3] Although he later made an equally strong impression on first meeting James's sister-in-law, Alice Howe Gibbens James, Andersen's attractiveness was typically experienced more by men than by women, according to Olivia Andersen.[4]

Following her husband Andreas's death in February 1902, after only one month of marriage, Olivia moved to Rome in 1903 to live with Hendrik and his mother for the last fourteen years of her life. In a never finished joint biography of her husband the painter and her brother-in-law the sculptor, Olivia muses on why Hendrik "drew such men toward him as a [sic] by a magnet":

> There is with certain intellectual men a special charm and attraction about an intellectual youth, which they seem not to find in their contemporaries or in the opposite sex. There is of course a freedom about their intercourse that leaves them quite uncompromised, and the physical and mental are so . . . interwoven that it becomes difficult to say whether the attraction is chiefly physical or mental.[5]

This passage precedes Olivia's account of "the warmest attachment" felt for Andersen by two particular men, Henry James and Lord Ronald Sutherland Gower.

In January 1897 Andersen came under the eye of the travelling Lord Gower, the accomplished and wealthy English sculptor and art critic.[6] Yet Gower's few diary references to his "Norwegian sculptor friend" are all matter-of-fact passages that offer little evidence for what Olivia describes as his "closest attentions" to and growing intimacy with Andersen.[7] Were Gower's discreet diaries the sole record of the relationship, there would be little to tell. But, despite the air of equanimity in which Olivia cloaks her

3. The description is from HJ's 20 July 1899 letter to Maud Howe Elliott, qtd. in Elliott's *John Elliott: The Story of an Artist* (Boston: Houghton Mifflin, 1930), 113.

4. Writing to Henry from Rome on 1 January 1901, William James noted that when Andersen called on Alice she "saw him and fell in love. I haven't seen her so pleased with anyone for a long time." See *William and Henry, 1897–1910,* ed. Ignas Skrupskelis and Elizabeth Berkeley, in *The Correspondence of William James* (Charlottesville: University of Virginia Press, 1992–), 3:154.

5. "(H[endrik]—Rome '96–97)," pp. 10, 9.

6. Lord Ronald Sutherland Gower (1845–1916), was a politician, sculptor, art critic, and biographer.

7. Ronald Gower, *Old Diaries, 1881–1901* (New York: Charles Scribner's Sons, 1902), 293, 279, 302–3.

brother-in-law, Andersen's acquaintance with the fifty-two-year-old Gower only shortly before his meeting with James had to have been one of the more disquieting episodes in his youthful life.

Gower enjoyed not merely an artistic but a licentious reputation: he was an openly homosexual English peer who had consorted with Oscar Wilde and his circle since 1876 (providing Wilde with one of the principal models for Lord Henry Wotton in *The Picture of Dorian Gray*) and whose numerous affairs had included one with W. Morton Fullerton, a close friend of James's and later the lover of Edith Wharton.[8] As Olivia Andersen tells the story, Gower courted her brother-in-law assiduously: "Once he had found his way to Hendrik's studio, he was continually calling there, sending notes, inviting the young man to lunch or dinner, introducing him to other intellectual men, treating him, indeed, with the warmth of attention that men are wont to bestow on women." Hendrik was not unaware, according to Olivia, that "Lord R.'[s] attentions were almost such as a lover bestows on his loved one": "Gradually it dawned upon him the hunt [kind?] of man that L.R. probably was—a phase of his character however which seemed in no way to inpair [*sic*] the other's social standing on [i.e., or?] to shut any doors on his face."[9]

While the doors to Andersen's studio were certainly not closed to Gower, the temptation to construe his interest in the relationship as a sexual one—or as solely a sexual one—ignores what was in Andersen a certain measure of opportunism, or perhaps simply naive optimism.[10] Gower's generous luncheons and dinners and his "range of acquaintance" were "convenient," but his potential generosity extended far beyond meals and introductions. According to Olivia, Gower "brought to his studio

---

8. See Phyllis Grosskurth, *John Addington Symonds* (London: Longman's, 1964), 266–67, 311; Kaplan, *Henry James*, 447. Rupert Croft-Cooke offers a less documented but more salacious portrait of Gower in *The Unrecorded Life of Oscar Wilde* (London: W. H. Allen, 1972), 41: "a mundane and talented man who followed the life of a promiscuous homosexual and shocked more discreet friends by openly whoring after guardsmen and other male prostitutes in the underpaid Services."

9. "(H[endrik]—Rome '96–97)," pp. 11, 13.

10. The most that can be confidently asserted about Andersen's sexuality is that he chafed at conventionality and considered himself superior to the common laws: "It is hard for a man to give vent and full expression to his natural and normal physical or sexual necessities without offending the laws of nature or those that control people. . . . What is right is to hold sacred every act with a full consciousness of its meaning, morally, intellectually, and spiritually. Laws are made for people who do not know or value thier [*sic*] souls and must be controlled" (diary entry for 28 November 1914, HCA Papers, LC: Box 1, Folder 1).

large photographs of a beautiful estate in England, which since he had no legal heirs, should go [to] the heir of his choice."[11] How close Andersen came to being the beneficiary of Gower's largesse will never be known, but two details in Olivia's account—Maud Elliott's surprise and Olivia's sense of injustice—suggest genuine disappointment when Andersen was supplanted in Gower's affections by another young man. The twenty-four-year-old Frank Hird, Roman correspondent for the *Morning Post*, arrived in Rome and was soon adopted, first figuratively and then legally, by Gower.[12]

This summary of the Gower-Andersen episode, wherein Andersen loses a patron, an English estate, and, most importantly, the affections of an older and artistically sensitive man who would accept him as a son, is a necessary prelude to any discussion of the events in the spring of 1899, when James entered the drawing room of Maud Elliott and the life of Hendrik Andersen.

James was not drawn to Andersen by the latter's sculptural predilections, which tended relentlessly—megalomaniacally, James would later say—toward the colossal nude and the monumental public figure. As early as 19 August 1899, during Andersen's first visit to Lamb House, James was already writing sardonically to Edmund Gosse of Andersen's "altogether alternative vision," of how "the over-trousered & over-crinolined race had not remained his immediate inspiration."[13] But James sufficiently valued either Andersen's continuing friendship or his artistic promise to become a modest patron, purchasing a terra cotta bust of Count Alberto Bevilacqua that he installed as a kind of tutelary spirit in his Lamb House dining room. And he soon set about promoting, in letters of experienced advice if not in action, what he saw as Andersen's professional and personal interests—promotion that involved increasingly strenuous attempts to dissuade Andersen from his monumentalist schemes.

---

11. "(H[endrik]—Rome '96–97)," p. 13.

12. The journalist Frank Hird (b. 1873) was also the author of disparate books, including *The Cry of the Children: An Exposure of Certain British Industries in Which Children are Iniquitously Employed* (1898), *Rosa Bonheur* (1904), *Victoria the Woman* (1908), *Lancashire Stories* (1912), *The Bannantyne Sapphires* (1928), and *H. M. Stanley; The Authorized Life* (1935). Lord Gower's diary entry for 2 February 1898 celebrates the imminent adoption: "My heart is very happy to-night, for I have just received a letter from Frank accepting the offer I made him . . . last week . . . of becoming my adopted son" (*Old Diaries*, 323).

13. *Selected Letters of Henry James to Edmund Gosse, 1882–1915: A Literary Friendship*, ed. Rayburn S. Moore (Baton Rouge: Louisiana State University Press, 1988), 166.

Andersen's new patron lacked Gower's degree of influence in Parisian art circles, just as he lacked any title to English estates, but the new and proud owner of Lamb House was able to offer Andersen the quiet hospitality of Rye—as a northern retreat from the summer heat of Rome, as a rural respite from his typically unremitting work pace, and as a convenient resting point in his travels to and from America. Perhaps most importantly, though, James offered him in Lamb House a semblance of a much simpler home life. For after 1902 Andersen was a principal supporter of his alcoholic father in Norway as well as the mainstay of a complicated Roman household—a shifting and populous ménage that included his mother; his sister-in-law, Olivia; occasionally Olivia's brother, Howard Cushing; occasionally his own brother, Arthur; and the orphaned Lucia, companion to his mother and occasional model and future step-sister.

Andersen accepted James's hospitality on an annual basis in the first five years of their friendship, and then only once thereafter. He first visited Lamb House for three days in August 1899 while en route to America, and he sojourned there again in December 1900, in September 1901, in February 1902, in October 1903, and finally in October 1908. On his part, James visited Andersen in Rome once again in June 1907. And their simultaneous presence in America in 1905 allowed for a Newport reunion that James afterward recalled in tender and loving terms.

These visits always passed too quickly to satisfy James. Less ephemeral, though, was the correspondence that the two men conducted for almost sixteen years, from at least 19 July 1899 until at least 16 March 1915. James's frequent letters bore sufficient affection and admiration and, as called for, sympathy that Andersen preserved them and, in the 1930s, unsuccessfully attempted to publish them.[14] Although Andersen's own letters to James have not survived, his side of the relationship is not wholly a matter of speculation. From letters to and by family members, from Hendrik's and Olivia's diaries, and from Hendrik's successive but ultimately unsuccessful efforts to write his own memoir about James one can begin to grasp the relationship as Andersen felt it.

---

14. Seventy-six letters from HJ are preserved in the Clifton Waller Barrett Library at the University of Virginia, but there may have been many more. Amid the late Leon Edel's professional papers is a note of 5 September 1939 from Adele Neville, a former clerical assistant to Hendrik Andersen, claiming that he possessed hundreds of James letters that he planned to publish. A subsequent letter to Edel from Andersen noted that Harry James had refused him publication permission (Edel Archive, McGill University: tls, Neville to Edel, 5 September 1939 and tls, Andersen to Edel, 23 October 1939).

Andersen's initial attraction to James was anything but a literary one. Even as the friendship deepened between 1899 and 1904, Andersen became more and more dismissive of James's intricate work, just as James was unresponsive to Andersen's increasingly colossal schemes. Instead, Andersen seemingly sought in James a kindred spirit who could understand the range and complexity of his bifurcated emotions. In Emersonian terms, the "party of memory" contested with the "party of hope" for control of Andersen's temperament.

On the one hand, Andersen lived in the imminent expectation, even conviction, of a better life. Such is the tenor of his invariably cheerful letters home to Newport while establishing himself as a sculptor in Rome: the assurance that he would someday be able to send his mother not ten thousand kisses but ten thousand dollars, that the health of his beloved but doomed Andreas would improve, that the family's fortunes would change once he repatriated his alcoholic father to a distant life in Norway. Such is the tenor of the idée fixe of his adult years, the belief that with the establishment of a new city, of a World Centre of Communication, he could hasten in a new era of peace and happiness in the postwar West. And such a temperament perhaps explains his willingness to be courted by Lord Gower, who held at least the earthly keys to a better life. Alongside this persistent and ultimately transcendent optimism, however, there was in Andersen a significant residue of painful experience: a youth spent with an alcoholic father, his early dependence on Newport sponsors whose belief in his talent gradually waned, the loneliness and poverty of his student years in Europe, what must have been guilt over his inability to contribute to the support of his mother while pursuing his art, his devastation over the death of Andreas, the inevitable frustration and self-doubt of an artist wrestling not just with clay but with a largely indifferent public.

Writing to Olivia in 1902, in the year of Andreas's death, Andersen lamented that he had "very few friends, and *no one* that I can really talk to, dearest Andreas was the only one. And often when there comes [*sic*] moments that I want to talk to someone I can only think of him as one who would understand and feel what I me[a]nt."[15] When Andersen later tried to write about James, he cast the elder writer in the roles of sympathetic confidant and understanding lover. Extant in the Andersen Papers are five overlapping, incomplete versions of a memoir that Andersen seemingly intended as a preface to his envisioned edition of James's letters.

---

15. Als, 14 October 1902, HCA Papers, LC: Box 11, Folder 9.

Therein he attempted to write of the "brotherly love" that he felt for the writer and mentor who "never failed to guide me with with [*sic*] the most delicate and sympathetic understanding over the rough and deceptive road that leads to success."[16] Although James's letters were "very intemite and personal," Andersen considered their publication to be a duty he owed "to the writer whose love and sympathy, as well as his continued friendship and affection gave comfort and incouragement through the many years I struggled on alone indevering to create and infuse strength beauity and the dignity as well as the sacred meaning of life into, marble and Bronze."[17] The point is reiterated in his elegiac remarks on James:

> Deeply as the loss of Henry James was felt by his innumerable friends and the literary world at large, to me it was an unutterable sorrow, for no one had ever understood me as he had done, or sympathised so sincerely with my struggle and my aim in life.

Andersen then recalled visits to Lamb House, with its delightful garden, where "sometimes we would sit far into the summer night talking over our experiences of our past lives, both sweet and bitter; experiences so different in their details but often set in the same background of Boston, Newport, Paris and Rome."[18]

If Andersen's primary interest in James was to find a "father" or an elder "brother" in whom he could confide about the past even as he anticipated a better future, he had picked the wrong man on several counts. Andersen's melioristic and ultimately transcendent visions met with little patience

---

16. From Version 2 of five unpublished mss. and tss., HCA Papers, LC: Box 17, Folder 4. We identify version 1 as twenty pencilled pages that, after opening remarks on meeting HJ, turn to anecdotes from Andersen's early Roman years. Version 2 consists of nine double-spaced typed pages that essentially recast version 1. Version 3, four pencilled sheets, focuses more consistently on Andersen's relationship with HJ. Version 4, two typescript pages numbered "41" and "42," is a less prolix version of 3. In Version 5, ten typed pages, Andersen observes that "Henry James alone knew the bitterness and hardship that crushed my spirit from early childhood" and then focuses on his mother's difficult life and disappointing marriage in Norway before the family's 1873 immigration to Newport. Version 5 also provides an approximate date of composition—c. 1932 or slightly later—as Andersen recalls his birth in 1872, some "sixty odd years ago." All of the manuscript and typescript versions are heavily edited, in Andersen's or at least one other person's hand, and no effort is made here to retain canceled passages or to distinguish inserted text. Andersen's erratic spelling is maintained, however.
17. From version 3 of five unpublished mss. and tss., HCA Papers, LC: Box 17, Folder 4.
18. From version 4 of five unpublished mss. and tss., HCA Papers, LC: Box 17, Folder 4.

from Henry James, whose signature stoicism little consorted with an un-critical optimism, who did not expect or seek a heaven on earth, whose health declined precipitously within a decade of their meeting, and for whom the outbreak of war marked not an opportunity for renewal but the end of so many valued things. It is hardly surprising, therefore, that An-dersen's criticism of James's writings eventually turned into criticism of the writer himself. In October 1908, when he last saw James, he wrote to Olivia from Lamb House excoriating the rainy weather, the "quiet sleepy little town" of Rye, the "dullness and almost cruel hardness that one sees in the faces" of the unemotional English. From a critique of the stolid English—"some of the freshest and most human instincts in them are dead"—Andersen moved without pause into an equally critical description of James:

> I have had long walks and talks with Henry James who is as you know a mountain of technical ability and form; yet I cannot help feeling that the mountain stands directly in his own way. and it is impossible for him to climb over it, even though he is often assured of the brightness and freshness there is to be had on the other side. What he knows, he knows deeply and thoroughly. But he knows too much. He handles every subject with the same material. He builds with ease and his inexaustable supply of material is ever growing. but I do not care to go into detail or point out limitations which would not change the face of things in the least.[19]

Fred Kaplan suggests that although James was more emotionally open and expressive beginning in the late 1890s, this "was not a public openness, and it had its private ambivalences and disguises."[20] One of those disguises was surely the "self-satisfied assurance" that Andersen complained of to Olivia in October 1904 and then singled out again in June 1907:

> I do not miss the absence of H.J. as he got just a bit heavy and a bit tiresome with his absolute cock sure penetration. Yet he is always kind and I must say that I have gotten to know him better. which means that I see cleerer where the gates are that open and shut and how narrow the roads are that lead up to his shrine. and all this is for the best.[21]

Had he not cared so deeply for Andersen, James would surely have appreci-ated the irony: the sculptor devoted to lifeless depictions of monumentally

19. Als, 15 October 1908, HCA Papers, LC: Box 12, Folder 4.
20. Kaplan, *Henry James*, 403.
21. Als to Olivia Cushing Andersen, 30 June 1907, HCA Papers, LC: Box 12, Folder 4.

scaled figures would at last dismiss James from his emotional life by re-fashioning him into a "mountain" of an artist, into an inaccessible shrine to a life and an art devoid of "some of the freshest and most human instincts."

In a 1955 article on the James-Andersen relationship Michael Swan quoted at length from the letters and concluded that they revealed a "strong paternal feeling in James," that "Andersen had become one of the family of 'son-figures' which James gathered round him during the remaining years of his life."[22] But in truth James could never be an adequate father to Andersen, no more than the alcoholic Anders Andersen or the profligate Lord Gower. Their correspondence continued intermittently for another eight years, but by June 1907 Hendrik Andersen was already able to write to Olivia that "I am getting on well with James but James is meens nothing to me."[23]

22. Michael Swan, "Henry James and the Heroic Young Master," *Harper's Bazaar,* September 1955, 227.

23. Als, 1–3 June 1907, HCA Papers, LC: Box 12, Folder 4.

My dear Hans Anderson.[24]   July 19*th* 1899.

You must have wondered at not hearing from me—& I found your letter here on my arrival, from Italy some twelve days ago. But I thought it better to wait, to answer you, till your box & its precious contents had arrived—to give you news of it, & its condition; & this happy event has only *just* taken place. I have been for 3 or 4 days in London, & in my absence the box turned up; so that yesterday, on my return, I could have it carefully, tenderly unpacked & its burden, with every precaution, laid bare & lifted out. It is, the beautiful bust, I rejoice to tell you, in perfect condition (it was admirably packed,) without a flaw or a nick—& is more charming and delightful to [see?] even than it was in Rome.[25] I heartily rejoice to possess it—& I am by this post writing to my bankers in London for a draft on Rome of the amount of $250—that is Fifty Pounds—which will immediately reach me & which I will instantly, on its arrival, transmit to you. I find the sum modest for the admirable & exquisite work. I have perched the latter on the chimney-piece of my dining room—the position I have that best lends itself, all things carefully considered—where he commands the scene & has a broad base to rest on & the arch of a little niche to enshrine him, & where, moreover, as I sit at meat, I shall have him constantly before me as a loved companion & friend. He is so living, so human, so sympathetic & sociable & curious, that I foresee it will be a lifelong attachment. Brave little Bevilacqua and braver still big Maestro Anderson! You will both make many friends here. So I thank you again, & give you a good & grateful stretta di mano [It.: handshake], which I will repeat 2 or 3 days hence. I think very kindly of our too few but so interesting hours together, & I send you my benediction & my heartiest good wishes. Lift up your heart, keep up your head, & don't sacrifice your

---

24. In this first letter to Hendrik Andersen HJ consistently misspells his name as "Anderson."

25. In his letter of 20 July 1899 to Maud Howe Elliott HJ writes that his dreaming of Italy "has just been brought more intimately home to me by the arrival of a charming object I, at the last hour, made bold to purchase (on very modest terms) from our wonderful young friend, H. C. Andersen—the colored terra cotta bust of the Bevilacqua which struck me, on the whole, more than anything in his studio. It perches now on my chimney-piece and diffuses extraordinary life, expression and charm. It bids fair to be a delightful possession, and without you I shouldn't have had it, nor known the touchingly interesting youth" (Elliott, *John Elliott,* 113).

health. I hope you are not roasting before a slow fire or shivering in a clammy shade. Yours, my dear Anderson, most faithfully

Henry James

ALS: Virginia MSS 6251 (1)

LAMB HOUSE, RYE.

My dear Andersen. August 9*th* 1899.

May this promptly meet you! I have your letter of Rome of the other day. You say "Cook & Sons, London"—but in point of fact they have ½ a dozen offices there. However, I shall direct this to the principal one, Ludgate Circus—& pray it be to *that* one you first go. Perhaps I will send another line to the other most likely one—in Pall Mall. Take, to come down here, the 5.15 p.m. from *St. Paul's Station,* which is just beyond (east of) Blackfriars' Bridge, 15 minutes drive in a hansom from Charing X (*more* if you come by the Strand, the Embankment—on the Thames—the short & straight way—being perhaps still blocked—as it was 10 days ago—by repairs.) Buy—if you want to be thrifty—a 3d class *return* to Rye, & be sure you get into a Rye carriage—the *forward* part of the train; the backward part, at Ashford, going off at a tangent. Write or wire me in advance—& I will meet you at this station (train due at 7.9, but at this season, alas, usually *late;*) which is but 5 minutes' walk from my house. I feel you to be formidable, fresh from your St. Peterses, Vaticans & Trattorie Fiorentine [It.: Florentine restaurants]—formidable to my small red British cottage & & [*sic*] small plain British cuisine—but you will be very welcome to yours ever[26]

Henry James

ALS: Virginia MSS 6251 (4)

---

26. Andersen's response to Lamb House is recorded in his letter of 16 August 1899, written to his mother and father on Lamb House stationery: "I am now with Henry James. . . . The english country is perfectly beautiful. I never thought it would be so lovely and fresh. . . . I will spend a few quite [i.e., quiet] days with Henry James, who is kindness itself and whom I care very much for. He has such a pretty little red brick cottage, very old, but beautifully arranged, with a little garden of fresh green grass, and pretty flowers, every thing both inside and outeside of the house as cleen and neat as a pin, with such excellent taste for furniture and color. only a few things in each room but just the things that one needs, and I have one of the most beautiful rooms I ever slept in, with rich old oak walls in pannells polished so that they look like strong iron and in every way I am in a little Paradise here" (HCA Papers, LC: Box 11, Folder 6).

September *7th 1899*

My dearest little Hans: without prejudice to your magnificent stature! Your note of this morning is exactly what I had been hoping for, & it gives me the liveliest pleasure. I hereby "ask" you, with all my heart. *Do,* unfailingly and delightfully, come back next summer & let me put you up for as long as you can possibly stay. There, mind you—it's an engagement. I was absurdly sorry to lose you when, that afternoon of last month we walked sadly to the innocent & kindly little station together & our common fate growled out the harsh false note of whirling you, untimely, away. Since then I have *missed* you out of all proportion to the three meagre little days (for it seems strange they were only *that*) that we had together. I have never (& I've done it 3 or 4 times,) passed the little corner where we came up Udimore hill (from Winchelsea,) in the eventide on our bicycles, without thinking ever so tenderly of our charming spin homeward in the twilight & feeling again the strange perversity it made of that sort of thing being so soon *over*. Never mind—we *shall* have more, lots more, of that sort of thing! If things go well with me I'm by no means without hope of having been able, meanwhile, to take the studio so in hand that I shall be ready to put you into it comfortably for a little artistic habitation.[27] Rye, alas, is not sculpturesque, nor of a sculpturesque inspiration—but what's good for the man is, in the long run, good for the artist—& we shall be good for eachother [*sic*]; & the studio good for both of us. May the terrific U.S.A. be meanwhile not a brute to you. I feel in you a *confidence,* dear Boy— which to show is a joy to me. My hopes & desires and sympathies right heartily, & most firmly, go with you. So keep up *your* heart, & tell me, as it shapes itself, your (inevitably, I imagine, more or less weird) American story. May, at any rate *tutta quella gente* [It.: all those people] be good to you. Yours, my dear Hans, right constantly

Henry James

ALS: Virginia MSS 6251 (5)

My dear Hans Boy. Oct. 23. *1899.*

Your letter from Brookline much interests & touches me—& makes me feel, as I do with joy, the reality of the possibility, as it were, of your being

---

27. The Lamb House property included a small studio on Watchbell Street, adjoining the garden.

with me for a while next summer. *Work* for it, strive for it, my dear Boy, do—before all else—make it a motive & a spur! It *was,* last August,—our meeting—all too brief, too fleeting & too sad. You merely brushed me with your elbow & turned me your back. I walked up from the station, that soft summer morning of your departure, much more lonely than I should have thought 3 days of companionship could, in their extinction, have made me. So, most assuredly, boil the pot by every art & every cunning you can contrive & cultivate. Of *course* you must do portrait-busts, and mighty good things they will be to do, with the style & mastery that you will put into them. I hope to God people will have the Sense to come to you & the wit to bring others. For this I pray, and it's an end to which I wish I could more actively contribute. But I feel, here, millions of miles away from your strange American scene of action. Your impressions, expressions, of the big, formidable country penetrate to the centre of my intelligence—& I stand there with you & hear you "draw your breath in pain," & squeeze your arm, & pat your back—oh, so affectionately & tenderly!—& stuff you (so far as your own admirable pluck leaves room for it,) with my conception of your required courage & patience. These things won't fail you—&, as you have the greater things still, *nothing* will. My confidence in you is a satisfaction to me that is made perfect by the sense of your being touched by it. I continue to have long talks with little Bevilacqua about you & we help each other to bear up. The autumn here is all russet & purple & brown—all rich, thick, golden atmospheric tones & pleasant, friendly pictures. I shall be *infinitely* interested when I hear of your having opened shop in New York—do, my dear Boy, let me know before too long how it goes. Write me ten words when you can't write me twenty. I should be, myself, were I there, very kind to those—to any one—whom you find kind to you. I should show them how I feel it. It is late, more than bedtime, & I scribble this in my little brown parlour. It takes you, my dear Boy, a great deal of remembrance & goodwill. I respond with all my heart to the manner in which you put your own sentiments to *me.* I wrote weeks ago to Mrs. Elliott[28]—but she is silent & estranged! I'm very glad her mother[29] is good to you. Gird your strong young loins, nurse your

---

28. See the biographical register for Maud Howe Elliott.

29. Julia Ward (Mrs. Samuel Gridley) Howe (1819–1910), was a Newport writer, editor, social activist, and lecturer whose bust Hendrik Andersen sculpted in 1898.

brave visions, bear with your stupid sitters, gouge in your master-thumb, and continue to believe in the ever-affectionate interest of yours always

Henry James

ALS: Virginia MSS 6251 (6)

My dear boy Hans. December 22: *1899*.

If I had acknowledged your last touching letter on the spot—when I got it—this might be sailing in towards you just in time to lie on your table as a Xmas greeting. But I've been pressed, squeezed, worried, bothered, anxious—ill circumstanced to write immediately; besides wanting *you* yourself not to feel that I am one of those fearful persons so quick on the trigger that correspondence is cheated of its natural & comfortable languors & leisures. May these words bring you my tender good wishes for the dawn of a good New Year! I gather that your installation & start in New York are a grimmishly up-hill matter & I think of you with infinite sympathy & understanding. Hard the conditions & rough & cold & ugly much of the way. But throw yourself hard on your youth, your courage & your genius; believe they constitute a solid, golden capital, and *use* them to such advantage that they will start up results. I don't, I can't for the life of me see how such extraordinarily individual & distinguished portrait-busts as you have the secret of shouldn't be ferociously wanted as soon as people *have begun to become aware of them. Make them* aware—& then wait. You won't have to wait too long. I shall be delighted to hear of *any* symptom of awakening work for you. The year wanes to its last drops & finds me still here. I *may* go to London for 2 or 3 months early in 1900 (gruesome date!) but I don't yet know. I have let my apartment there (for a year,) for pressing financial reasons & have thereby no town refuge.[30] These same reasons may keep me here straight away, & will, I fear, at any rate, put out of the question any sneaking hope for me of going to Italy again this spring. My elder brother & his wife are with me—he gravely ill, with career & work interrupted,—which causes me much anxiety.[31] But he hopes soon to get off to the South of France, which may bring him, in time, relief, & me, in

---

30. After purchasing Lamb House in July 1899, HJ leased his London flat, 34 De Vere Gardens, to the Stopford Brookses.

31. An October 1899 visit to Lamb House by William James, his wife Alice, and their daughter Peggy was HJ's first sight of his brother in seven years. The visit was shadowed by the onset earlier that year of the heart disease that would afflict William until his death in 1910.

that case, cheer. These are cold, dark days—though this ripe little old corner has its small secrets of winter beauty as well as the friendly brightness & homeliness that you saw & liked—that you must see & like soon again. Work stoutly towards *that* admirable end—while I do the same on my side. It's a charming, cheering vision, & I keep your place for you hard—or rather soft. I read over, as I write, your letter, & nothing in it that is affectionate to me fails to move me to deep & hearty response. Allons [Fr.: Come now]—lift up your heart; & stick in your thumb, & start the procession, & hold fast to yours, my dear boy Hans, right cordially & constantly

Henry James

P.S. Mrs. Gardner[32] spent a day or two with me the other week, & she spoke to me most appreciatively & kindly of your brother the painter[33] whom she knows, I gathered, more than she has had a chance to know you, & whom she evidently much values. This makes me desire to hope things are well with him—to express to him, also, this hope, & that of my some day seeing him & knowing him. Good-night! I am sitting late—my usual letter-hour—into the winter-night stillness in which my huddled little town lies sleeping under as many blankets as it can muster.———

ALS: Virginia MSS 6251 (7)

LAMB HOUSE, RYE.

My dear (by which I mean my dear young,) old Hans!   March 9*th 1900.*

I've had your last good letter too long unacknowledged. Yet I've waited also on purpose, in order not to produce with you the feeling of pressure & overfrequent appeal—in respect to our interchange. All the same it's charming to hear from you, & I welcome & respond to every touch of your hand. "Charming" I say, in spite of my sense of your uphill winter, your alien & exiled state (as it were—after Rome the artists' *own,*) & your generally stiff conditions. I figure to myself these things & I figure you *in* them, & I sigh, & I think, & I hope; & I count the gleams of light that seem to spot a little your gloom. The biggest gleam, for both of us, will be having you here, a few months hence—if so be it that, when the time arrives, you *can* come; for which I shall earnestly pray. I've had, myself, (as you sympathetically guess,) a somewhat worried & bothered winter (wholly spent in this house;) but the lengthening days are bringing cheer &

32. See the biographical register for Isabella Stewart Gardner.
33. See the biographical register for Andreas M. Andersen.

change in some measure, & I hope that—as the hard year relents—some such process is also taking place with you. May your pall be lifted and your light diffuse itself. I don't see how this can fail. I've told you that before—& it may irritate you to hear me *bêtement* [Fr.: foolishly, stupidly] repeat it, while your fate does hang fire: & yet I do repeat it, while I pat you ever so tenderly on the back—as obstinately as if you had swallowed something & were choking. I'm afraid I've no news for you that will amuse you—no news, thank goodness (I myself feel,) of *any* kind. It's when nothing happens that one is most at ease. I'm very quiet, very busy, & very uncompanied. But I go up to London for a fortnight day after tomorrow. There I shall see some old friends & taste a little of the cup of the world. Then I shall come back here for a long go—another—of tranquillity & production. That's the only thing that makes life tolerable—to forget everything in some sort of creation. That's what *you* can do;—none better. It's probably what you *are,* a little, doing, *Dio vuole* [It.: God willing]! Only when you speak of "lessons" I groan. I'm glad you've got them if you need them—yet I gnash my teeth to think they've got *you.*——As the time comes round that makes the anniversary of my Italian journey of last year, a deep nostalgia seizes me, a melancholy yearning to be there again, to feel the Roman May & June. I think of the day you lunched & dined with me. But it's out of the question *this* spring, & when I go again you must be there. Good night, my dear Hans—lift up your heart. We shall again be shoulder to shoulder—or, better still, face to face, and I am yours always
                                                        Henry James
P.S. Forgive this stupid blank side—which I accidentally skipped. I would undertake still to cover it were it not one o'clk in the a.m. & my hand weary & weak. Felicissima notte [It.: the happiest of nights]!————
[On flap of envelope] Have stupidly lost your New York address and have to reach you thus *indirectly.*[34]
ALS: Virginia MSS 6251 (8)

Dearest Boy Hans.   March 20*th 1900.*
    You will have received, I think, my response to your last letter but one just after dispatching to me the so charming & tender letter (March 7th)

---

34. HJ addresses the letter to Andersen in Newport, with the request, *"Please forward."*
35. Although James is writing from London, he cancels the club address and indicates that Andersen should address letters to "Lamb House *Rye."*

which just reaches me here. My own answer (to the other) went to Newport—by reason of my having stupidly mislaid or destroyed, your New York address before transcribing it—but it will, I trust, have been promptly forwarded to you thence. It's a great joy to me to hear from you—& you obeyed a delightful impulse of kindness & sympathy in writing. But reassure yourself on the subject of my worries & incommodities. They have quite subsided & are not worth speaking of; I am always, thank heaven, well enough and happy enough (as *you* must be—as all artists are,) when work goes on without interruption & disaster, & one sees one stone of the little pyramid pile itself on another. Thanks, therefore—all affectionate, all equally tender, thanks for any anxiety you may have felt about me, & for your gentle, genial, graceful little gesture across the sea. I am perfectly well, the dark & dismal (particularly dismal this year,) winter is past, & every day softens & brightens the near prospect. I have been spending a week in London—I spend a few days more (these are the 1st for months & months;) & then I return to little restful, redroofed uncomplicated Rye. There I shall be for months (6 or 7) to follow. I don't go, I can't go, don't even desire to go, to Italy this particular year. There are all sorts of reasons against it, & all sorts for "sitting close" at home, & driving my pen & minding my business & keeping my engagements. So think of me as peaceful & productive—the 2 best things a man can be, & the 2 that *you* will be tending more & more, (through every vain appearance to the contrary that may temporarily seem to mock & worry you,) triumphantly to become. Only keep your hand to the plough, & your eye to the end of the furrow. You will "get there"—*be* there—even in the fulness of your youth. I think of you with hope in the big, kind, ugly country—so monstrous & yet so responsive—with hope, with confidence, as well as with compassion. It would be awful for always—but it will pay you for Now. I am glad dear Mrs. Jack[36] is kind to you—be kind, when you can, to *her*. No sound of Mrs. Elliott reaches me—it's like the stillness of prayer or of Death! I put, my dear boy, my arm around you, & I feel the pulsation, thereby, as it were, of your excellent future & your admirable endowment; & I am yours just so

Henry James

ALS: Virginia MSS 6251 (9)

---

36. See the biographical register for Isabella Stewart Gardner.

My dearest boy Hans. Sept. *7th* 1900.

I am distressed (as well as relieved, of course) by your letter received this a.m.—giving me news of you that I had begun a good deal to worry at the absence of. I have been, lately, repeatedly on the point of writing you again—but lately sent a kind of emissary to you (in New York) in the person of a young painter-cousin of mine,[37] who has been with me much this summer, who has just gone to America & promised me to knock at your door, see you, from me, if possible, & report to me on your situation—tell me, from ocular evidence, what had become of you. She will, however—the said "Bay" Emmet—have missed you, through your absence,[38] & meanwhile your letter fills, a little, the gap. I fear you've had a devil of a time, & it all sounds very horrid & hateful. You don't tell me what has been the matter with you, or what your operation was *for*, & I can only commiserate & congratulate you (on the issue,) in a kind of tender, unillumined way. But all's well that ends well—I devoutly hope that you are really & solidly set on your feet again. Stick to Newport, to your good mother & to those gallant little brothers (who, I am sure are not less good,) till you can go quite safely alone. Then come to *me,* & I will do all I can to give you a further lift. It consoles me for your non-appearance here this summer that my season has been rather a burdened, complicated & troubled time. Family duties & anxieties have been heavy on me; my little house always full—so constantly occupied that if you had turned up I should have had to keep you along, ungraciously & unhappily, at the inn or in a lodging. But I trust the worst is over, or will be next month or thereabouts. My brother & sister-in-law are much with me, & he is seriously ill. But I *shall* be here in November, & till Xmas. If you *do* make your way over I shall be delighted to see you. But I have doubts & fears. I understand your desire, God knows, to get back to Europe, but I also understand that the practical problem may meet, easily, many delays. But

---

37. See the biographical register for Ellen Gertrude "Bay" Emmet. Her 1900 portrait of the newly shaven HJ, plus a sketch discovered beneath the finished canvas, are now displayed in the National Portrait Gallery (Washington).

38. The envelope is addressed to Hendrik Andersen at "19 Calvert Street, Newport." *The Newport Directory 1900, Containing a Directory of the Citizens, Street Directory, the City Record and Business Directory, Also Directory of Summer Residents* (Providence: Sampson, Murdock, 1900) lists the three "Anderson" [*sic*] brothers—"Andreas M. artist," "Arthur O.," and "Hendrick C. sculptor"—as boarding at 19 Calvert Street.

Lamb House counts on you for *some* keeping of our tryst. Get well first of all, & keep up your heart. I shall be much interested in the fortunes, over there, of the poor J. Elliotts. I see miseries for *him*—but a bath of her native air, & of friends & relatives & kindness, will do *her* a world of good. Give her, please, when you see her, my particular love. Good night, dear Hans. It's, as usual with my letter-time, much past midnight. I think of you right heartily & helpfully; I renew my blessing to your brothers, & I am yours always

Henry James

P.S. I enclose a poor little kodak-thing of *my* brother & me. He is thin & changed & I am fat & *shaved!*[39]

ALS: Virginia MSS 6251 (10)

105 PALL MALL. S.W.[40]

My dear Boy Hans.   January 12 *1901*.

It has been a great joy to me to hear from you in such good sort, & I think of you, in your temple of art on the banks of the Tiber, with uncommon satisfaction & sympathy. I'm delighted to gather that you established yourself without great worry or wait, & I send you my blessing on all you do & are. If good old Lincoln does hang about you,[41] so much the better, & if you've really got him I pray you may hold him tight. And on all the bright company in which you take him to dwell with you, may peace & abundance descend. How jolly it must be to be restored to Rome & the old life & the old light, at least, & the old loves—I mean, more particularly, as regards the last-named, the pure & independent passions of the mind & of the imagination. I rejoice that you saw my admirable sister-

---

39. At the outset of 1900 HJ shaved the beard he had worn since he was twenty-one (Kaplan, *Henry James,* 430–31).

40. HJ canceled "Reform Club" on the letterhead and wrote "105" before Pall Mall, the address of one of the club's bed-sitting rooms that, after December 1900, he used while in London.

41. In November 1900 a Buffalo, New York, committee invited Andersen to submit sketches for a Lincoln statue (see als, Andersen to Helena Andersen, 2 November 1900, HCA Papers, LC: Box 11, Folder 7). He wrote to his mother and brother on the same day as HJ's letter, declaring his attention "to make a great statue of 'Lincoln' and it will make a name for me if it is a success" (als, Andersen to Helena and Arthur Andersen, 12 January 1901, HCA Papers, LC: Box 1, Folder 8).

in-law, who mentioned to me your visit with very marked appreciation.[42] She views you with extraordinary favour. But I hope you won't fail altogether of a sight of my brother himself—he has a wondrous sense of things plastic, things modelled, things wrought. And he is a very delightful man—better even than I! We have both, you see, you & I, such endowed brothers that we can boast of them.——I am not, as you see, at Lamb House; the winter there had ceased to be tolerable, & I've come up to town for 3 months. It's a very dusky, dingy, fog-smothered town just now; but it is also many other things else, & is the place in the world in which the state of the atmosphere, on the whole, least matters. But I shall revert, about April 1st, with a long breath & a great glee. I hope with all my heart that the summer will bring you to England. If it does I shall lay my hand on you firmly & expect you to have a good bit of a fairy tale to tell me. May the fairies meanwhile then—by which I mean the felicities that an artist knows when he doesn't know the black devils of despair—smother you with their favours. Think of me as thinking of you very tenderly & confidently, & believe me yours, my dear Hans, always & ever

Henry James

P.S. Don't think of this as a thing to be "answered"—*damn* answers!

ALS: Virginia MSS 6251 (13)

LAMB HOUSE, RYE.

Dearest Boy Hendrik. July *1st 1901*.

I am more shocked & grieved than I can say by the bad news I get from you tonight, & I hold out to you, (with open arms, as it were,) the assurance of my tender sympathy—my very tenderest.[43] What a sad & sorry upshot of a whole winter's work—of so many months of high hope & good faith! It is odious, it's utterly upsetting & I don't know—or

---

42. HJ's sister-in-law, Alice Howe Gibbens James, the wife of William, met Andersen in late December 1900; William James did not meet him until late January 1901. In a joint letter to HJ on 25 January 1901, Alice and William James comment on making "the acquaintance of your friend Andersen. William is much pleased with him and as soon as he is feeling better we shall ask him to dine with us when he will bring photographs of his work. [William James's hand] He has given me his male & female human beings harnessed abreast, and despite a certain dryness in the execution I find them strangely fascinating and uplifting" (Skrupskelis and Berkeley, *William and Henry*, 161).

43. The "bad news" apparently concerned the Lincoln commission: in April 1901 the Buffalo Committee rejected Andersen's statue of Lincoln but subsequently accepted two bronze figures, only to remove them because of concerns about their nudity (unpublished als, Hendrik Andersen to Andreas Andersen, 23 June 1901, HCA Papers, LC: Box 11, Folder 8).

scarce—what to say to you about it that won't seem too poorly comforting. Patience & courage you clearly have in high measure—& one can only feel sure that you are throwing yourself upon them. Do that, my dear Boy, as hard as ever you can—& may they bravely bear the weight; but press also, I beg you, with no less intensity, on my affectionate friendship—let me feel that it reaches you & that it sustains & penetrates. I had begun to worry at not hearing from you—had a vague suspicion that things mightn't be well, & had been saying to myself daily for the last 2 or 3 weeks that I *must* write you within the 24 hours. I don't even now make out whether you got my letter of about 2 months ago, addressed to Sebasti's Bank, & acknowledging your Lincoln photos.* I had lost & forgotten your Ripetta address,[44] & didn't know what to do, & my brother & his wife, who have been with me till this very day, suggested that Sebasti would be sure to get at you. If he *didn't* get at you, it must have seemed.to you indeed a terribly long time since I have (before *this,*) made you a sign. I hope this at least will reach you straight & soon. You are evidently very weary & worn, & small wonder; & your torrid Perugia strikes me as but scantily refreshing—though better, I doubt not, than your red-hot Rome. Better than either of these is little cool & bowery (& even flowery) Lamb House, where a small but secure apartment opens, from tonight, to its utmost width to you, & holds itself open till you come. Isn't it possible to you to come? Is the journey to England out of the question for you? Isn't there something I can do to help to make it feasible? What I should like is that you should come & stay with me till you are wholly rested & consoled & cheered—now [*sic*][45] matter how long it takes: the longer the better. You can't summer altogether in Italy—it would be the worst policy & the worst economy—& insanity into the bargain. Therefore, as you must get off somewhere, why not get off *here,* where the air & the conditions, let alone my personal solicitude, will be for you as a cool healing bath? I can give you a studio all to yourself—& would share with you my last crust! I am looking to a quiet summer & have no complications in prospect save that my brother & his wife, who sail for the U.S. on August 31st, come back here next month, for 2 or 3 weeks. (They left me this a.m. for Nauheim, where he is to go through a longish cure.) But that needn't interfere—I can *place* you, if not one way, then another, at *any* time. And *that* is long ahead. Only let me hear from you, & hear that

---

44. Andersen moved his studio from Via Margutta to 16 Passeggiatta di Ripetta, southwest of the Piazza del Popolo and closer to the Tiber.

45. HJ's misspelling of "no" as "now" perhaps suggests the urgency of his invitation to Andersen.

my proposal doesn't present insurmountable difficulties. So far as there *are* difficulties they must be flattened down. I interest myself greatly in your fountain & its figures;[46] but what a dismal doom for a sculptor to work for a great vulgar stupid community that revels in every hideous vulgarity & only quakes at the clean & blessed nude!—the last refuge of Honour! But it's late, as usual—I'm a midnight letter-writer only—and I give you my benediction. Yours, my dear Hendrik, very heartily & hopefully

Henry James

*These latter I found only *here,* on returning from 4 or 5 months (the whole winter,) spent in London. Hence my delay. They hadn't been forwarded to me, for some reason.

ALS: Virginia MSS 6251 (15)

LAMB HOUSE, RYE, SUSSEX.

My dear, dear Boy.   *Oct. 5. 1901.*

I won't hang the consciousness of a long letter round your neck like a millstone—I will only thank you, with a tenderer pat on the back than ever, for your prompt signal to me of your safety—after a woefully weary journey, I can well believe.[47] But now that you're the young priest within the great temple again, with the flame glowing on your altar & your idols, bless their brave limbs & blank eyes, ranged round about in its light—now that this is the case I feel easy & glad for you, I like to think of you so "fixed" for the long, soft Roman winter, & I wish you, my dear, dear Boy, such a high tide of inspiration & execution as will float you over every worry & land you in peace & renown. I miss you—keep on doing so—out of all proportion to the too few hours you were here—& even go so far as to ask myself whether visits so damnably short haven't more in them to groan, than to thank, for. However, the memory *is* a kind of beggarly stopgap till we can meet again. Only there abides with me the vision of your deep & damnable anxiety about your father[48]—in connection with

---

46. Andersen planned to use the figures rejected by Buffalo in "a large fountain. . . . which I [s]hall do with a big bold spirit" (als, Hendrik Andersen to Andreas Andersen, 23 June 1901, HCA Papers, LC: Box 11, Folder 8).

47. Andersen initially considered spending two weeks with HJ but finally stayed less than a week, appearing on 21 September and arriving back in Rome on 28 September (als, Hendrik Andersen to Mrs. Helene Andersen, [August 1901?] and 28 September 1901, HCA Papers, LC: Box 11, Folder 8).

48. Andersen was instrumental in separating his mother, Helene Monsen Andersen, and his brothers from the alcoholic Anders Andersen, returning his father to Norway in 1900 with a modest annual stipend.

which I feel as if I must have struck you as helpless & unconsoling. Yet I am full of the sense of your trouble, & when I think of you it's the 1st thing I think of. Don't let yourself get nervous about it—deal with it piecemeal, from month to month, as you can—& you will so break it into small pieces, so to speak—deprive it of mass & magnitude. Don't dream of *my* little squalid botheration, which is rapidly receding into the past.[49]——— Yea, verily, will we have some Italian walks & talks again! I foresee a real *crisis* of homesickness for the loved land looming ahead of me at no great distance & having, no long time hence, to be seriously reckoned with. Then you will be there to help me to reckon—more than I've ever helped *you*. Addio, caro—buon riposo, & above all, buon coragio [*sic*] & buona fede & buon lavoro & buona salute! [It.: Goodbye, dear—good rest, & above all, good courage & faith & work & health!] Do *tell* me if anything more occurs to trouble you in the Norway business. I can't bear not to know your nightmares. I hold you close & am ever your affectionate old friend

Henry James

ALS: Virginia MSS 6251 (18)

105 PALL MALL, S.W.

My dear, dear, dearest Hendrik.   Feb. *9th* 1902.

Your news fills me with horror & pity, & how can I express the tenderness with wh: it makes me think of you & the aching wish to be near you & put my arms round you? My heart fairly bleeds & breaks at the vision of you *alone,* in your wicked & indifferent old far-off Rome, with this haunting, blighting, unbearable sorrow.[50] The sense that I can't *help* you, see you, talk to you, touch you, hold you close & long, or do anything to make you rest on me, & feel my deep participation—this torments me, dearest boy, makes me ache for you, & for myself; makes me gnash my teeth & groan at the bitterness of things. I can only take refuge in hoping you are *not* utterly alone, that some human tenderness of *some* sort, some kindly

---

49. HJ refers to "the tragedy of the Doom of the Smiths," a domestic upheaval brewing at Lamb House during Andersen's October visit. See HJ's letters of 19–20 September 1901 to Jessie Allen and 26 September 1901 to Alice Howe Gibbens James (both in *Henry James Letters,* 4:202–4, 204–8) for accounts of HJ's dismissal, after sixteen years of service, of two household servants, husband and wife, for drunkenness.

50. HJ had received from Hendrik Andersen news of the 1 February 1902 death from tuberculosis of his brother Andreas, less than a month after his marriage to Olivia Cushing.

voice & hand *are* near you that may make a little the difference. What a dismal winter you must have had, with this staggering blow as the climax! I don't of course know *what* fragment of friendship there may be to draw near to you, & in my uncertainty my image of you is of the darkest, and my pity, as I say, feels so helpless. I wish I could go to Rome & put my hands on you (oh, how lovingly I should lay them!) but that, alas, is odiously impossible. (Not, moreover, that, apart from *you,* I should so much as like to be there now.) I find myself thrown back on anxiously, & doubtless vainly, wondering if there may not, after a while, [be] some possibility of your coming to England, of the current of your trouble inevitably carrying you here—so that I might take consoling, soothing, infinitely close & tender & affectionately-healing *possession* of you.[51] This is the one thought that relieves me about you a little—& I wish you might fix your eyes on it for the idea, just, of the possibility. I am in town for a few weeks, but I return to Rye April 1st, & sooner or later to *have* you there & do for you, to put my arm round you & *make* you lean on me as on a brother & a lover, & keep you on & on, slowly comforted or at least relieved of the first bitterness of pain—this I try to imagine as thinkable, attainable, not wholly out of the question. There I am, at any rate, & there is my house & my garden & my table, & my studio—such as it is!—& your room, & your welcome, & your place everywhere—& I press them upon you, oh so earnestly, dearest boy, if isolation & grief & the worries you are overdone with become intolerable to you. There they are, I say—to fall upon, to rest upon, to find whatever possible shade of oblivion in. I will *nurse* you through your dark passage. I wish I could do something *more*—something straighter & nearer & more immediate; but such as it is please let it sink into you. Let all my tenderness, dearest boy, do *that.* This is all now. I wired you 3 words an hour ago. I can't *think* of your sister-in-law—I brush her vision away and your history with your father, as I've feared it, has haunted me all winter. I embrace you with almost a passion of pity.

Henry James

ALS: Virginia MSS 6251 (19)

51. Andersen assured Olivia Cushing Andersen that he would be in America as soon after 1 June as possible, but managed to see HJ en route. "I find dear Henry James as good and as kind as ever, and I will spend another day with him here in his beautiful little house," he wrote to his mother on 22 May 1902 (HCA Papers, LC: Box 11, Folder 9).

Feb: 28*th 1902*

Dearest, dearest Boy, more tenderly embraced than I can say!—How woefully you must have wondered at my apparently horrid & heartless silence since your last so beautiful, noble, exquisite letter! *But,* dearest Boy, I've been dismally *ill*—as I was even when I wrote to you from town; & it's only within a day or two that free utterance has—to *this* poor extent—become possible to me. *Don't waste any pity, any words, on me now,* for it's, at last, blissfully over, I'm convalescent, on firm ground, safe, gaining daily—only weak & "down" & spent, & above all like a helpless pigmy before my accumulation of the mountain of a month's letters, &c. To make a long story of the shortest, I was taken in London, on Jan. 29th—2 days after getting there, with a malignant sudden attack, through a chill, of inflammation of the bowels; which threw me into bed, for a week, howling. Then I had a few days of false & apparent recuperation—*one* of which was the Sunday I wrote you from the Athenaeum on receipt of *your* direful letter. But I felt myself collapsing, *re*lapsing again, & hurried down here on Feb. 11th just in time to save, as it were, my life from another wretched siege out of my own house. I tumbled into bed here & had a dozen wretched days of complicated, aggravated relapse: but at least nursed, tended, cared for, with all zeal & needfulness. So I've pulled through—& am out—& surprisingly soon—of a very deep dark hole. *In* my deep hole, how I thought yearningly, helplessly, dearest Boy of *you* as your last letter gives you to me, & as I take you, to my heart. I determined, deliberately, *not* to *wire* you, for I felt it would but cruelly worry & alarm you; & each day I reached out to the hope of some scrawl—I mean toward some possibility of a word to you. But that has come only now. Now, at least, my weak arms still can fold you close. Infinitely, deeply, as deeply as you will have felt, for yourself, was I touched by your 2d letter. I respond to every throb of it, I participate in every pang. I've gone through Death, & Deaths, enough in my long life, to know how all that we *are,* all that we *have,* all that is best of us within, our genius, our imagination, our passion, our whole personal being, become then but aids & channels & open gates to suffering, to being flooded. But, it is better so. Let yourself go & *live,* even as a lacerated, mutilated lover, with your grief, your loss, your sore, unforgettable consciousness. *Possess* them & let them possess you, & life, so, will still hold you in her arms, & press you to her breast, & keep you, like the great merciless but still *most* enfolding and never disowning mighty Mother, on & on for things to come. Beautiful & unspeakable your acct. of relation to Andreas. Sacred & beyond tears. How I wish I had known him, admirable, loveable boy—but you make me: I *do*. Well, he is *all* yours now: he lives in you & out of all pain. Wait, & you will see; hold fast, sit tight, *stick hard,* & more things than I can tell you now will come back to you. But you know, in your courage, your genius & your patience, more of these things than I need try thus to stammer to you. And now I am tired & spent. I only, for goodnight, for five minutes, take you to my heart. And I'm better, better, better, dearest Boy; don't think of my having been ill. Think only of my love & that I am yours always & ever

Henry James.

ALS: Virginia MSS 6251 (20)

Torquay.

Beloved Boy! March 19*th*. [1902]⁵²

This is a small fond word you are not to acknowledge or notice by sound or sign, under penalty of having me come down on you straight & strong. The reason of it is, 1st: that I *can't* have your beautiful last letter without the necessity of putting my hand out & laying it upon you, touched as I am to the heart, with the tenderest, softest, most healing & soothing benediction. Let it rest on your shoulder, perch there, lightly, like a dove whose wing you may stroke with your cheek; & feel it there as long as possible. Then, 2d: You mustn't, absolutely, waste another thought on any recent & now quite past & done-with little trouble of mine. I am admirably, blessedly better, & only wanting to go back to work in a week or two. But I shall stick in a little more absence & patience—every day in this lovely place, & bland soft air, being meanwhile a remedy & a general boon. Think of me there as all yours—but only as I *ought* to be—your solidly convalescent & solidly fond & faithful

Henry James

ALS: Virginia MSS 6251 (76)

LAMB HOUSE, RYE, SUSSEX.

My dear, dear, my very dear Hendrik. August 13*th 1902*

I won't pretend that it isn't a blow to learn from you that you are passing so near me on the narrow seas without coming any nearer. How it makes me wish I could have put out a longer arm and grabbed you in your

---

52. The envelope has been clipped for the stamps, removing half of the cancellation, but the year is reckoned by HJ's presence in Torquay.

flight—have drawn you in & held you, for a little, close. Somehow I had been counting on you, waiting for you, promising myself your September visit, and now you are off in space & who knows when it will be? But of course I understand how natural it is that you should be making for Paris by the shortest cut. With your mother & your brother you can only want as few stops & complications as possible, & the straightest & simplest way. I only wish I might have seen *them* too. But these things must still—they *will* still, be. May you get to Rome again, & to work, with as little delay as possible, & as much relief & ease & success. I wish I could speak with any definiteness of my getting to Italy this winter. All I can say is that the time has come round again when I yearn, constantly, to be there for a longish stay, when I keep thinking of it & desiring it & planning—though as yet rather ineffectually—for it. But it will *come*—it's only a question of time. I should be unhappy indeed if I didn't believe that I should sometime come & pick you up there & take you off with me for a turn among some dear old places—seen in dreams—that I want to go to & never *have*—a really romantic little *giro* [It.: tour]. Be sure that I shall put my hand upon you the first moment I can; & meantime heaven speed the day. It's a good deal of a torment to hear from you of the so "strange" & so busy time you've had in America & to know nothing more of it—& to feel only, in vain, how I should have liked to have you here to tell me of it in detail, for comfort & sympathy, for all understanding & participation. But I hope what you mean is that you have been, with whatever toil & trouble, able to put something solid under your feet & something bright before your eyes. Good night, dearest boy; it *is* a pang that I'm not to see you. But we must make it up as soon as we can & as fully, & meantime you must march to glory with lengthening strides. I send my blessing to your mother—may she find peace & comfort in being with you & being able to help you & be helped by you. Yours, dearest boy, always & ever

Henry James

ALS: Virginia MSS 6251 (21)

LAMB HOUSE, RYE, SUSSEX.

My dear dear Hendrik.   November 15*th 1902*

I have been systematically silent since the receipt of your last good letter—I haven't, believe me, dear Boy, been thoughtlessly so. I thought it really kinder & tenderer not to come down on you too instantly with a reply & so leave you with a sense that I must soon again be written to. I felt that I could make you think of me almost more by not writing, & I can

41

assure you that it has been a means for me of thinking every day, & ever so longingly, of *you*. But I think we have now been subjected to discipline enough, & I lay my hands affectionately on your shoulders, so to hold you well & firmly before me, & myself scarcely less before *you*. You wrote me in so cheerful & hopeful a strain & spoke so well of being peacefully settled & launched in work, & of having your mother[53] so conveniently established with you, that I have been cultivating optimism, & almost rose-colour, about you, & indulging in none but soothing images. I earnestly hope I have not been wrong in this & that peace & ease have been your portion in some decent degree. I have been taking the greatest comfort in the fact of your mother's presence, in your having her to break your solitude, create your home, & generally care for you, & be cared for (which is better for you still;) I was *haunted,* all last winter, by the vision of your lonely labours & lonely misery, & feel that I must never again think of you that way. What I almost mainly hope is that your mother is herself happy, that she likes Rome, "appreciates" it, as they say, & that it above all agrees with her & keeps her well. Surely the beautiful Italian autumn ought to be to her a benediction—for I assume the season *has* been beautiful this year. Much of it has been so even in this grey northern corner. Here I am, where you left me & where I was when I last wrote you, & here I shall be till some time early in January, when I go for 3 or 4 months up to town. I am infinitely touched by your delightful response to what I said of my lively desire that we shall before too long get some time together in Italy; but as I read you over I wince under a fear that I may have seemed to say to you that that time might be, definitely, this spring, so that you may be disappointed, or think me a broken reed, if I say that, as matters now stand, I have little hope of being able to spend these next months out of England. I am *always* yearning for Italy, & I am distinctly, I think, working *nearer* to the prospect of going back there for a good big generous mouthful, even if it be the last of my life. But circumstances just now don't favour; the thing is in truth, as an *actuality,* (for sordid but pressing reasons that I needn't trouble you with,) impossible. The dream, on the other hand, is always there, & you are always *in* the dream, & the fact of your being so counts immensely in making me work & strive & pray, & say to you Hold on tight & have patience with me & I will repay you tenfold. I quite gloat over the idea that you must be *always* more or less in Rome. I call down blessings on the

---

53. Helene Monsen Andersen came to live with Andersen in Rome in the fall of 1902 after the death of Andreas and the "resettlement" of Anders Andersen.

42

particular work your letter tells me of, heroic young master of the grand style that you are. It all sounds terribly beautiful & big & difficult, but I well know that therein, exactly, is the interest & the honour. Tell me when you *easily* can that things are not ill with you & that your ideas take shape & your shapes take solidity. At present good night; I am wholly alone now, & I sit scribbling to you, past midnight, in my little upstairs green room where we have sat together. Here too may we sit again. I send my hearty good wishes to your mother & I am, my dear, dear Hendrik, yours always & ever

Henry James.

P.S. I am forgetting to say that *now*—only now—my ponderous & long winded book[54] goes to you, since you so gallantly ask for it. I haven't thought it *fair* to send it sooner—fair, I mean, to the fact that you may possibly attempt, really, to read it. But *don't,* my dear Hendrik, do that—it will lay you low in the flower of your youth. Put it on your table, if you like, that the world may see I've sent it to you; but don't think [it] necessary to plough *through* it. It has to go from London, as I haven't a copy in the house; otherwise I would write to your name in it. But that I shall yet live to do. Yours again—& again!

H.J.

ALS: Virginia MSS 6251 (22)

LAMB HOUSE, RYE, SUSSEX.

My dearest Hendrik.   June 13*th* 1903

It was a melancholy satisfaction to get your good letter a few days since: a satisfaction because it told me of your splendid activity, production & courage; but a melancholy one because of the sad vision of your confinement all summer to the torrid Rome, & of the anxiety I can't help feeling about you. It wouldn't do for *me;* but you know what you are in for, & I hope you won't be too damnably the worse for it. May your path be cheered by your seeing your work grow & exult & triumph: also by your not finding that your mother, your sister in law & your brother rise up (or lie down) & curse you for what you are doing to them. Please assure them of my very earnest sympathy with them. Your devotion (& theirs,) makes me long indeed to see what you are doing & *have* done. I wish you didn't follow so little portable & so much payable a trade: but since you do, I hold

---

54. HJ's "ponderous & long winded book" was *The Wings of the Dove,* published in England on 30 August 1902.

43

you fast to your promise to send me your photographs both of your creatures & their creator—the latter especially if, as I understand you, it includes the portrait of your mother, which I shall be very glad to possess. Your creatures *sound* magnificent, & I pray that fame & fortune may await them. I send you meanwhile a slightly dreary portrait of myself. Keep it, all the same, before you & let it remind you that avenging angels will scourge you if your words about coming to this country at the summer's end are— turn out to be—words of hollowness & mockery! Don't put me off with such, but show that you *believe* I await you. Come & stay with me here as long as you can—not for the poor few hours of your former passings. I sit fast in this place from now to Christmas next—so you can't say I don't give you time. If you reach the end of your long roast alive, this will really be the *only* thing for you, the blessed & beneficent, the cooling, resting, healing thing. So I bid you good night on it, &, always grasping you hard & holding you close, am yours, dearest Hendrik, immensely

Henry James

ALS: Virginia MSS 6251 (24)

My dear, dear Hendrik.   August 23*d 1903*

I send forth this rocket as a signal—not exactly from a ship in the last distress, but from a vessel drifting rather drearily & aimlessly in respect to the hope you held out to me (in I trust no mocking & treacherous spirit,) at the beginning of the summer. You beguiled me then with fair words of promise, with the assurance that you counted on being able to be in England in September; with the shining intimation that the said September would, in part, at least, roll over your head under this very roof. I needn't tell you how fondly, since then, I have thought of this possibility, & with what lively pleasure I should learn that the vision hasn't been shattered by anything that has happened since. I don't want to goad you, to prod you, even to hurry you, or in any way whatever to harry you: I only want to let you know, after so many weeks of silence, that my spirit hangs tenderly about you—so that if your idea still holds good you may be reminded of how warm my welcome will be. You must have had an heroic summer—& it would be horrible to me to have to take it from you that your reward is *not* to be in some liberal taste of our northern freshness. I know your complications—they are all part of the heroic life. But I hope they rather *make* for your getting away a while from Rome. You will all be worth 3 times as much to yourselves for returning there—or certainly you individually will—if you breathe for a few weeks an air as different as possible. Let off at me at any rate—however simply & singly—a little red—or rather a sweet little rose-pink—rocket, a little answering signal. Don't use up the dregs of your spent nervous fluid on a letter that you'll hate to have to write, but send me ten affectionate words—not taking time & strength about me even if you have to give me bad news. All I want is *some* news—a scrap; in which I shall jubilate if it's good. We've had a horrible wintry, drenching summer here—I hope you've had thereby something of a cool one & that your mother & sister have happily resisted & are not the worse for it. I send you all my benediction, & I am, my dear dear Hendrik, always right affectionately yours

Henry James

ALS: Virginia MSS 6251 (25)

Beloved Hendrik!   [3 December 1903]

The "pedestal of the young count" has not come, but your good letter has (it sounds—that does—like a phrase out of Ollendorf[55]—& if you don't know what Ollendorf is, ask your sister, & she will tell you.) The pedestal meanwhile was announced to me some days ago (by the express-agents) as about to arrive, so that unless the custom house is sitting over it in solemn conclave, as a tribute to its inordinate value & beauty, I suppose it may turn up any hour. Yet I don't wait for it to write you—I shall make my thanks a separate business after it has come; but send this off in immediate gratitude for your letter. I rejoice, affectionately, to hear from you, but wasn't in the least "missing" it—compared, I mean, with my so perfectly knowing, always, how much else you have to do than drive the stiff steel pen. I wasn't even waiting for it to write to you—for all my native disposition to do *that* was even now rapidly coming to a head. I have been wanting you to know how often & how tenderly my thoughts hover about you, & how still more after you had gone than while you were here it came over me (as I fear I didn't half decently express at the time,) that your generosity in pushing all the way from Paris & across the sickening Channel for 4 or 5 mere dull days at L[amb]. H[ouse]. was infinitely touching to me. Well, wait till opportunity favours, & I'll do as much, & more, for you. I've been pretty well alone since then, except for 3 or 4 short absences,

---

55. Heinrich Gottfried Ollendorf (1803–1865) published numerous self-help guides to rapid language acquisition.

& my walks are solitary & my evenings severe. But the autumn ebbs fast, & the New Year, which will bring some changes of life for me with it is approaching with strides. (I mean that I go up to London for 3 or 4 months sometime in January.) Nothing could please me more than your telling me that you are robust & mighty for your heroic labour. Out of such turmoil & travail are the creations of genius born. But if you are in your studio before dawn I hope you are in your bed not much after sunset! Give my kindest regards, please, to Mrs. Andreas & tell her that I will with great pleasure & sympathy give my best attention to anything she may feel disposed to send me—as a matter of writing to be looked at.[56] May your winter together—& I mean for your mother too—be balmy alike for soul & sense. Good night, dear boy—I respond immensely to your wish that we might have an hour, again, in my little old oak parlour together. But that we assuredly *shall,* when the good day comes back, & I meanwhile pat you affectionately on the back, across Alps & Appennines [*sic*]. I draw you close, I hold you long, & I am ever so tenderly, dearest Hendrik, yours

Henry James
Dec. 3. 1903

ALS: Virginia MSS 6251 (28)

LAMB HOUSE, RYE, SUSSEX.

My dear dear Hendrik.   [4 June 1904]

I bade good-bye to Arthur yesterday a.m., after too short a visit (only from the previous afternoon;) & I haven't had a moment to write since.[57] His return ticket was by Newhaven & Dieppe (not Dover & Calais;) so that he *had* to go back to London, &, in short, had very little time. But he

---

56. Olivia Cushing Andersen had already heard from Hendrik of HJ's proffered help. See her 4 October 1903 diary entry: "I had a good letter from Henry [i.e., Hendrik] from Henry James' and he says that H.J. is willing to correct any manuscript I wish to send him and do anything he can to make the book a success." The entry for 3 August 1904 voices an ambivalence toward HJ's work that was shared by Hendrik: "H.J. didn't write at all complimentarily, evidently he sees I have no talent and as he cares more, much more for the way a thing is said than for its meaning and intention, from his point of view I shall do nothing. What I succeed in doing, I know seems to him thin and bodiless. His own work is wonderfully full and solid yet suggests nothing, for the reason I suppose he has nothing to suggest" (HCA Papers, LC: Box 28, Folders 3 and 4, Vols. 14 and 15).

57. Arthur O. Andersen, Hendrik's brother, was a musician. HJ's letter of 6 June 1904 to William Dean Howells, who visited Lamb House on 31 May, contains only an oblique reference to Arthur's visit: "my young man who followed you was only a night & a day!" (Michael Anesko, *Letters, Fictions, Lives: Henry James and William Dean Howells* [New York: Oxford University Press, 1997], 405]).

dined & spent the night, & I was as kind to him as I could be—he won't tell you, I think, the contrary. I liked him greatly, found him a most delightful, engaging & charming youth, full of simplicity & sincerity, as well as, evidently, the love of his subject & the love of work. There is even something rather pathetic to me in seeing him thrown all alone, so young & so ingenuous, on that great fierce battlefield, or tropical artistic wilderness, of Paris; but on the other hand, with the evident beauty of his nature & seriousness of his inspiration, he makes one *believe* in him—believe that such clean & straight young geniuses carry with them their talisman. I shall always be glad to see him again, as I assured him; & shall watch, with interest, what becomes of him. All this will sufficiently tell you that I rejoice in your having sent him to me. For part of what I liked in him, too, was *you*, to whom his resemblance of look, tone, voice, expression, is at moments extraordinary. He brought you back to my side, at these moments—& that has made up to me a little for our long, & inevitably soundless, separation. Your letter broke this interval quite blessedly—but of course you know, on your side, why I haven't harassed you with postal matter that has had to be noticed & acknowledged. I have known you were leading a life of heroic concentration & that is really, always, a spell that one hesitates to break in upon. I, on my side, have been very motionless & adventureless—3 or 4 months of the winter in London, & the rest here, which is charming now. I have been very decently well & seem to continue so; but I greatly regret to hear of your vertigo & other penalties of over-work.[58] They worry me truly, & make me immensely wish I could see you. Arthur spoke of them (his impression of them) too, & they are the only blot on the joy of hearing from you of such a magnificent record of work. This is beautiful, admirable, to know of, but you mustn't pay too much for it. You will say, I know, that you can't do otherwise—& I shall not know what to answer, properly, to that till I *see* you & can talk with you. This must somehow occur—isn't there any chance of your coming to England this summer? I go, definitely, to America on *Aug. 24th*—for the autumn, winter & spring. Arthur tells me you have an urgent proposal to go there & "teach"—in a way that will give you a basis & a certainty. I hope you are *thinking* of it, seriously—if only because I shall then see you there &

---

58. HJ learned details of Hendrik's condition from Olivia Cushing Andersen in Boston. In a series of almost daily letters to her written from 13 June until 25 October 1904 from Turin's Instituto Gradenico, Hendrik described a regimen of electrical shocks, nasal surgery, and regular doses of quinine to treat his Ménière's disease, the cause of recurring vertigo, nausea, and headaches since he was eighteen. See HCA Papers, LC: Box 12, Folder 1.

perhaps be able to help you to bear it. I am going there (partly) for indispensable money—do *you* the same. I am too far off from you, of course, very *finally* to advise; but there are things I should like to say to you. The 1st is, at any rate, the vertigo question. Isn't that the result of long *foodless* hours of work—too long intervals on too little food? It used to be so with me—*stomachic* & digestive. Watch that frequent cause well. And have you any small photos of your new figures? I yearn to see them. Find a moment to write me something of your general & particular outlook for these next months. Tell me the American idea does count for you. Tell me you *may* be near enough to come to see me before I go. Tell me you see light for a cessation of your physical ills. Give my hearty blessing to your mother & sister—tell Mrs. Olivia that I congratulate her on her consoling & absorbing work. And believe me, dearest Hendrik, your fond & faithful old friend

Henry James
June 4th 1904.

ALS: Virginia MSS 6251 (30)

LAMB HOUSE, RYE, SUSSEX.

My dear dear Hendrik.   August 10*th 1904*

No letter from you was ever more charming & touching to me than your last from Montefiascone[59]—wonderful romantic spot of which I envy you (even till I *ache* with it,) the so intimate & friendly knowledge. Every word of you is as soothing as a caress of your hand, & the sense of the whole as sweet to me as being able to lay my own upon *you*. It's so much money in my pocket—that of my otherwise so baffled spirit—to know you are at your ease in a good high place, with rest & peace & idleness & cool airs & brown cheeks & glorious wine all keeping you company; to say nothing of your still more human companions,—whose being with you I more & more rejoice in & to whom I am particularly glad (both for him & for you,) to know that your brother Arthur is added. Make him a sign of my ever so kindly remembrance. Stay as long & lie as loose as you by a stretched possibility can—you will be of ever so much more value to yourself & to the world in the end—to say nothing of your being of more, my dear, dear Hendrik, to your poor fond old H.J. I only groan over its being so beastly long, of necessity, before I can hope to get from your lips

---

59. Montefiascone is a central Italian town near the southeastern edge of Lake Bolsena, approximately fifty miles northwest of Rome.

the charming echo & side-wind of your Italian summer—even as I had from you so beautifully, last year, the story of your primitive Norcia. I "sail", heaven help me, on Aug. 24th—not to return, very probably, till late in the spring—all of which means, doesn't it?—dreary and deadly postponements. But may the time be full, for you, of triumphant completions & consummations—without a solitary blink of giddiness. It was after I last wrote you that your photos. arrived, & I haven't as yet so much as thanked you for them directly. But I find them, dear Hendrik, difficult to speak of to you—they terrify me so with their evidence as of *madness* (almost) in the scale on which you are working! It is magnificent—it is sublime, it is heroic; & the idea & composition of your group-circled fountain, evidently a very big thing. Only I feel as if it were let loose into space like a blazing comet—with you, personally, dangling after like the tail, & I ask myself where my poor dear confident reckless Hendrik is being whirled, through the dark future, & where he is going to be dropped. I want to be there, wherever it is, to catch you in my arms—for my nerves, at all events, give way, with the too-long tension of your effort, even if yours don't. And I yearn, too, for the *smaller* masterpiece; the condensed, consummate, caressed, intensely filled-out thing. But forgive this obscure, this wild & wandering talk. The photographs are admirably interesting & give the impression of an immense effect; but to know where I am, & where *you* are, I ought to *be* there, in front of each group, with my questions to ask & your brave answers to take, while my arm is over your shoulder; & for all that *ci vuol' tempo* [It.: it takes time], alas. Meanwhile, at any rate, my dear boy, I pat you on the back lovingly, tenderly, tenderly— & I am, with every kindest message to your blessed companions, yours, my Hendrik, always and ever

Henry James

ALS: Virginia MSS 6251 (32)

21 East Eleventh St. New York:[60]

My dear dear Hendrik.

Dec. 9th 1904.

Three days ago, in Boston, I saw your sister Olivia, & talking with her brought to a head the intensity of my long desire to write to you; a desire you will scoff at, most justly, in the face of the silence I have so horribly kept. I have before me your beautiful & touching letter of the last days of

---

60. Twenty-one East Eleventh Street, New York, was the home of Mary Cadwalader Jones (1850–1935), the wife of Edith Wharton's brother and one of HJ's most intimate female friends since 1883.

August (21st,) which I have repeatedly re-read (to taste, as it were, the tenderness of it,) & if in spite of this I have remained so miserably mute you must put it all down to the explanation of *all* the delays & shortcomings & embarrassments that I now treat myself to—that complicating, devouring "America" that is the scapegoat of my conscience from day to day & hour to hour. But I won't take time for vain demonstrations: if I hadn't ever so constantly & affectionately *thought* of you, *that* monstrosity would be worth my elucidating: but nothing else. Seeing Mrs. Andreas, dear graceful & gentle lady, was an immense interest to me, & being able to ask her 500 questions a great joy. She will perhaps write you of our talk & of the fond intensity with which it hung about you—but she won't perhaps have understood even herself what a shock it was to me to learn that you had had to make that troubled pilgrimage to Turin,[61] in consequence of your not having been as much set up by your summer as I was stupidly taking for granted. You must have had[,] dearest boy, an anxious & a weary time—I can measure what you will have been through by my sense of your infinite capacity for not breaking down till the screw (of the unbearable) has really turned once too often. Olivia tells me you were better before she left, that your Turin specialist had advised you to good purpose &c—as to which I trust her report isn't all too rose-coloured. But, for God's sake, dear, dear boy, work gently & *sanely* (sanely;)[62] watch yourself well, put on the brake, twiddle your thumbs, merely, as much as possible, & *always* merely twiddle them (lying back in a chair) when you think of your poor helpless far-off but all devoted H.J., who seems condemned almost never to be near you, yet who, if he *were,* would lay upon you a pair of hands soothing, sustaining, positively *healing,* in the quality of their pressure. Mrs. Andreas showed me, in a delicious fat album-book, a perfect treasure of photographs, documents & illustrations of all your recent life & work, & as I hung over them yearningly (for all the vividness of Italy and of *you* that came up out of them,) I found myself (in the deadly—yet so goodly!—Boston street,) fairly envying you your conditions, in spite of the element of darkness & difficulty mixed with them. All the photos. of your work (& there were more & newer ones than I had seen before) quickened my conception of its greatness & its beauty—of the big,

---

61. Her diary entry for 4 October 1904 records, "We're again in Rome, but tomorrow H[endrik] and A[rthur] and Gustavo leave—the first to see a doctor in Turin." The entry for 1 November 1904 notes that "H. is back" (HCA Papers, LC: Box 28, Folder 4, Vol. 15).

62. HJ repeats the barely legible word for clarity's sake.

brave, sustained & magnificent conception that you're allowing to "chaw" you up. Well, you are killing yourself in a splendid cause, if you *are* killing yourself. (If I really *believed* you were I would of course come & smash a few dozen statues for you—smash them for brazen Idols feeding on your flesh—smash them to clear the air.) And then all the sweet snapshots of your villeggiatura [It.: country holidays] days and groups!—they filled me with a nostalgia (3 or 4 happy ones—so loveable and touchable—of you in your habit as you live!) that brought the tears to my eyes. I wanted to borrow the volume & live with it for a week! But I came on here the next day, where I am to spend these several weeks to come! I have been since my arrival (in the U.S.) only in New England; very happily, all the autumn, in different country regions, wh: struck me, for the most part as lovely in their way—little as their way is that of Montefiascone. I mean now to try to see what I can of the rest of the land—with some literary & bookmaking purpose—which will keep me on till late in the spring; that is if I don't break down for weariness & nostalgia. New York affects me rather fearfully, just on this 1st blush, & I am full of all sorts of homesicknesses & bewilderments. Nevertheless I am interested too; every one is extraordinary kind and friendly, the months rush away—*and* you must come to me at dear little old L[amb] H[ouse] next summer. Think of me there with an easy mind, & let me only yearn for your enabling me to think in somewhat the same way of *you*. I hold you, dearest boy, in my innermost love, & count on your feeling me—in every throb of your soul & sense—so do it. Keep up your heart & swing your hammer wide, & we will have good days together again yet. Yours, my dear, dear Hendrik, always & more than ever

Henry James

P.S. My address is always:
95 Irving St.
Cambridge, Mass.
ALS: Virginia MSS 6251 (34)

21, EAST ELEVENTH STREET. NEW YORK

My dear, dear Hendrik.   May 11*th 1905*.

Heaven send that this may reach you before you leave Rome, though it is nothing more than a poor pale word to ease you a little, & urge you & bless you & lift your heavy, weary wings for you, as you begin your course. I saw Olivia Andersen a few days since in Boston, & she told me about you much, & it was not very cheering—apart from the photographs of your magnificent figures, which it was a joy to me to behold.[63] They are an immense stride forward on what you had done before, fine as that too was, & they make me very proud of your genius & very happy in it. But it has gone hard with me to hear of your continued states of the head & attacks of vertigo, & I can't resist a certain uneasiness in thinking of your solitary voyage & your possibly being affected unfavourably by *that*. But I am sustained by this idea that I shan't (if you do sail at the beginning of June,) quite wholly fail to see you.[64] I sail myself, for England, on July 4th, & I expect to be in Boston, or near by, from *about* the 10th June to that date. Therefore God grant we can meet, for if we don't when & where the devil shall we later on or elsewhere? Mrs. Olivia tells me of the plan for your sailing again for Genoa early in the summer. I shall be back at Lamb House by July 15th (heaven send!) but what good will that do either of us if you are streaking off to 3000 miles away? However, we will talk of these things, dear boy, when I really can lay my hands on you—& how I *shall* lay them!—& then we can thresh out some sort of hope for the future. Your monuments are over the head of all the stupid here, but there are individuals who are not impenetrable, & I greatly hope that for *them* you are bringing some *larger* photos than those I saw. The man stretching his mighty arms is a very great triumph—the finest thing, to my sense, that you have ever done. But good bye—& may your voyage be easy & your courage worthy of your genius. I put all my affection into a strong spiritual tug to pull you close to yours, dear Hendrik, ever

Henry James

ALS: Virginia MSS 6251 (35)

---

63. Her diary for 4 May 1905 notes that she "Skipped Radcliffe to see H. James, who spent an hour here." On 22 May she went "to hear H.J. speak on Balzac. . . . Had an amusing time watching from gallery the potentates of Radcliffe and Harvard—atmosphere tense with good behavior. H.J. sprucer, stocky, bald-headed, gracious." She had availed herself of an earlier opportunity to learn about HJ from his brother, according to her 28 April 1905 entry: "I took Olivia to Concord Wednesday, and had an interesting day with Mr. [Robertson] James, a man full of talent and temperament, subsided with half humorous observations upon the world and himself. Says his brother Henry was born finished—never had a temptation in his life" (HCA Papers, LC: Box 28, Folder 4, Vol. 15).

64. Hendrik saw HJ soon after landing in America c. 16 June 1905. Writing to Olivia from Newport on "Thursday eve" of 22 June 1905, he remarked that "Henry James is as good and charming as ever and we have enjoyed some little walks together along Kay Street etc., now and then taking a gost out of the closit of some of those little doll looking houses that peek out of the green foliage at one! Today [23 June?] we are off to the Davises together, where we will lunch and get a little eygptilogican sauce on our ice cream" (als, HCA Papers, LC: Box 12, Folder 2).

My dear, dear Hendrik!   August *6th 1905.*

Your letter from Gibraltar is a sad enough story—which I bear a little less badly, however, for having felt myself, as the days have gone on, prepared for it. That I *should* have you here at this lovely moment (for it is of the loveliest here) was somehow too good to be true, & as your silence lengthened out I felt, more & more, that I was losing you. It is very horrible—but I understand well how difficult, how not to be managed, with your so much more direct & economic road to Italy it must have been for you to come this way. It was only that, in those last hours at Newport, you seemed to believe the thing possible. So *I* believed for a while—& I looked forward, & the pang of the loss is sharp; but, clearly, you have done the right thing. Short & scant—pitifully—with this annihilation, do those few American moments seem to me—& lighted with the strange light of our common uneasiness & outsideness there. But I remember ever so tenderly our first hour together in Boston, & our drive to the Railroad with my trap & then our other & better & longer drive at Newport (which was quite lovely,)—coloured with the beauty of our seeming then destined soon to meet again. When the Devil *shall* we meet, at this rate?—& when, ah when, shall I be able to go back again, at the right moment & in the right way, to the loved Italy? The grim years pass, & don't bring me that boon! Still, we *must* meet, & I must somehow arrange. What consoles me a little is to hear that your weeks in America did tend, did eventuate, in some way, to your profit & your gain—though I wish to heaven I were near enough for you to tell me more without the impossible trouble of your writing it. *That,* about nothing, must you have. Yet it's all pretty wretched, this non-communication—for there are long & weighty things—about your work, your plan, your perversity, your fountain, your building on & on, & up & up, *in the air,* as it were, *& out of relation to possibilities & actualities,* that I wanted to say to you. We could have *talked* them beautifully & intimately here, these things—but now it's as if they had to wait & wait. Yet they mustn't wait too long. *Make the pot boil at any price, as the only real basis* of freedom & sanity. Stop building in the air for a while & build on the ground. *Earn* the money that will give you the right to conceptions (and still more to executions,) like your fountain—though I am still wondering *what* American community is going to want to pay for 30 & 40 stark naked men & women, of whatever beauty, lifted into the raw light of one of their public places. Keep in relation to the *possible* possibilities, dearest boy, & hold on tight, at any rate, till I can get to you somehow & somewhere & have you *bust* me. But good night, dearest boy; it's ever so late, & it's hideous that you're not here & that you won't be. How long & close, in imagination & affection, I hold you! Feel, Hendrik, the force & the benediction of it & all the applied tenderness of your constant old friend

Henry James

P.S. It's a delight to me that you can speak of yourself as so cleared off, physically, & so confident, & oh, how I yearn after you to Montefiascone! ALS: Virginia MSS 6251 (37)

LAMB HOUSE, RYE, SUSSEX.

Carissimo Enrico mio! *November 5th* 1905.

It is very horrible that I have been so silent, so brutally, damnably dumb. *Everything* that I have had from you, the dear beautiful letter of so many, many weeks ago from—or rather *about*—Capo di Monte[65] in especial, & all the charming little annotated picture-cards—*all, in somma* [It.: in sum], that has come from you has been most gratefully, most responsively & tenderly received & has been a joy to me as expressing your thought of me; & yet I have let the time go by, thinking of *you,* heaven knows, my dear, dear Hendrik, but thinking in this dark & soundless way. The truth is, my dear boy, that our letters are grand little moments, little *bellissime feste* [It.: fine holidays], for us, & that we are capable of the wisdom of not expecting that there shall be a festa [It.: holiday], with shops closed & with red & yellow damask hung out of the windows, *every* week. I have it at heart to be ever so tenderly *easy* with you over the whole pen-question & not lay upon you the consciousness of a writing-job on *your* side to be tackled. So I have been content, & even careful, to remain magnificently in your debt, & only write at last because—well, because I now awfully want to. Your little inquiry about the D'Annunzio matter[66] came to me a few days ago in London, where I have been spending a month & whence I have just returned—& I would have answered that on the spot save that I have wanted to send it—my article, which you ask of—to you with this, & that the number of the *Quarterly Review* containing it was put away *here,* where no hand could get at it till my return. I shall put it into an envelope separately from this, & only ask you to be careful of it for me, as it is the

---

65. Capodimonte is a central Italian village on the southern shore of Lake Bolsena, in the province of Viterbo, approximately fifty-five miles northwest of Rome.

66. HJ's review-essay of translations of works by Gabriele D'Annunzio appeared in *Quarterly Review* in April 1904.

only copy I have—also I take it, tear it out of the very fat, bulky & heavy Review, for convenience of carriage. If (as I seem to guess,) Mrs. Olivia, being with you, desires to read it, please say to her for me that my blessing goes with it & that I hope it won't bore her too much! I imagine you restored these many weeks to Rome; &, I devoutly hope, in good vigour & felicity—though when I think of you confronted again with your horribly expensive family of naked sons & daughters, of all sizes & ages (to say nothing of prancing animals,) I know not in truth *what* to imagine, & only lose myself in the dark & troubled vision of your having to feed & clothe them. And then I reflect that you are always (terrible fellow!) begetting new ones as fast as possible—& I do lie awake at night asking myself what will become either of them or of you. But "that way madness lies",[67] as we say, & I won't bore you about them any more than I can help if I may only have still another gentle word from you, before too long, to the effect that your head keeps right & that you retain some general sense of how & where you are. This isn't, even now, to force your nose, your *bel naso* [It.: handsome nose], down to the grindstone of a sheet of letter-paper—it's only to suggest that you put it for me in the corner of another picture-card if you can (& even if the damned thing has to be a view of Piazza del Popolo or whatever) that you are clear in your head & firm on your pins—that at least *that* decent advantage is fighting on your side. And so I heartily pray.——But meanwhile I am omitting to tell you that those various little messengers from the Montefiascone land fluttered duly into my lap, like birds of rare plumage, from far off, resting their wings there—very rare plumage, all your strong Italian romanticisms, in this homely little British corner—& the more so for my having then had, even here, the queer American sights & sounds still stamped on my senses. Your charming long letter from Villa Codini, after your return from Capo di Monte, delighted me—except for the terrible way it made your homeless *gente nuda* [It.: nude people] loom before me & mock at me; it lies before me now, & I have just been reading it over & holding my nose & picking my steps through your vivid account of Montefiascone proper, or rather improper—as to the safe distance from which of your villa one draws a long breath.[68] You express admirably the natural beauty—the unique &

---

67. See *King Lear,* 3:4.

68. HJ's phrasing here is repeated in Hendrik Andersen's 26 August 1906 letter to Olivia from Porto Santo Stefano, perhaps suggesting how Hendrik had earlier described Montefiascone: "Pots are skillfully emptied from the windows, and the children of the family are sent out to have their morning passage near the front door, where they squat down in threes

exquisite charm of all that old, once loved & known Italian world—
making me groan with homesickness for it, & yet with a homesickness that
leaves cumbersome little Lamb House on my hands to take care of very
much as you have your Forty on yours. At any rate, dearest Hendrik, I
applaud your courage & gallantry of purpose, your patience & concentration, with all my heart, & I pray the Powers it may be still given to my aged
eyes to see you successfully through. I wish with all my heart that, instead
of the formidable Forty, I had 40 snug little potboilers to impose on you—
or even 4: how I would cram down them your throat! It is more than bedtime (& mine is late); so goodnight, with a long embrace. I hope, earnestly,
that your Roman winter announces itself comfortably for all of you. I find
myself thinking ever so tenderly of our too few American hours—which
seemed so meagre at the time: our first meeting in those Boston halls of
Art, our drive together to the railway station & quaffings of queer American *bibite* [It.: drinks] (what were we doing there?)—& above all, afterwards, the beautiful day of our Newport pilgrimage out to that far kind
Mr. Davis's.[69] It all seems romantic now, & I am, carissimo Enrico mio [It.:
my dearest Hendrik], your always affectionate old friend
Henry James

ALS: Virginia MSS 6251 (39)

LAMB HOUSE, RYE, SUSSEX.

My dear dear Hendrik.   [28 December 1905]
    This is but a bare, mean word—one only—to hold out my hand to
you, & feel for yours, & remind you of my love, & give you my tenderly
affectionate blessing. It is only a scrawled substitute for a horrible New
Year's card, which I can't dishonour myself, or you, by sending you. But
send me *you*, dearest Hendrik, a cartolina postale [It.: postcard], with no

---

and fours and race to see who can pee the furthest or make the most monumental chocolate
cream cake. One has to pick one's way as H. James would say" (als, HCA Papers, LC: Box
12, Folder 3).
    69. The luncheon with the Newport picture collector and archaeological patron took
place on 23 June 1905 at "The Reef," the Brenton Point estate of Theodore Monroe Davis
(1837–1915). Andersen recalled the day in his letter of 24 June 1905 to Olivia Cushing
Andersen: "I took James about and we had some pleasant talks and he spoke of Newport of
fifty years ago, and his father's house and many of the old families here" (als, HCA Papers,
LC: Box 12, Folder 2). For more on the man who William James described in 1898 as "a sort
of eccentric grand Seigneur" (*Correspondence of William James*, 3:42, 42n), see John Larsen,
"Theodore M. Davis: Pioneer to the Past," *KMT: A Modern Journal of Ancient Egypt* 1
(Spring 1990): 48–53, 60–61 and (Summer 1990): 43–46. John Romer's *Valley of the Kings*
(New York: Morrow, 1981) also contains a chapter on Davis.

matter what Roman view on it, & a scribbled word added to tell me how much you don't hate me. That is all—that will do; for we must hold on in one way or another till we can meet. It is miserable how little, as the months and the years go on, we *do*. Tell me, above all, that you are well, or at least are not ill—for I *need* that; tell me that your strength is equal to your work & your courage equal to your life. I wish to heaven I could help you somehow, but I seem to have all I can do to help myself—& the only sign of aid & comfort I can make you is to hold out my arms as wide to you here as you know—to show you how they are capable of closing round you. I hope your work grows & *lives*. I hope you are having the decentest possible winter, & that your mother & sister thrive & bear up. I send Mrs. Olivia my kindest remembrance, & all my good will to your mother. Ti abbraccio bene, Enrico caro, ti stringo caramente [It.: I embrace you well, dear Hendrik, I squeeze you dearly], & am always your tender old friend

Henry James

Dec: 28th *1905*.

ALS: Virginia MSS 6251 (40)

LAMB HOUSE, RYE, SUSSEX.

January 31*st* *1906*.

Bravo, bravo, dearest Hendrik, for the vivid little note & the still vivider little photos. of the vividest big group: a more than adequate & altogether beautiful response to my poor New Year's letter, which was only meant to bless & cheer you & never to hurry & worry you at all. Noble & admirable your two Lovers united in their long embrace, & quite, to my sense, the finest of all your fine contributions to this wonderful (& interminable!) series![70] It won't, by its nature, help the great nude Army to encamp in the heart of the American city, but when I have said *that,* I shall have exhausted the sum of my strictures upon it—with the exception perhaps of saying that I don't think I find the *hands,* on the backs, *living* enough & participant enough in the kiss. They would be, in life, very participant—to their finger-tips & would show it in many ways. But this you know, & the thing is very strong & (otherwise) complete. There is more flesh & *pulp* in it, more life of *surface* & of blood-flow *under* the surface, than you have hitherto, in your powerful simplifications, gone in for. So keep at *that*—at

---

70. HJ seemingly refers to Andersen's *Il Bacio* (The Kiss), a part of the larger group, *La notte* (1904–11). For a photograph of Andersen seated before the embracing figures, see *Amato ragazzo: lettere a Hendrik C. Andersen 1899–1915,* ed. Rosella Mamoli Zorzi (Venice: Marsilio, 2000), Illustration 7.

the flesh & the devil & the rest of it; make the creatures palpitate, & their flesh tingle & flush, & their internal economy proceed, & their bellies ache & their bladders fill—all in the mystery of your art! How I wish (to God!) I could stand there with you in your crowded workshop & talk of these things. But patience, patience; that *still* will happen! You say no word of your head & your health—so I try to take the Kissers for favourable evidence, & I scan the so handsome fatigued face of the rabbit-picture for signs reassuring & veracious.[71] I don't know to what extent I make them out: you're so beautiful in it that I only hope you're really exempt from physical woe. I take hold of you ever so tenderly & am yours ever so faithfully

Henry James

[On back of envelope] *His* hand is the better & his knees ever so interesting & *magnificent.*

ALS: Virginia MSS 6251 (41)

LAMB HOUSE, RYE, SUSSEX.

My dearest old Boy. *July: 20: 1906*

Charming to me your little note; very interesting your 2 little pictures; very touching your telling me that you affectionately think of me & reach out toward me. Yet formidable too, I confess, the vision of your pegging away there through the Roman summer at the rate of a pair of twins, or even triplets, a month, & with no other reward, for the time, than the sight of your so expensive family. My brain reels, dearest Hendrik, for the thought of you, & the mad dance of your lusty images makes me fear they may whirl you back into *your* old "blind staggers." But you say nothing of that, & God forbid it. Only you say nothing either of any chance of your getting away into country coolness for a bit, & I would willingly sacrifice ½ a twin or the 3d of a triplet to think you might. It eased me off, when you were at Montefiascone &c, to feel that there you *couldn't* add to your family—splendid family as it is. But you must live as you can, & as you will, & I can only pray for you. Your fertility & power seem to me marvellous, & the 2 Kodak-figures of your note to testify to that as wondrously as ever. They are very beautiful to me, as to everything but their faces—I am quite impertinently unhappy (as I told you, offensively, the last time,) about your system of face. Also I sometimes find your sexes

---

71. For a photograph of Andersen sitting in his studio and holding a rabbit, see Zorzi, illustration 5.

(putting *the* indispensable sign apart!) not quite intensely enough differentiated—I mean through the ladies resembling a shade too much the gentlemen (perhaps, as in the case of this last *ballerina,* through your not allowing her a quite sufficient luxury—to my taste—of hip, or, to speak plainly, Bottom. She hasn't *much* more of that than her husband, & I should like her to have a good deal more.) But no matter—they are both full of life & beauty & power—though I fear they will presently, in the mazes of the dance, tear their baby limb from limb. How many babies they do have—how they do keep at it, making you, to a tremendous tune, a grandfather! Admirable this back view of them in especial. But who, all this while, is *seeing* them, Enrico mio? & to what degree is the world the wiser? But you can't write me any answer to that—remember well how little pressure I *ever* put on you to write, spent as you eternally are with all this fierce creation. Therefore you *must* come & tell me about all such matters, about everything, here, & we must absolutely arrange it for the autumn. The only thing is that I *may* be very little alone in September, & I like to have you to myself. But there will probably be times, too! Write to me at the first real gleam of your seeing your way, & I'll be hanged if I shan't be able to help—! I rejoice your Mother is well, & I send her my blessing. I trust that Arthur really prospers. I take you, my dear old Boy, to my heart, & beg you to feel my arms round you. Your *devotissimo* [It.: most faithful]
H.J.

ALS: Virginia MSS 6251 (43)

LAMB HOUSE, RYE, SUSSEX.

My dear dear Hendrik.   [18 October 1906]

Very touching to me your distracted little card, which brings tears to my eyes. My dear, dear boy, I understand everything & much as I hoped for you had no confidence whatever in your being able to come. I knew in fact that too many things, on your own side, were against it—& my own original idea had never been that you should incur *any* expense or make the effort unaided. When we last wrote I thought I saw my way to make it possible to you, & indeed *could* have done so if everything here hadn't taken an unfavourable turn—I mean in the way, 1st of my not having been *alone,* or appearing likely to be, for 2 days together, these many weeks, & then of my house being plunged, as now, into rude, *pulling-up,* disturbing labour for the introduction of a heating-apparatus (hot-water pipes,) to combat the rigour of the winter cold (a thing I have been meaning to do ever since I first came here.) It makes the place possible meanwhile only to me. Relations & invaders have, till 5 days ago, encompassed me, & I reached out to you in thought—wondering, fearing, asking myself if you hadn't some *independent necessity* perhaps for coming as far as Paris (your last allusion had somehow suggested it;) in which case the rest could have been easily managed. In fact if we could only have been in more intimate communication before you left Venice (but too many things were against it,) I could, & *would,* absolutely have wired you (or otherwise sent you,) your Return-ticket from that place (Venice—or rather your Return back to Rome.) *Now* it's too late to dream of proposing to you to make the formidable journey for a poor few days! I should, oh I should, have planned & settled this with you, definitely, earlier—but I wanted you *to myself,* & I seemed to risk not having you so, if you should come—& meanwhile the weeks have ebbed away—& you are further off than ever. Trust me however a little longer for *still* getting at you. Alas that my own travels have of late *had* so utterly to shrink & die out. Rome & its *people* scare me—but I shall absolutely go to the Continent this winter for a month—& *something* will come, for us, of that. So hold on tight, dearest boy—there will be better days. I hope with all my heart that your holiday has done you good & that you return to Rome fortified & refreshed. When you speak of your Poverty, however, I could howl—howl with anguish— over your continued *parti-pris* [Fr.: set purpose] never apparently to do any blessed helpful pot-boilers—but only your vast stripped stark sublime Family—on whose myriads of penises & bottoms & other private orna- ments how can you *ever* financially "realise" in America?? Forgive this anxious cry from your tenderest

H.J.

ALS: Virginia MSS 6251 (45)

My dear, dear Hendrik. *November 25th 1906.*

I have *had* to wait to acknowledge your touching, quite harrowing letter: a friend had just arrived (from Paris) to spend a week with me;[72] complications of work piled themselves on top of that, & in short every minute was taken. Now the friend has departed, the air is a little clearer, & I seize the pen to tell you that I yearn all tenderly over you & your new

---

72. HJ's letter to William James of 17–18 November 1906 identifies the "friend from Paris" as the American scholar Thomas Sergeant Perry, then traveling on the Continent and in England (*Correspondence of William James,* 3:327–28).

visitation—I mean the indigestion & dyspepsia you tell me about. I wish to goodness I could get *near* to you for a while & intervene somehow between you & these sorry fates which your manner of life & of work seem so disturbingly (& by no *intentional* perversity of your own, I fully recognise,) to draw down upon you. I am *trying,* all the while—I am laying out plans for our coming together somehow—somehow that will permit of my laying the firmest & kindest & closest of all arms about you & talking to you, "for your good," for three uninterrupted days & nights. For the root of these afflictions & disasters strikes me as lying in the *lonely insanity* (permit me the expression, dearest boy,) of your manner of work: the long, unbroken tension of your Scheme itself, the scheme of piling up into the air this fantastic number of figures on which you are *realizing nothing* (neither money, nor judgement—the practical judgement, practical attitude towards them, of the purchasing, paying, supporting, rewarding world;) on which you are not even realizing that benefit of *friction with the market* which is so true a one for solitary artists too much steeped in their mere personal dreams, & which wakes them up to a measure of where they are and what they are doing & not doing—for practical value or no-value. You are attempting what no young artist *ever* did—to live on air indefinitely, by what I can make out, putting all your eggs into one extremely precarious & perforated basket, & declining the aid of the thing done meanwhile *to live,* to bring in its assistance from month to month: the potboiler call it if you like, the potboiler which represents, in the lives of all artists, some of the most beautiful things ever done by them. Stop your multiplication of unsaleable nakednesses for a while & hurl yourself, by every cunning art you can command, into the production of the interesting, the charming, the vendible, the *placeable* small thing. With your talent you easily *can*—& if I were but near you now I should take you by the throat & squeeze it till you howled & make you do *my Bust!* You ought absolutely to get at Busts, at any cost of ingenuity—for it is fatal for you to go on indefinitely neglecting the *Face,* never doing one, only adding Belly to Belly—however beautiful—& Bottom to Bottom, however sublime. It is only by the Face that the artist—the sculptor—can hope *predominantly* & steadily to live—& it is so supremely & exquisitely interesting to do! The impossible effort to *ignore* all this wisdom that I thus pour out on you is what is working havoc in your nerves & digestion by the abnormal sort of tension & fever (the *monstrous* nature of the effort,) it requires. Dear, dear Hendrik, have patience with my words & shut yourself up with them a while & judge of the affection that prompts them. I want extremely to see

Mrs. Gardner,[73] who has seen you so lately, & who will give me news of you—for I *shall* see her a week hence in London, whither she comes, from Paris, on her way home. I am to go up on purpose, & I shall learn from her what she suggested to you (as you mention,) in the way of small placeable figures, &, blessing her for doing so, shall throw my weight into the same scale, as hard, dear boy, as ever I can—& all the harder if I see you still insensible. Heaven grant that meanwhile (since you announce to me a slight improvement,) you are less tormented than when you came back to Rome. I wonder if I couldn't make you adopt the precious system of "Fletcherization" which for the last 2 or 3 years has renewed my own life & worked off all my ailments of dire & lifelong indigestion, gout & rheumatism: the system of absolutely complete & exhaustive "mouth treatment" of one's food before swallowing it; of masticating it & *insalivating* it (saturating it with one's saliva,) till *all* its taste is extracted & enjoyed, & then letting it leak away, in a state of thinnest liquid pulp, down one's throat, taking care of itself utterly & being handed over to one's stomach & intestines in a condition *immeasurably* more easy for them to deal with than before, & that they repay tenfold by their active & immediate gratitude. It makes eating of course *slower,* much slower; but that is a pure boon, & one eats just half as much—food so treated giving one the sense of satisfaction & satiety in much smaller quantities & simpler sorts. One gets *all* the taste (as never before,) of the simplest & most familiar things, & *enjoys* as never before. Take care not (of course) to really *under-eat,* & try it, dearest boy—*try it! It has renewed my elderly life!* If you are sufficiently interested to want to know more (as I hope & pray!) make me, dear Hendrik, some simple sign, & I will be more explicit still; though what I tell you is of the essence & contains the gist of the matter. Treat your *liquids* the same way—take the mouthful & retain it, make it at home in your mouth as long as possible, thoroughly *tasting* it, thoroughly saturating it with saliva & gently, as it were, *breathing* it. By that time, the time *all* the taste has gone, the liquid, the coffee, the tea, the wine (in single, isolated *bouchées* [Fr.: mouthfuls],) will have leaked away of itself down your throat & be all *prepared* for easy assimilation in your insides. Do you *see,* dearest boy? My dinner of one or two dishes takes me thus *40 minutes*—but it takes all the time *then,* & none afterwards in *getting over* it & losing days with illness & pain. *Eat what you desire & as much*—but *treat* it, religiously so: the habit forms itself, with attention & patience, easily, the relief is

---

73. See the biographical register for Isabella Stewart (Mrs. John L.) Gardner.

extraordinary, & the return to the shocking sensation of bolted & gobbled morsels, taken practically *entire* into one's stomach & abdomen, impossible![74] But enough for this occasion. With what formidable & ferocious advice you will feel me drenching you! However, I'm not really afraid that you won't see in it, my dear dear Hendrik, all the tenderest tenderness of your insufferable old friend

Henry James

ALS: Virginia MSS 6251 (46)

Dearest Hendrik. *July 18th 1907.*

Horribly have I delayed to thank you for your generous packet of photographs accompanied by your gentle words. They all make those romantic Roman days of ours together live again for me; for they—our happy studio hours & all the rest—are already romantic, from *this* prosy point of view, as they become, in spite of their recent nearness, far & faint & fabulous. Now that the vulgar world that's not Italy has seized me again I can scarce believe that Italy, that Rome & you & the cool arched workshop, & the slowly-breathing bust, the subtle Ettore[75] & t'other *model-chap*, & the mild sessions at Aragno's,[76] & above all that wondrous terrace-dinner of my last night, unforgettably sweet in the cool high Roman evening[77]—that all these brave things were only of *last* month. I spent 12 days—admirable ones—in Venice; but those too are already all a dream—& what has happened *since* then, in this dull bourgeois other world, isn't worthy to be named to you dwellers amid greatness. Never had coming

---

74. From May 1904 until 1910, when he was beset by nervous and emotional disorders, HJ was a disciple of Horace Fletcher, the Progressive Era dietary reformer known—for reasons made clear in the letter—as "The Great Masticator."

75. Ettore was one of Andersen's male models.

76. Aragno's was apparently a Roman restaurant.

77. This final dinner is remembered by HJ in *Italian Hours,* ed. John Auchard (University Park: Pennsylvania State University Press, 1992), 203–4: "another impression I was to owe" to a sculptor friend was "that of an evening meal spread, in the warm still darkness that made no candle flicker, on the wide high space of an old loggia that overhung, in one quarter, the great obelisked Square preceding one of the Gates, and in the other the Tiber and the far Trastavere and more things than I can say—above all, as it were, the whole backward past, the mild confused romance of the Rome one had loved and of which one was exactly taking leave under protection of the friendly lanterned and garlanded feast and the commanding, all-embracing roof-garden. It was indeed a reconciling, it was an altogether penetrating last hour."

back here (after the greatness) seemed so flat & common & humiliating.[78] But here I am—& in my little deep-green garden, where the roses are almost as good as the Roman, & the lawn is almost as smooth beneath the feet as your floors of No. 3[79]—I try to forget what I've lost. Please thank Lucia[80] very kindly for her labour over so many of my ugly images. No, I don't "come out" well—& it isn't her fault, or yours, or Ettore's, or that of anything but my own deadly & unmanageable mug. *Your* mug, dearest Hendrik, is much sweeter & shines as silver beside heavy pewter. You don't tell me how you are, as to your troubled *physics*—but I devoutly pray that the summer be melting your pains & disabilities away. I delight to think of your admirable home-quarters, & if I don't believe in the great statued studio (I mean in its air & its influence) quite so much, I won't worry you about that now. And as for the brave bust—but I must write you *separately,* as soon as possible, about that. All affectionately yours, dearest Hendrik,

H.J.

Tanti saluti [It.: regards, all good wishes] to your Mother & Baccareisis[81]—is that the way to spell him?—who I hope continues faithful!

ALS: Virginia MSS 6251 (50)

LAMB HOUSE. RYE. SUSSEX.
My dear dear Hendrik! *January 24th* 1908.
   It's very horrible that your kind & charming & interesting letter should have waited so many days for an acknowledgement. But I have had times—bad times—especially just now—I mean, for letter-writing; when one kind of pressure of work holds me all the morning, & another all the evening, & between the two I feel so spent & *voided* that I can only stare

---

78. Cf. HJ's remarks of 31 May 1907 to William James on his "equivocal 'jaunt'" to Italy: "I now want no more jaunts whatever, for all time—but only to get 'safely home' & mind my proper business (much enriched indeed by my recent experience, but resenting more and more the lavish squanderment of golden Time—to say nothing of golden gold. . . . I am straining to get off from day to day. . . . But I've been let in for sitting for my bust to Hendrik Andersen, & have promised him 3 or 4 sitting[s] more—they make a vast hole in the day" (Skrupskelis and Berkeley, *William and Henry,* 342).

79. Andersen now resided on the "ultima piano"—the top floor—at 3 Piazza del Popolo, Rome.

80. Companion to Andersen's mother and occasional model for him, the orphaned Lucia Elise became his foster sister when she was adopted in April 1918 (see his 26 April 1918 diary entry, HCA Papers, LC: Box 1, Folder 2).

81. HJ consistently misspells the name of the Spanish painter Gustave Bacarisas (1873–1971).

with a jaundiced eye at my drawer-full of neglected postal matter. You will understand, dearest Hendrik; but the great thing is Don't estimate *by* my rude silence the extreme pleasure it is to me to hear from you. Thank God we can trust each other to do always as we can, & to *be* always as we must, & in short to be the tender & close old friends we have so long been. Your news affects me as good & brave & easy, inasmuch as you don't *say* you've been unwell, don't mention any of those bad days you were, to my great distress, having last May, & *do* mention that you have been keeping at work. Heaven grant that things *are* well & comfortable & convenient for you. The two photographic heads (one thrown back, the other bent down, most charmingly,) have come, & I continue to hold my breath over the extraordinary abundance of your inspiration & the magnificence of your faith in the *placing* of *tutti quei bravi signori, belle signore & graziosi bambini* [It.: all the clever gentlemen, beautiful ladies, and gentle babies]. We shall have to build a big bold city on purpose to take them in—but I daresay you would take a contract for that, too, yourself. I am extremely interested in the casting of the Bust—though rather scared & abashed that you should think me worthy (even though I think *you* so,) of imperial & eternal bronze. I shall be infinitely anxious to hear how I come out, and am rather hoping, if you will pass me the indiscretion, that I shan't be in very yellow or shiny metal. However, I shall be in whatever you think good & fit, & grateful for any form or hue my poor old struggling sleepyhead (with which you had such generous patience, though you must have so hated it,) will take. Beautiful, dearest Hendrik, your saying the thing is to be a gift to me. That will never do in the world; I shall not be in the *least* able to appropriate coolly & unrequitingly that amount of your ardent living labour, & if you will have a little *more* of the same long patience with me you will duly receive the well-earned wage of your toil. This you should already have done had it not happened that, truth to tell, my poor old perforated pocket has been this autumn & winter exceptionally empty of ready money. I came back from my 4 or 5 months' foreign tour last summer decidedly depleted—& haven't as yet quite got on my feet again in the sense of having "realized". But I shall now, before long, *be* realizing, & then you shall distinctly hear from me in a form that will give *me,* dearest Hendrik, great pleasure, whatever it may do to you.——As for showing the Bust in London, I am already—from old observation & knowledge— sufficiently master of the subject to be able to inform you definitely. There is no use *whatever* in trying to get the thing into—in sending it, as a stranger & foreigner unknown here, *to* the Royal Academy. That is practically for British artists alone; the accommodation for sculpture is small, the flood of things sent huge, & I've *never known* any "outside" thing to get in (having had frequent occasion to watch & hope, on behalf of friends.) Your one chance is to try for the New Gallery. To that end the bust must be seen in London, privately, by Comyns Carr or Charles Hallé,[82] & then they if thereto moved, will *invite* you to send it. I myself would really (for my own interest in it) rather you *didn't* send it; & I don't quite know where to ask, or to tell you to address it, in London, so that it may be on view by those—or one of those—gentlemen. But if it *were* where they could see it, I should be able to manage that they come—though of course quite unable to answer for their often unaccountable & quite irresponsible *decision.* The thing is first, I think, to get it cast—& then if possible photographed (without too high lights;) & then to send me the photograph. I *might* be able to do something with that; & would willingly *try* (if the photograph seems favourable or fortunate.) But I must end, dearest Hendrik, this long & a little *weary* letter. Forgive its crookedness & jadedness. That will pass. It's one o'clock (& past) in the morning, & my bed calls to me whiningly. I hope you are peacefully & restfully tucked away in yours. I greet your Mother & Olivia very faithfully & send them affectionate remembrance. The thought of your grand old apartment, & of your spacious settlement in it, has kept doing me, whenever I have thought of you, a world of good. I hope it has had its fine points for winter as well as for those wondrous May-June weeks. Commend me kindly to the brave Baccarisis (is that the way to spell his name?) Good night—felicissima notte! [It.: happiest of nights!] Ever, dearest H., your tenderly affectionate old friend

Henry James

[On envelope flap] P.S. I send you by bookpost registered, with my blessing, a copy of *The American Scene.*[83]

ALS: Virginia MSS 6251 (51)

REFORM CLUB, PALL MALL. S.W.

Dearest Hendrik.   June 3*d 1909.*

I have horribly delayed to thank you, all faithfully & tenderly, as I ought to have done before this, for your delightful little note of some, of too

---

82. Joseph William Comyns Carr (1849–1916), one of the cofounders of the New Gallery, was art critic for the *Pall Mall Gazette* as well as founder and editor of the *English Illustrated Magazine.* Charles Hallé (1846–1919) was director and manager of the New Gallery.

83. *The American Scene* was published 30 January 1907.

many, days ago. But London & Life are complicated for me—& in the midst of complications I haven't the less thought of you. All good news of you is always welcome & cheering to me. I wish you weren't a thousand miles away—or that I weren't—but so the weary Fates have perversely appointed. I rejoice in your health, your work & in everything that is yours. I haven't had, myself, a very brilliant winter & spring—but then I am ninety-nine years old, & in point of fact am in better form at present than for many months past. I have been in London these 3 weeks—but go home again before long, & just now a cold wet time rages, & the town is really more workable than the supposed kindly breast of nature; which is detestable when chilly & sodden. I yearn over your Roman beauty & geniality at this moment of the year & would gladly struggle with stupid sleep again, for 2 hours on end, in that upright sitter's chair of yours, of 2 years ago, if so I might be *with* you, & with Piazza del Popolo, & the Tiber-edge, & all the rest of dear impossible old Rome. Give my love to it all, & especially to Olivia & your Mother. Recall me kindly to Baccarisis. The grand green bronze, beautifully placed in my dining room niche, looks down upon me 3 times a day with all *your* kindness & spirit, much more, I feel, than with any character of my own, in its fine blank green eyes. However, we talk about you together—&, you see, as we are thus two to remember & love you it doubles the affection, dearest Hendrik, of your faithfullest old

Henry James

ALS: Virginia MSS 6251 (55)

LAMB HOUSE, RYE, SUSSEX.

Dearest Hendrik   [3 August 1909]

I lately had a pleasant—a picturesque—little signal from you—which I have been meaning from day to day to acknowledge. What I allude to so is the small image of your place of villeggiatura [It.: country holidays]—a Naples suburb, as I gather; which looks very charming in its way, but rather in the eye of your terrible Southern sun.[84] However, you are all sala-manders by now, clearly—or you would long since have yielded to the forces of perspiration. Therefore I hope with all my heart you like it, your wondrous Vico Equense; whence, to save yourselves, walks & efforts for the Bath, you appear quite able to throw yourselves—or lazily to tumble—

---

84. HJ addresses the letter to Andersen at "Ferma Posta, *Vico Equense,* Presso Napoli." Vico Equense is a rocky seaside village overlooking the Gulf of Naples, approximately midway between Pompeii and Sorrento.

from your romantic heights straight into the sea. May you at any rate get all refreshment & break no bones. I trust it's doing your Mother & Olivia, to whom I send very cordial greetings, all sorts of good. I like to think of your being out of the dusty Rome of these weeks—& you, dearest Hendrik, barred of your bristling studio, to which you will return with more gallantry for the temporary rupture. Of the magnificence of your gallantry & the scale of your production the photographs you lately sent me give me renewed evidence. They speak to me of your being in health & heart—for which I love you! They seem to represent to me the bravest & biggest & finest work you have yet done—& suggest marked progress & increase of power. I see less then ever where you are *"coming out"*, but admire more than ever, my dear boy, your plastic passion & your confidence & courage. As I sit—or rather stand (for it's too cold & damp here this damnable summer to loll about much,) in my quiet little green garden I think of you all-affectionately, dearest Hendrik & wish I had my hand in your arm, as we *have* had arm & hand—in the old good days that don't seem in a hurry to recur. Let us pray at any rate, for something like them again—*ci vuol' pazienza!* [It.: one must be patient!] & believe me ever your all-faithful & fond old friend

Henry James
August 3*d 1909.*

ALS: Virginia MSS 6251 (56)

LAMB HOUSE, RYE, SUSSEX.
Dearest Hendrik.   [1 January 1910]
    Your tender little letter awakens in me the most tender response,—& I greet you all affectionately & faithfully. I put out my arms & hold you fast, across Channel & Alps & Appenines [*sic*]. I seem to feel that your words express a certain assured well-being, & I marvel again, as so often before, at your heroic assiduity & concentration of labour. You're magnificent—if you can stand it—but very few men could. Therefore, clearly, you are made of steel & gold & shining agate. Well, I *see* you, as you come & go, & I put my arm into yours to go with you—& I sit again in your high cool studio with all your brilliant creations about. Those were delightful hours, & I recall them ever so fondly. Above all, however, I rejoice in your telling me of your plan of coming to Paris this spring & of the happy chance of your coming to *me* by the same stroke. The only cloud on that picture is that I may not be—I almost never am—spending the month of March in this place—& yet that it is in this place only that I want to receive you, &

shall be able to. However, I shall *probably* then not be further away than London & in that case I will rush down again to open door, & my arms, wide to you. I have promised (also) to go to Paris & stay with a friend[85] a fortnight or so—but that *probably* (also) won't be till later. It is no use whatever our attempting—or consenting—to meet in Paris—we shld. be able to see nothing of each other there. Let me know in advance—won't you—as much in advance as possible—when your journey northward is likely to begin. I greet your Mother & Olivia very cordially. I thank Bacarisis kindly, please tell him, for his Xmas remembrance. And please tell yourself that I am yours, dearest Hendrik, all affectionately ever

Henry James

New Years Night. 1910.

ALS: Virginia MSS 6251 (57)

Lowland House. *Nahant. Mass.*[86]

Dearest Hendrik. *June 11th 1911*

Your telegram has reached me here—away from Cambridge, where I am spending the greater part of this month with an old friend. I am delighted to feel you so much nearer to me,[87] & yet I don't know how to propose or arrange (at least till I hear a bit more from you) to see you & embrace you. I am greatly better than I *have* been—but still at times very inconveniently unwell—I am so even just now—& much hindered & hampered thereby; so that I haven't much freedom of range or of suggestion. If you are to be nearer to Boston—& I rather assume you are *not*—I cld. come up from here to see you (if you cld. come out to Cambridge;) I don't suggest you shld. come out *here*—at much inconvenience perhaps—for many reasons. I go up to Cambridge for a few hours at any rate on *Tuesday*—I seem to make out; but that is so soon that it gives us no time to turn round, & I am much at a loss. What becomes of you? where do you go? and how long stay? Write me *here.* I wish you all ease & peace—so far

---

85. The Parisian friend has not been identified.

86. The letter is written on black-bordered letterhead from 95 Irving Street, Cambridge, the home of Alice and the late William James, but HJ canceled that address and substituted the seaside address of George Abbott James (b. 1838), an acquaintance (no relation) from his 1862 stint at Harvard Law School.

87. Andersen landed in New York on 8 June 1911. HJ's letter is addressed to him at 121 East Seventieth Street, New York, the home of Howard Cushing, brother of Olivia Cushing Andersen.

as these formidable American conditions permit; & am yours, dearest Hendrik, all affectionately

Henry James

ALS: Virginia MSS 6251 (60)

HILL THEYDON MOUNT EPPING.[88]

TELEPHONE: 21 EPPING

Dearest Hendrik.   Sept. *4th 1911.*

This must be but a poor & ragged word—but an all tender & affection-ate one—of response to your gentle & touching signal to me from the bosky Saltino.[89] I am glad indeed to think of you on that high safe shelf—after the nightmare, as I shld. think you would all feel it, of your wild American adventure. Yet I could wish you, after those horrors, in a cooler place still, & can't but lament that you had so quickly to plunge into the boiling caldron of Tuscany. However, everything is relative & the Val-lombrosa shades are probably quite as cool as those I have taken refuge in here (Epping Forest, so called—20 miles from London,) from the glare & heat & drought of poor South Coast little Rye. England too has been for weeks & weeks torrid & rainless—& with railway strikes & rumours of War & other abominations to add to the sinister effect.[90] But don't waste sympathy on me—I'm unutterably glad to have escaped from the Awful-ness beyond sea—for truly all *that* was an immense trial. I rejoice, dearest Hendrik, in every word of your letter save your allusion to our not having done what we might toward seeing each other—in those so few & so impossible days. I bear great heat not at all—it makes me deadly ill—& the conditions of temperature added to the conditions of general distance & difficulty, the hustled & crowded confusion of *all* the elements, made it all the while simply & horribly *inevitable* that we failed of contact. I was hanging on to the hospitality of friends & had no place of my own to receive you in where we shld. have been in the least really together. I look back on all those days as a true nightmare—a large part of the evil of which was the sense that you *were,* wildly & distractedly, somewhere about the

88. HJ writes from Hill Hall, Theydon Bois, Epping, the Essex home of Charles and Mary Smyth Hunter.

89. Saltino is a summer resort in the Pratomagno hills of Tuscany, approximately two kilometers from Vallombrosa.

90. See chapter 4 of George Dangerfield's *The Strange Death of Liberal England, 1910–1914* (New York: Smith and Haas, 1935) on the labor strikes throughout England from June 1911 onward. Amid this domestic turmoil, England confronted the possibility of a European war when Germany tested French interests in Morocco.

land, but that the abnormal circumstances made all establishment of relations a mockery & a derision. I couldn't moreover, as I say, have had you to myself, & didn't want to meet you in a mere sweating crowd—still less to *ask* any single step of another *journey* from you—after the awfulness of your Chicago & back &c. But so, dearest Hendrik, it goes—the time, & the years & the troubles, & the dire process of growing older, go; & we don't meet at all—& nothing seems able to help it. For, alas, my travelling days are over now; the trains, the hotels, the American & German crowds that infest Italy, are, with the fatigues & expenses & wastes of time by the way, all finally prohibitive to me. The only chance for the future will be our being able to arrange somehow that you do actually come to England to pay me a brave little visit. *That* I shall work for, tooth & nail, & we'll bring it off before it's too late. Meanwhile *this* sort of thing is poor work—who knows it better & more lamentingly than your faithfully fond old

Henry James.

P.S. May Rome open out her great maternal arms to you, in due course, protectingly & claspingly again! I hope the long absence from your studio will have refreshed your splendid senses & eased off your tired but still so gallant genius. Love to your companions both.

ALS: Virginia MSS 6251 (63)

105, PALL MALL, S.W.

Dearest Hendrik. April 14*th 1912*

Not another day do I delay to answer (with such difficulty!) your long & interesting letter. I have waited these ten days or so just *because* of the difficulty: so little, (as you may imagine or realise on thinking a little) is it a soft & simple matter to stagger out from under such an avalanche of information & announcement as you let drop on me with this terrific story of your working so in the colossal & in the void & in the air! Brace yourself for my telling you that (*having*, these days, scrambled a little from under the avalanche,) I now, staggering to my feet again, just simply flee before the horrific mass, lest I start the remainder (what is hanging in the air) afresh to overwhelm me. I say "brace yourself", though I don't quite see why I need, having showed you in the past, so again & again, that your mania for the colossal, the swelling & the huge, the monotonously & repeatedly huge, breaks the heart of me for you, so convinced have I been all along that it means your simply burying yourself & all your products & belongings, & everything & Every One that is yours, in the most bottomless & thankless & fatal of sandbanks. There is no use or application or

71

power of absorption or assimilation for these enormities, beloved Hendrik, anywhere on the whole surface of the practicable, or, as I should rather say, impracticable globe; & when you write me that you are now lavishing time & money on a colossal ready-made City, I simply cover my head with my mantle & turn my face to the wall, & there, dearest Hendrik, just bitterly *weep* for you—just desperately & dismally & helplessly water that dim refuge with a salt flood. I have practically said these things to you before— though perhaps never in so dreadfully straight & sore a form as today: when this culmination of your madness, to the tune of five hundred millions of tons of weight, simply squeezes it out of me. For that, dearest boy, is the dread Delusion to warn you against—what is called in Medical Science *Megalomania* (look it up in the Dictionary;) in French *la folie des grandeurs,* the infatuated & disproportionate love & pursuit of, & attempt at, the Big, the Bigger, the Biggest, the Immensest Immensity, with all sense of proportion, application, relation & possibility madly *submerged.* What am I to say to you, gentle & dearest Hendrik, *but* these things, cruel as they may seem to you, when you write me (with so little *spelling* even— though that was always your wild grace!) that you are extemporizing a World-City from top to toe, & employing 40 architects to see you through with it &c? How can I throw myself on your side to the extent of employ- ing to back you a single letter of the Alphabet when you break to me anything so fantastic or out of relation to any reality of any kind in all the weary world??? The idea, my dear old Friend, fills me with mere pitying Dismay, the unutterable Waste of it all makes me retire into my room & lock the door to howl! Think of me as doing so, as howling for hours on end, & as not coming out till I hear from you that you have just gone straight out on to the Ripetta[91] & chucked the total mass of your Para- phernalia, planned to that end, bravely over the parapet & well into the Tiber. As *if,* beloved boy, any use on all the mad earth can be found for a ready-made city, made-while-one-waits, as they say, & which is the more preposterous & the more delirious, the more elaborate & the more "com- plete" & the more magnificent you have made it. Cities are *living* organ- isms, that grow from within & by experience & piece by piece; they are not bought, all hanging together, in *any* inspired studio anywhere whatsoever, and to attempt to plank one down on its area prepared, or even just merely projected, for use is to—well, it's to go forth into the deadly Desert & talk

---

91. Passeggiata di Ripetta parallels Lungotevere in Augusta and is proximate to the Tiber.

to the winds. Dearest Hendrik, don't ask me to *help* you so to talk—don't, don't, don't; I should be so playing to you the part of the falsest, *fatallest* friend. But do *this*—realise how dismally unspeakably much these cold, hard, desperate words, withholding sympathy, cost your ever-affectionate, your terribly tender old friend

Henry James

ALS: Virginia MSS 6251 (65)

[*Dictated*]

LAMB HOUSE RYE SUSSEX

TELEPHONE 51 RYE

Dearest Hendrik.   November 28th., 1912.

This is only a scrap of a blessing on you, in the roundabout form to which you see me still condemned, for your beautiful letter this morning received, and which I have read with as much admiration and wonder, as much appreciation and bewilderment, as you may charitably imagine. Everything you evoke for me in it is charming and interesting to me as being *yours,* as being part of a fond and devoted dream, in which you are spending your life, as some Prince in a fairy-tale might spend *his* if he had been locked up in a boundless palace by some perverse wizard, and, shut out thus from the world and its realities and complications, were able to pass his time in wandering from room to room and dashing off, on each large wall-surface, as it came, "This is the great Temple of the Arts," or "This is the prodigious Stadium," and "This," in the next room of the interminable series, "is the Temple of Religions."[92] The patience and ingenuity, not to say the shining splendour, of your dream, touch me more than I can say; but what I don't see is the *application* of the vast puzzle, or the steps which, in this world of such sharp intricate actual living facts and bristling problems and overwhelming actualities, are to convert the affair into the Reality which is needed for giving it a Sense. You see, dearest Hendrik, I live myself in the very intensity of reality and can only conceive of any art-work as producing itself piece by piece and touch by touch, in close relation to some immediate form of life that may be open to it—I do this so much, I say, that I think of colossal aggregations of the multiplied and the continuous and the piled up, as brilliant castles in the air, brilliant as you will, cut off from all root-taking in this terribly crowded and

---

92. A reference to Andersen's envisioned city, the Centre of World Communication, which was to feature "palaces" devoted to, among other "ideals," Nations, Art, and Religion.

smothered and overbuilt ground that stretches under the feet of the for the most part raging and would-be throat-cutting & mutually dynamiting nations. I don't, in fine, see where your vision, subject to such murderous obstruction and control and annihilating criticism, "comes in"; the very law of our difficult human sphere being that things struggle into life, even the very best of them, by slow steps and stages and rages and convulsions of experience, and utterly refuse to be taken over ready-made or *en bloc*. But here I am douching you with cold water again, when I only meant to spray on you, and on your sublime good faith and splendid imagination, a mixture, soothing and satisfying, of all the "perfumes of Araby." This is only a momentary sign of affectionate remembrance, of tender recognition *quand même* [Fr.: all the same]. I am fit for nothing more, for I grieve to say I am still in these accursèd throes. Three days hence I shall have entered into my tenth week of them, and, frankly, I don't know what to make of that—any more than my helpless doctors do. However, they, these abominable Shingles, have been known to last 3 months on end, and I am perhaps but a fine three-months case. I could well dispense with the honour of being to that extent a "pathological" curiosity—which means, to simplify, medical freak or monstrous specimen. I envy you the rapid clearing off of your own indisposition. My doctor too is "dull and pleasant"—but not dull enough if that's what's wanted to cure me, like yours (for you)—nor pleasant enough to console me for this endless woe. Set down to my continued bedevilment anything in this that may have rubbed you the wrong way, and believe me yours affectionately, all,

Henry James

P.S. I feel how you know that I can't by that impersonal machinery, dearest Hendrik, touch you, & draw you close, half as tenderly as I would on better & above all on nearer ground.[93]

TL/ALS: Virginia MSS 6251 (67)

21, CARLYLE MANSIONS, CHEYNE WALK. S.W.

2417 KENSINGTON.

Dearest Hendrik.   March 5*th* 1913

Yes, I have been silent—because I have been endlessly *ill* & the writing of letters a burden & effort beyond my power. I throw myself on your mercy, & thought I had more explicitly done so at my last writing— though I am rather vague—as a consequence of my too much physical

---

93. The postscript is in HJ's hand.

woe—about when that was. At any rate, dearest Hendrik, be easy with me, & think of me as old & afflicted & much stricken—think of me so in the pride of your own so preserved youth & splendid activity. Above all don't, dearest Hendrik, write to put me such ghastly questions as whether I'm "offended" with you. That's verily more than I can bear. I thought I remembered reporting to you of my atrocious autumn illness & its pernicious train of consequences—but I must have made nothing clear. I got sufficiently better early in January to escape from Rye & come up to this small Flat, as a better London refuge than I have had for a long time; but I was soon laid low again—& though my Nurse departed a week ago & the Doctor interspaces, I am still a poor thing, & this explanation must be feeble & faint. However, I have been out 3 times in a Bath chair—& I do hope really to emerge. Let this dismal tale serve you for the present if possible, but bear in mind that I [am] at the best aged & blighted & disabled. I can't, I see, have really brought it home to you—as indeed why should I bring anything so dreary?—that the dreadful illness that broke upon me at the New Year of 1910 is a thing I have never but very imperfectly recovered from, & never *shall,* completely; & let that plead with you for my sorry old shortcomings. If I could only have a good go of your blest climate I should be the better for it—but one doesn't live by climate alone & the attainment of such a boon is impossible for me. I thank you for your desire to *know*—it was faithful & beautiful of you & I am yours, dearest Hendrik, all as faithfully & tenderly as ever

Henry James

ALS: Virginia MSS 6251 (68)

21, CARLYLE MANSIONS, CHEYNE WALK.S.W.

2417 KENSINGTON.

Dearest Hendrik.   [15 March 1913]

This isn't an "answer" to your lovely & generous letter—it's only a mere little, & yet all intensely appreciative, hand-waggle. Most beautiful & unspeakable your open arms, your grand beckonings *to* you & across Channel & Alps & Appenni[n]es—& I can't leave my sense of them unexpressed—if these feeble signs are expression. Alas, I am no more fit for journeys & transmigrations than for *tours de force* [Fr.: feats of strength] or other acrobatic feats in the market-place. My travel-power of every sort is dead & buried & I don't even weep on its tomb. You will come in your young might to England—& then we will meet (& still embracingly) over the abyss of our difference in years & conditions. I do so greatly rejoice in yours. And I *bear* my own—really quite well. And I am, dearest Hendrik, your all-affectionate old

Henry James

March 15. 1913.

ALS: Virginia MSS 6251 (69)

21, CARLYLE MANSIONS, CHEYNE WALK.S.W.

2417 KENSINGTON.

Dearest Hendrik. March 25*th 1913.*

I am touched more than I can say by your tender participation—but you must think of me as better now. I have a compromised life—as one may well have at my age, but still I *have* a life, of sorts—& I kind of get on, I don't despair of doing so better yet. Only the old freedom of range (so far indeed as I ever had it) has gone—though truly I don't miss it. I can live as I am—if I can only *stay* as I am—toward which I will do *mio possibile* [It.: my best]. So let us buck up together—& feel my arm about you. I have just received certain splendid printed sheets from you which I must pull myself together a little more yet to dip into—they seem to stretch into so vast a sea. However the water seems a warm, *kind* tide, & I shall presently, no doubt, make bold to kick it about. Only, dearest Hendrik, I feel moved to plead with you, as a bookmaker myself, against a *format,* a size of page that defies human handling. People won't read (they can't) huge folios. However, it's very handsome as a—well, as an *expanse;* & I judge also as an expense.[94] Pardon my depressed tone. I can't leap & bound, but I can think of you all fondly & be your all-faithful old

Henry James

ALS: Virginia MSS 6251 (70)

LAMB HOUSE RYE SUSSEX

Dearest Hendrik. September 4*th 1913.*

If I have been silent so long it is because distress & embarrassment have kept me so; & now your letter today received makes me write, makes me unable *not* to write even with this regret at having to—having to about the matter you insist on my speaking of, I mean, & in the only sense in which, with my hand so forced, I *can.* I seem to remember that I some time ago wrote you more or less in that sense, & under your pressure—after you had

---

94. HJ refers to the sheets for Andersen's "volume de grand luxe" of architectural and sculptural plans for the World Centre of Communication. Printed in Paris and published in early 1913, the limited-edition volume featured handmade sheets sized 17⁹⁄₁₆″ × 12½.″

sent me your plan of a "World Centre" & then again your 1st instalment of your pamphlet on a "World Conscience"; wrote you in a manner expressive of my pain in having to pronounce on these things which I understand & enter into so little. But you appear to have forgotten the impression I tried then to give you—or I seem quite to have failed of giving it; for you urge me again as if I had said nothing—had uttered no warning. Do you think, dearest Hendrik, I *like* telling you that I don't, & can't possibly, go *with* you, that I don't, & can't possibly, understand, congratulate you on, or enter into, projects & plans so vast & vague & meaning to me simply nothing whatever? You take too much for granted, & take it too sublimely so, of the poor old friend who left you such a comparatively short time since making in all contentment, as he supposed, in a happy Roman studio, statues interesting & limited, even if a little alarming in scale & number, & who then at the turn of a hand finds you appeal to him & press him hard on such totally different ground altogether & as if this were what he had ever gone in for. Evidently, my dear boy, I can only give you pain that it gives *me* pain to be forced to give you, by telling you that I don't so much as *understand* your very terms of "World" this & "World" the other & can neither think myself, nor *want* to think, in any such vain & false & presumptuous, any such idle & deplorable & delirious connections—*as they seem to me,* & as nothing will suit you, rash youth, but that I should definitely let you *know* they seem to me. They would so seem even if I were not old & ill & detached, & reduced to ending my life in a very restricted way—the ground on which I begged you to let me off, some time back, from a participation impossible to me, & in spite of my plea of which you again ask for what you call my *help.* You see, dear Hendrik, to be utterly & unsparingly frank, & not to drag out a statement I wd. so much rather not have had to make, I simply *loathe* such pretensious [*sic*] forms of words as "World" anything—they are to me mere monstrous sound without sense. The World is a prodigious & portentous & immeasurable affair, & I can't for a moment pretend to sit in my little corner here & "sympathise with" proposals for dealing with it. It is so far vaster in all its appalling complexity than you or me, or than anything we can pretend without the imputation of absurdity & insanity to do to it, that I content myself, & inevitably *must* (so far as I can do anything at all now,) with living in the realities of things, with "cultivating my garden" (morally & intellectually speaking,) & with referring my questions to a Conscience (my own poor little personal,) less inconceivable than that of the globe. There—see what you have made me write, & ask yourself if I enjoy distressing you as (from the immensities that you assume to the contrary,) it utterly must. If it weren't that I don't want to add another word I would beseech you to return, yourself, to sound & sane Reality, to recover the proportions of things & to dread as the hugest evil of all the forces of evil the dark danger of Megalomania. For *that* way, my dear boy, Madness simply lies. Reality, Reality, the seeing of things as they *are,* & not in the light of the loosest simplifications—come back to *that* with me, & then, even now, we can talk! I say "even now," for it's late at night & the pen drops from the hand of your poor old weary & sorrowing & yet always so personally & faithfully tender old

Henry James

ALS: Virginia MSS 6251 (71)

21 CARLYLE MANSIONS CHEYNE WALK S.W.

TELEPHONE 2417 KENSINGTON.

Dearest Hendrik.   December 1*st 1913.*

The little (or rather the very big!) signs of your bustling prosperity give me great pleasure, & I congratulate you most affectionately on having leaped so into the saddle—in which may you ride far! Your friend Albert[95] looks like a most amiable monarch; I rejoice greatly that he was kind to you, & hope you now will proceed to the fascination of each of the others. Only when you come over to polish off our George,[96] do keep a little time at the disposal of a much older & clearer friend. May the Paris lecture be in every way delightful—& thus though the view of your Future City affects me alas with (again the most affectionate) Horror! However, this is of no consequence to me at all, so long as *you* go on affecting me as always, dearest Hendrik, in such a way that I can only be your poor old devotissimo [It.: most faithful]

Henry James

ALS: Virginia MSS 6251 (72)

21 CARLYLE MANSIONS CHEYNE WALK S.W.

TELEPHONE 2417 KENSINGTON.

Dearest old Hendrik   December 8*th 1913.*

I shall scarce know where to address this note—for fear you may already have left Paris; but wherever it reaches you let it open out its poor page wide enough to wrap you up in its embrace. *What* an idiot certainly the Sovereign of these realms—not to understand how tremendously in his

---

95. "Albert" has not been identified.
96. Presumably George V, British king from 1910 to 1936.

interest (& in mine above all,) to give you that beautiful reason for coming here. In spite of the paralyzing chill of age & infirmity I am very sorry indeed to miss the chance of you that I had so hoped for. But you are apparently having a lovely time & I rejoice in it for you. To console me for your failure to materialize I hang up *here,* in my room, that admirable sidelong photograph of you that I have had at Lamb House these several years & place under it the Jacob wrestling with the Angel[97]—so I feebly have you about. It *is* a pity that you melt away—for once with me again as of old you would never know, & never *believe,* that I'm horrid & detached. That wd. be all right, for such terms don't really apply to me at all. I envy you the commerce of all those charming demonstrative French people— who will give you fine words without end; & I bless the wish of your heart & the abundance of your genius. Above all dearest old boy I am all faithfully & & [*sic*] tenderly yours

Henry James

ALS: Virginia MSS 6251 (73)

LAMB HOUSE RYE SUSSEX

TELEPHONE 2417 KENSINGTON.

Dearest old Hendrik. July 16*th* 1914

This is just a scrabble of thanks & affectionate recognition. I am touched by your having found time & thought to make me the gentle sign from Washington in your conditions of stress & strain, of complication & perspiration.[98] What a devil of a life you appear to be leading, & what wonders you will have to pour out on me when you turn up again here, as I trust indeed you will be able to, toward the end of next month. A very affectionate greeting will await you & much revival of old memories. You will perhaps be cultivating a few of those even at haunted old Newport even now, I gather—whence the sense again of that drive of ours together out to lunch far away by the sea with the opulent collector & charming host whose name I have forgotten[99] comes strangely, sadly & yet valuably back to me. Advise me further, when you are able to, as to my time for

---

97. HJ apparently refers to a photograph of Andersen's *Giacobbe et l'angelo* (1909–11), a gesso version of which is on display at the Museo Hendrik Christian Andersen in Rome.

98. Andersen was in New York and Washington from late June until early December, seeking audiences with the secretary of the interior and others to show his "volume de grand luxe" of plans for the World Centre of Communication.

99. See the letters of 6 August 1905 and 5 November 1905, and accompanying notes, for references to the Newport drive that took HJ and Andersen to the Davises.

counting on a night or two of you here. I am rather a hampered old entertainer now, while you spread your wings, & powerfully agitate them, at these greater & greater rates; but I shall rejoice in the sight of you & am, dearest Hendrik, your affectionate old

Henry James

ALS: Virginia MSS 6251 (74)

21 CARLYLE MANSIONS CHEYNE WALK S.W.

TELEPHONE 2417 KENSINGTON.

Dearest Hendrik. March 16*th* *1915.*

Yes, I have indeed heard from you in your great goodness & fidelity, & by every law of ancient truth & honour you should long since have been thanked. You were going to be yet, I assure you, even if your kind little word of inquiry hadn't come in; but meanwhile I have suffered, & caused you, dearest gentle Hendrik, to suffer, from the fact that everything in my life now is at the mercy of our horrific public situation, which has in my aged & dilapidated frame, struck at the very roots of letter-writing. Nothing is as it ever was before, & the strain & stress under which we live has brought about for me a kind of leak of nervous force—through the mere tension of anxiety & resistance—which leaves me only the dregs of that article for all the other uses of life. One does (or at least *I* do,) nothing that one used to be able to; *all* one's effort goes to simply living through the long nightmare of this black consciousness. That, with a damnable fact of ill-health, to say nothing of the accumulated years, aiding, keeps me exhausted & done; so that though I try not to let everything go, a part of the nightmare *is,* truly, that I sit among the ruins of every pretension to virtue that I ever possessed, surrounded by the grim ghosts of neglected friends & unwritten letters. I feel that you will understand all this—or partly will, if I put it to you; though you would do that much better if you had been breathing our air & living our life a little, since the War settled on us. If it has so miserably reduced my supply of response to everything but its terrible self, however, it hasn't made me cease to *feel* other things & other relations, even if I don't do them or appear to "keep them up"; & I was thoroughly interested & deeply touched by your writing to me in the thick of your own agitations & adventures. I thought with horror of your being whirled about the globe at such a rate & at such a time (the very name of the awful American, or America, proposition goes far toward appalling me *quest'oggi* [It.: this very day];) & it was a relief to hear of your return to that blest terrace over the Tiber where I last saw you so splendidly at peace & at ease. I hope it spreads under (& over) you all at present in the same fine old protecting & refreshing way—I say "over" by reason of my remembrance of certain grand tentlike awnings or gorgeous canopies (aren't they?) that flung a benignant shade. I myself hold as fast as I can to London now, you see; I spent last summer at Lamb House, but came early in the autumn back to town—unable, under the great oppression & obsession, to bear for any length of time the solitude, & the prospect of the winter confinement, of country conditions. I have lent L[amb]. H[ouse]., with gladness, to the unfortunate, the war-unfortunate, to live in for the present, & shall return only when I see what next summer brings forth. Of course the interest of our War-state (& I get the full force of it here,) is as hideously great as the dreadfulness, & of course the passion of one's sympathy with the cause for which the Allies are fighting gives a tremendous savour to life in spite of all the pity & the horror & the general fierce agitation of mind in which one lives. It is in fact that interest, exactly, & that sympathy & pity & uncertainty from day to day that have the depleting effect (not to speak of the depletion of one's poor old apology for a pocket,) that I have tried to express to you. Up to lately all possibility of work has been blighted & blasted for me—but during these very last weeks I have been trying to get hold of it again, & I feel the good effect so far as I have done so. I trust with all my heart the case is the same with you. I don't break ground on the terrible question of what Italy is going to do—which you must have enough of at home, which the grand old terrace must in fact heave & shake with; but I will yet just say that if on the one hand I would welcome with joy any and every degree of support you may be moved to give us, I hold a country that *can* by hook or crook keep out of the misery & abomination of war the biggest kind of a fool to plunge into it without some utter overwhelmingness of reason, some life-&-death necessity, such as this country & France & Russia have had.

March 17th. I wrote the above last night—then I had to go to bed. Now it's night again—my letter has had alas to wait over too many hours; which have brought forth nothing but the old monotony of pretendedly good newses [*sic*] that see us so little forwarder. I don't mean to say all the same that the general feeling of confidence in spite of everything isn't greater than it has ever been. It is, distinctly, for it is only now at last that this country—after nearly 8 months—begins to feel army'd & equipped & ready. And the same is true of France, & will be probably, in the course of some weeks, for Russia; whereby the assurance of the Allies can only be still in a long War. This is very horrible—but that things are horrible at present only seems to make them the more true. Yet let us remember, also, for truth, that it isn't horrible that I am very fondly faithful to you, dearest Hendrik, that I send my kindest remembrance to your Mother & Olivia, & that I am your all-affectionate old

Henry James

ALS: Virginia MSS 6251 (75)

Jocelyn Persse

Leon Edel in *The Master* called James's relationship with Dudley Jocelyn Persse (1873–1943) "a case of love at first sight."[1] In fact, of all the younger men he befriended and nurtured, James may have loved his Jocelyn best. Persse professedly never understood the grounds for James's affection, but he made him an excellent private companion. Like the three other young men in this edition, he adored the aging writer, testifying to James's magnetic appeal when he told Leon Edel on 31 August 1937, "H.J. was the dearest human being I have ever known. Why he liked me so much I cannot say."[2]

There were several different Dudley Jocelyn Persses in the Persse family, and it is difficult to differentiate among them in the few sources that reference the name. James's friend Persse was the brother of the heir of the Persse family estate, Roxborough in Ireland, and the Irish nephew of Irish playwright Lady Isabella Augusta Persse Gregory (1852–1932), founder of the Irish National Theatre with Yeats. James knew her socially for many years, and she thought well of James. Persse himself was a passionate and knowledgeable devotee of the theater.[3] He inherited the Primrose Club in

---

1. *Henry James, 1901–1916: The Master* (Philadelphia: J. B. Lippincott, 1972), 183.

2. This citation and subsequent ones from Jocelyn Persse to Leon Edel are by permission of McGill University Libraries, holder of the Leon Edel Papers.

3. We are indebted to Jocelyn Persse's descendants for the information on his life and that of Lorna Hutton Black included in this introduction: Mrs. Jarzebowska, Mrs. Black's daughter and subsequently Persse's stepdaughter; Yvonne Jarzebowska and Michael Jarzebowski of England, Persse's step-grandchildren and the grandchildren of Lorna Hutton Black; and Richard H. Persse of Northumberland, Persse's grandnephew. All generously shared considerable information about their family as well as the wedding photo of Mrs. Black and Persse.

London from his father, living above it at 4 Park Place, St. James. By all accounts he was a witty, warm, and companionable individual who walked his dog in Hyde Park and socialized with his many friends, who included Henry Ainley, Max Beerbohm, Algernon Blackwood, Mrs. Patrick Campbell, Ernest Theisiger, and Evelyn Waugh.[4]

Though reports circulated of his affairs with women, there were no rumors of same-sex liaisons for Persse. His closest long-term friend, whom he met in 1903, was Lorna Hutton Black, who in her twenties had married a delicate, intellectual man, Florance Black. As Mr. Black had no objection to his wife's friendship with Persse, Mrs. Black and Persse attended plays together frequently in London and also traveled abroad together to Berlin, Hamburg, and Paris, evidently content in one another's company. He in fact made his second home with the Blacks in their various houses, such as the White Hermitage at Windsor. Mrs. Black called her companion by his first name, Dudley, while her children nicknamed him "Daky." Mrs. Black, a striking fair-haired woman who was presented at court, had a flair for interior decorating, and loved the theater, maintained a relationship of mutual respect and enjoyment with Persse for decades. The family thought of her as "chic but not bizarre." After her husband's death, though, this friendship changed, as she married Persse in December 1938.

The two men met at the wedding of Frances Sitwell and Sir Sidney Colvin in 1903,[5] and the sixty-year-old James was instantly captivated by the thirty-year-old Persse's blond good looks and social aplomb. James wooed him in letters and in person, sending him photographs and accolades. The letters to Persse are perhaps the most erotic he ever penned. The more than eighty letters that James wrote to his young friend reveal a sexually liberated, free, even bawdy James, who used his powerful pen to write his way into intimacy. References to "shackled bondage," Persse's "promiscuous social exercise," and intimate evenings together indicate the degree and intensity of the friendship: "I remember how when I last saw you I wanted to breathe upon you an entirely *cooling* affection."[6] On 3 March 1904 he longed for Persse to return from his travels:

---

4. Mrs. Jarzebowska recalls these men visiting Persse at the Blacks' various homes.

5. The two men narrowly missed meeting nine years earlier, for Lady Gregory's diary entry for 9 November 1894 records having Persse to tea and later that day receiving HJ (*Lady Gregory's Diaries, 1882–1902,* ed. James Pethica [New York: Oxford University Press, 1996]).

6. Als, HJ to Jocelyn Persse, 9 July 1908.

God grant accordingly that I be here when you turn up with the rich glow of travel on your manly cheek and the oaths of all the Mediterranean peoples on your your [*sic*] moustachioed lips: (as I hope, at least; I shld. like so to hear you rip them out[)]. But I yearn, dear Jocelyn, for all your sensations & notations, & think with joy of your coming to me for a couple of days, near at hand a little later on, shaking the dew of Parnassus from your hair.[7]

This is the language of someone well aware of the rich variety of sexual behaviors possible between two loving adults, behaviors not dependent upon gender.

James was one of Persse's sponsors when he wanted to join James's own club, the Athenaeum, whose members traditionally were drawn from Britain's political, literary, and religious aristocracy. James told him,

As for the other matter (which you oughtn't to have chucked like that into a (*misspelled!*) postscript, but made the subject, given the honours, of a communication by itself.) I will my dear Jocelyn, with the greatest joy, second you at the *Athenaeum* (not "Ethaneum"—horror of horrors!) though I could wish, in view of the amount of waiting involved, I fear, that you had a younger & more blooming sponsor. . . . Meanwhile, dearest Jocelyn, get it well into your head that the institution in question takes its name from *Athena,* otherwise (Romanly) Minerva, the goddess of wisdom & patroness of *Athens* who took *its* name from *her,* & practice writing *Athenaeum* 10 times a day.[8]

They dined frequently in London, often concluding their evenings by attending plays, sometimes something of the music hall variety.[9] James admired, even perhaps envied, Persse's "genius for personally, & all so successfully, existing!,"[10] while Persse admired James's writing, noting in particular the first volume of James's autobiography, *A Small Boy and Others:* "I think this [the autobiography] is a very beautiful work. He told me how much the boys envied C[oquelin] going home to the jam tarts!"[11]

---

7. Als, HJ to Jocelyn Persse.

8. Als, HJ to Jocelyn Persse, n.d., Houghton bMS Am 1094.1.

9. Persse told Leon Edel in a letter dated 31 August 1937 that the "low" music hall they attended together from time to time was "the Middlesex, Walter Sickert painted it so often. I took H.J. there as the primitive audience appealed to him." Edel Archive, McGill University.

10. Als, HJ to Jocelyn Persse, 21 September 1905.

11. Als, Jocelyn Persse to Leon Edel, 1 October 1937, Edel Archive, McGill University.

Although their friendship waned after 1906 or 1907, James continued to see and to support Persse. He included Persse's friend Mrs. Black in at least one invitation to the theater, apparently not at all threatened by their heterosexual friendship. By 1908, when James traveled much less frequently, he participated vicariously in Persse's exotic adventures, which included trips to France, Italy, Greece, and then Algiers:

> [S]tick very fast for a bit & take deep draughts of what I suppose (in my poor inexperience) to be a beautiful mixture of the East & the South, golden air & shining landscape & handsome orientation of every kind with French cooking & café-concerts thrown in. May it do you a lot of good, & may you bring back endlessly charming things to tell me about it. Take notes, take notes always & intensely, for your old stick-in-the-mud friend, & above all go to Biskrah if you can & work him up, on your return, with *that*. He has nothing wonderful to regale you with on his own side.[12]

They celebrated a glorious weekend together at Lady Lovelace's estate, Ockham, in November 1909, a time James recalled a year later as "our rather odd & melancholy, but also exquisite, Sunday at Ockham—Nov. 27th–29th, *1909*—in those fantastic contiguous apartments."[13]

By 1911 James's love had expanded to an all-embracing, effusive outpouring of deep affection and regard for all these young men. He was proud when Persse joined the Royal Welch Fuseliers in 1914, and he wrote him cheering letters when Persse evidently had difficulties adjusting to the rigors of boot camp, recalling Whitman, who loved and nursed Civil War soldiers more than a generation before, telling Persse that camp would improve him.

His love and concern for Persse transcended death, as he left him one hundred pounds in his will.

---

12. Als, HJ to Jocelyn Persse, 22 February 1908, Houghton bMS Am 1094.1.
13. Als, HJ to Jocelyn Persse, 27 October 1910.

My dear Jocelyn.

[Monday p.m. (1903?)]

This is but a poor word, omitted 3 days ago, very stupidly, to say that I have written to have a copy of *The Ambassadors* sent you—every copy I have succeeded in being possessed of here having successively melted away.[14] Don't write to "thank" me for it—but if you are able successfully to struggle with it try to like the poor old hero, in whom you will perhaps find a vague resemblance (though not facial!) to yours always

Henry James.

Monday p.m.

ALS: Houghton bMS Am 1094.1

My dear Jocelyn.

September 15*th* *1903*

Had I obeyed the impulse of the moment, on receipt of your letter from Norfolk I would have acknowledged it on the spot & with the liveliest signs of appreciation. "This, my dear Jocelyn, is charming—this is liberal & lovely—this does equal credit to your head & heart!"—some such bundle of compliments would I have sent flying at you by return of post. You wrote to me in a manner that gave me great pleasure—& all my *disposition* was that you should straightway know it. But I have it always on my conscience to play fair in these matters, & I stayed my hand in order that you shouldn't too soon be crushed to earth by the sense of again *owing* a letter (not indeed that I believe this is a consciousness that so very utterly flattens you out!) I preferred that you should have the pleasure (such as it is for you,) of *my* owing you one, & I have left that to you, these days, to make the most of. May it have counted a little among the familiar joys of your actual romantic (as it so strikes me) career! I seem to see you roll, triumphant, from one scene of amiable hospitality & promiscuous social exercise to another; &, sitting here, on my side, as tight as I can, with a complete avoidance of personal rolling, I quite rejoice in the bright brave vision of you, who are willing to do these things (that I *can't* do) for my mind, & to take me with you, so to speak, in thought—so that, even while I crouch in my corner, I get, through you, more or less, the vibration of adventure & the side-wind of the unfolding panorama. May you, to the end of the feast, retain a stout young stomach! Which is a means of saying

---

14. The gift of *The Ambassadors* (London: Methuen, 1903), one of the three great novels of HJ's major phase, makes 1903 the likely year of this letter.

may you suffer yourself to be pelted with as many of the flowers of experience as you can (we won't talk just now of the thorns;) so that when next we meet you shall have at least some of the withered leaves to show me & let me sniff. I meanwhile am also a good deal pelted, (pelted, not petted!) but I feel as if my experience were mere thorn & bramble. I sit (as I say,) as tight as I can, but it hasn't prevented these last weeks here from being a time of really rather sharp discipline for me—in the way of making some sort of terms with invasions, interruptions, complications, that I seem powerless to prevent. I have been pressed with retarded work (which greatly interests me,)[15] & have had at the same time to keep putting up & "doing for" visitor after visitor, & running a crowded & quite unlucrative little hotel. People *chez moi* [Fr.: at my house] & howling storms (*chez moi,* quite enough, too;) these have been the chief of my diet ever since you left me; & the end is not yet. The rest of this month threatens to be much compromised & complicated, & I have been anxiously studying your remark about the probability of your being accessible to me in town (for the question of our evening together,) "about September 25th or October 1st." It looks at present (to my great regret,) as if I should be tied here by entanglements straight *over* the 25th; & it also looks as if a friend abroad, who comes to me for a week within the next 3 or 4, would precisely choose for his visit the time *from* Oct 1st.[16] That will force me to wait, for my little rush to London, for his departure. However I take it that you mean that you come back there for more or less *permanence* on that later date—not that you are merely there between a couple of prolonged absences. This simplifies & only makes necessary a short delay. I will write you of the earliest date in October that I shall be able to propose—I mean I will write as soon as I see my way a little clearer. I pat you affectionately on the back meanwhile & am yours, my dear Jocelyn, always & ever

Henry James

ALS: Houghton bMS Am 1094.1

LAMB HOUSE, RYE, SUSSEX.
October 23*d 1903*.

My dear dear Jocelyn!

I almost wish your mystic *malaise* were justified, so that I might have

---

15. HJ was trying to complete his last great novel, *The Golden Bowl,* published in New York by Scribner's in 1904 and in London by Methuen in 1905.

16. "The friend abroad" may be Hendrik Andersen, who had been in Italy and Paris and planned to visit Lamb House on October 12. Here again is an instance of HJ's "juggling" his friends' visits.

even reason[17] for being touched & charmed by it. I mean that I would almost *be* ill to add the deeper note to our harmony. But I am no worse than usual, & I hope with all my heart (being, after all, inconsistent here) that your charming Irish presentiment—a real brush of the Banshee![18]— proving you the Celtic man of imagination like myself—doesn't mean that I'm *going* to come any sort of cropper. I shall try hard not to, for I want to hold on to *you*. All thanks at any rate for your beautiful & blessed suspicion, & for your acting upon it, which makes us for the moment communicate—to my extreme joy. We shall do so in London again before too long—for excellent to me is the memory of the other evening, & the new chance will turn up for me to snatch it. But don't, my dear boy, afflict me again by talking of my "sacrifices." There is, for me, something admirable and absolute between us which waves away all that. But these things are beyond words—words almost vulgarize them. Yet the last ones of your note infinitely move me, & I am, my dear Jocelyn, yours ever so tenderly

Henry James

ALS: Houghton bMS Am 1094.1

REFORM CLUB, PALL MALL. S.W.[19]

My dear Jocelyn.   March *3d 1904*

The benevolence of your letter, very happily inspired at this moment, consoles me a little—a *very* little—for your prolonged & continued absence. I have been three times to Park Place—fairly haunted it—in search of news of you, & it has been only the assurance given me there (in compassion for my long face,) that you would now at last "very soon be back" that has kept me from attacking you by letter. The last time I was there—it was but 4 days ago—I wrote a message on a card for you; & really it is rather as if that fond act had, by a magic sympathy, determined in you at the same moment, Feb. 29th, the impulse to write to me. The

---

17. The page is torn here and two words are partially destroyed. The second word is "reason" and the first word may be "better," but too much of it is missing to be certain.

18. A banshee, in Gaelic folklore, is a female spirit whose appearance or wailing warns families that one of their members will die.

19. Awkward transitions, changes in letterhead and pen, and other contextual references all suggest this may be more than one letter, though it is included here because its contents further illuminate the relationship between the two men. Pages 5–8 of the holograph may come from a letter later than 3 March 1904 but prior to May 1904. This would help account for the awkward transition in "Je t'embrasse tendressement—that I spent the greater part of that month . . ." as well as other peculiarities in the letter's references.

charming coincidence delights me. And your letter, moreover, clears up a little your mystery; for the Park Place people have only vouchsafed me the information that you are "abroad"—& I was too discreet to ask how or where. But I rejoiced to know. I have dodged or refused every mundane solicitation, & I stay here till this week's end. Then I go away for 10 days, but I expect to be in town again from the 1st to the 15th May. (Mrs. Wharton, by the way, will be here I think, for the whole of the month of May—or about. So you won't, if I can arrange it, fail of seeing her.) I am invited to the Academy Dinner this year,[20] to my surprise, having declined the last time I was asked & not supposing I ever shld. be asked again. This is on May 5th—& I expect, as I say, to stay on over it to about the 15th. God grant accordingly that I be here when you turn up with the rich glow of travel on your manly cheek & the oaths of all the Mediterranean peoples on your your [*sic*] moustachioed lips: (as I hope, at least; I shld. like so to hear you rip them out[)]. But I yearn, dear Jocelyn, for all your sensations & notations, & think with joy of your coming to me for a couple of days, near at hand a little later on, shaking the dews of Parnassus from your hair.[21] When I think you are living with Phidias & the Hermes,[22] with the divine Muse, in short, I am ashamed of writing you a prosy Pall Mall note. Je t'embrasse bien tendressement [Fr: I embrace you tenderly]—that I spent the greater part of that month in bed (& in my chair,) under a dire visitation of gout, unfit for human intercourse & with my whole situation rendered still more impossible by the eternal, desolating, torrential rain. I was too demoralized to make you any sign, & shouldn't have had the courage to ask you to share my moist & melancholy life. I came up to town the 1st days of Feb.; but no sooner had I got here than I had a relapse (into the arms of the gout-devil;) & had to go back home again for another (luckily a much shorter) nursing. Now I seem fairly firm on my afflicted extremities (for both feet were engaged;) & I shall be here (D[eo].V[olente]. [Lt.: God willing]) till about April 7th. I hate to say a word in the sense of anticipating the end of your sunbath—a cup that I like to think of your draining to the dregs; but it will be a very jolly

---

20. HJ does not specify which academy this is. In 1901 the British Academy was formed to promote literature, history, and philosophy.

21. Parnassus is, of course, Mount Parnassus at Delphi, sacred to letters, learning, and art. The references in the letter suggest Persse has been in Greece.

22. Phidias was considered the greatest sculptor in ancient Greece. Hermes was an Olympian god, the son of Zeus and Maia, who corresponds to the Roman god Mercury. The gods' messenger, he conducted souls to Hades.

circumstance if you do turn up before my departure. I shall be back again, later on, but only in a few small patches. As soon as you begin to see your way, make me some sign preliminary—that I may have the pleasure of counting & calculating—of consciously watching & waiting. Heaven speed, at any rate, the event. London seems very peopled, & I've been twice to the Monument, where, between Colvin & Colvina,[23] our meeting of last summer, there, always comes romantically back to yours, my dear Jocelyn, always,

Henry James.

ALS: Houghton bMS Am 1094.1

REFORM CLUB, PALL MALL. S.W.
My dear Jocelyn.
[21 March 1904]
    This has been sorry news for me, & you must think of me as, these 3 or 4 days, since your letter came, as very much overdarkened by it. I very actively, I quite lamentably miss you, but I am trying to throw off that aching sense by fixing my thought on your being in a place, & in many conditions, which many unfortunates would give their eyes for a breath, the shortest sniff, of—on your being perhaps, that is, a little in prison, but in a gorgeous, gilded, flowery, bowery prison—& with the term of your liberation not so very far off. Unfortunately the furthest limit of my present stay in London seems to be about the date of your leaving Cannes—if you leave very punctually. But I feel that I shall find it impossible to go without first greeting you here. However, we shall have time to talk of that, & I congratulate you in the meanwhile on being able to render your mother the service of your care & company—not an hour of which, in your future, but you will look back to rejoice in. I am greatly touched by her kind message to me, & shall always make haste to embrace any opportunity that may present itself of seeing her. London, *my* London, goes on smoothly, but too swiftly & there is already a faint premonition of spring in the lengthening days & the milder air. Unfortunately the mildness has, after a blessed little interval of bright & rather hard cold, brought a return of rather muggy moisture. But Easter is close, & I revel in the fact that I "go" nowhere. I sit tight in town thanking my stars for the same.——Just after I last wrote you I met at dinner Mrs. Mond, your very genial & charming

---

23. HJ met Persse for the first time at the wedding of Sir Sidney Colvin (1845–1927), British art and literary critic, and Frances Sitwell (1839–1924), a notable British society woman. Hugh Walpole was also in attendance.

(about *you,*) friend (the dinner was at the James Bryces'.)[24] I found her decidedly interesting & pleasing & hoped I should see her again—till I "twigged" her husband—who is surely a shock of the 1st magnitude. How can one *taste* of a woman when one has more or less to swallow such a man (or a slice of him) off the same dish? However, we got on, she & I, beautifully together & we pulled you famously to pieces. On Saturday I am going to some Stephen Gwynne [*sic*] Irish play again[25]—where I shall miss you, afresh, very acutely—& not have, this time, Violet Hunt to console yours,[26] my dear Jocelyn, forever & ever

Henry James

3.21.04.

ALS: Houghton bMS Am 1094.1

LAMB HOUSE, RYE, SUSSEX.

My dear boy Jocelyn. Aug: 10*th* *1904.*

My struggles, as you imagine them, with the sense of your penstrokes (& my own, by the same token, are none too luminous,) don't prevent my being peculiarly touched by every letter of yours that reaches me. Always remember that. It is the first I ever open, no matter what others arrive with it. And the record of your eternal Bacchanalia (do you know what Bacchanalia are?)[27] continue to excite my vague envy, or at least my lively admiration, of your social genius, social good health, the mysterious genial power that guides & sustains you through the multitude of your contacts & the mazes of your dance. What I do envy you is the magnificent *ease* with which you circulate & revolve—spinning round like a brightly-painted top that emits, as it goes, only the most musical hum. You don't *creak.* ⟨Two pages are missing here⟩ the "bawdy" Grosvenor Club at 8.15—

---

24. Mrs. Mond is Lady Violet Florence Mabel Goetze (1867–1945), wife of Alfred Mond, Baron Melchett. She formed a Women's Liberal Association in Chester in 1906 and was active in war relief from 1914 on. "The James Bryces" were First Viscount James Bryce (1838–1922)—British statesman, jurist, and author—and his wife, Elizabeth Marion Ashton Bryce (1853–1939). It was Bryce who brought the Order of Merit to HJ's bedside in January 1916.

25. Stephen Lucius Gwynn (1864–1950), a prolific Irish biographer and literary historian whose works included the well-known *Masters of English Literature* (1904), was a journalist in London from 1896 to 1904.

26. Violet Hunt (1862–1942), British writer, was a friend of both HJ and Jocelyn Persse.

27. Originally a Roman religious ceremony in honor of Bacchus, the god of wine, the Bacchanalia became a drunken orgy and was finally outlawed.

the Reform Club being closed then for cleaning. I will, however, be damnably definite. Only make me the sign of assent.

ALS: Houghton bMS Am 1094.1

LAMB HOUSE, RYE, SUSSEX.
September *21st 1905.*

I don't know, my dear Jocelyn, where this will find you, but I desire it to carry you my fondest blessing. I begin to suppose your return to London may be in sight, & want you to know, again (for I wrote you—to Park Place—rather copiously, & ever so responsively, in answer to yours from somewhere in Scotland) that I think all yearningly of the pleasure of having you here for a couple of days at no distant date; & beg you to remember that you are to work me in. My "book," thank heaven, is very clear—I've only a man coming for the 30th et & c.—that is between the 29th & Oct. 2d—& any time after that my door is pressingly open to you. I have to go up to town for 3 or 4 days—but that is some time or other only, & can wait: I welcome in fact excuses & postponements, anything that will keep that hanging on—or off. And so, my dear, dear boy, I bid you my late goodnight. I don't so much "wish" you may have flourished in the light of life, these last weeks, as feel sure that you have *done* so, possessing as you do the admirable & infallible faculty. Come to me therefore with your cup of experience overflowing, & let me taste in you, as always (for envy without a pang,) this genius for personally, & all so successfully, existing! It's one of your ways of doing good, dear Jocelyn, to your affectionate old friend, ever & always,

Henry James

ALS: Houghton bMS Am 1094.1

LAMB HOUSE, RYE, SUSSEX.
My dear Jocelyn.
[22 November 1905]

A word to say that I have settled for the *Imperial* on Friday p.m. next[28]—so please don't deflower our pure young virginal evening together by seeing the "Perfect Lover"[29] *before* that. Won't you dine with me first at the Reform, in simple sociability, & adjourn thence to the Theatre? We

---

28. London's Imperial Theatre was open from 1876 to 1907. First called the Aquarium Theatre, in 1901 it was converted into the Imperial Theatre by Lily Langtry, who modeled it on a Greek temple.

29. This undoubtedly refers to the play, *The Perfect Lover: A New and Original Play in Five Acts,* by Alfred Sutro (1863–1933).

should dine at *7.30*, I think—& if I don't hear from you otherwise I shall expect you. I pestered you over the B[ernard]. Shaw,[30] but you will have felt, yourself, that the source of this was the very tenderness of my consideration. Suppose I *had,* unwittingly, dragged you there a 4th time! I veil my face at the thought. But I *shall* drag you to the Sesame on Feb. 12th.[31] Those amiable Furies have been at me directly & insistently & I have succumbed. But you must *take* me; you must guide the steps of yours, my dear Jocelyn, ever

Henry James

Nov. 22*d 1905.*

ALS: Houghton bMS Am 1094.1

LAMB HOUSE, RYE, SUSSEX.

My dear Jocelyn. [December 1905–January 1906?]

Only a word to remind that you dine with me (very frugally!) on Tuesday 6th, at the R[eform].C[lub]., before our Theatre (Court)[32] of that evening. The play is at 8.15—& I fear we ought really (with my slowly ruminating food-system) to dine at a hideous 7. So you will eat with a Cow in a Beargarden—for that is what the Reform—with this Liberal Flood[33]—will have become. Unfortunately the Strangers' Coffeeroom isn't open there till Parliament meets. So we must pig in with the promiscuous horde; in spite of which, however, I am impatiently yours

Henry James

P.S. And don't forget either that you are due to me on the 12th—the Sesame Night!

ALS: Houghton bMS Am 1094.1

---

30. The Shaw play that ran in 1905 was *Major Barbara.* Jocelyn Persse wrote Edel, "No I do not remember his views about Shaw but I think that he thought the plays were provocative and stimulating. He was exasperated by the English Theatre and I do not think he had a very high opinion of the mentality of actors!" (1 October 1937, Edel Archive, McGill University).

31. Sesame may be the name of a London theater.

32. The "Theatre (Court)" is London's Royal Court Theatre, whose title is abbreviated to Court Theatre in some sources. Harley Granville-Barker (1877–1946) was manager from 1904 to 1907. Many of the first English productions by playwrights such as George Bernard Shaw, Maurice Maeterlinck, and Henrik Ibsen were staged there.

33. The "Liberal Flood" must refer to the growth of the Liberal Party in England. The letter is undated, so it is difficult to say when this is—probably the early 1900s. In 1906 the Liberals returned to power, largely as a result of Chamberlain's challenge to free trade.

Dear, dear Jocelyn. April 4*th 1906*.

The least sign or word from you, or intimated wish, makes me vibrate with response & readiness—so attached am I to your ineffaceable image: wherefore I send this off to Venice to meet you on your returning way & drench you (so far as it poorly may,) with my benediction. I am visited by the pangs of envy & yearning at the sight of your Perugian image[34] (the pretty picture-card received:) my imagination hangs about you & dogs your happy steps across the Italian scene—& the days when I too was young & Italy-haunting came back in their *troublant* [Fr.: disquieting] swarm. Well, drink as deep of the cup as you may, & come back to me here & breathe forth something of the scent and the taste. Lay up a treasure of impressions for me, & be prepared to hand them over when we meet. I hope you're having the right sort of time & no friction from any source— or sauce! You are well out of this grey island of the North, where the eastwind blows & the newspapers think between whiles[35] a little, my dear Jocelyn of your always & ever

Henry James

ALS: Houghton bMS Am 1094.1

My dear Jocelyn. [17 June 1906]

Yes indeed, the charming little reddy-brown porous object arrived, & I began immediately to dip it into the (as it were) water of your benevolence, so as to let the same trickle over & off me & cool & comfort my battered surface. It is a brave little memento, associated (as I'm a fairly clean creature) with one of the most frequent & regular acts of life, & yet promising, I judge, to be stout & *durable* in spite of it—so as to help to make me feel you about me the longer. I should like to have your Paris from you—keep a plum or two for me from the anecdotic pudding. Yes, Mrs. Mond swam into my ken (she has really a swanlike motor) with Mrs. Clifford on Friday,[36] & was lovely & graceful & charming & made the best of all the hardships & called you "dear old J" (which made me feel her quite a link— charmingly & rather funnily,) & in short much beautified, for the hour,

---

34. Perugia is a province in Umbria, in central Italy. HJ first went to Italy in summer of 1869.

35. The sense of "whiles" here seems to be to an archaic Scottish adverb meaning "sometimes"; "between whiles" thus might be "sometimes."

36. See the biographical register for Sophia Lucy Lane Clifford.

the homely little scene. Today I have an American friend & Mrs. Charles Hunter has come down to the George but feeds here.[37] Only this word—my cares are considerable. Yours, dear, dear boy, always

Henry James

June 17*th* 1906.

ALS: Houghton bMS Am 1094.1

LAMB HOUSE, RYE, SUSSEX.

Dearest Jocelyn! November 27*th* *1906.*

I just get your good note, & I scrabble of [*sic*] this for a bare catch of the post.

I come up to town Friday evening, for 3 or 4 nights, but go into the country on Saturday till Monday. I am submerged in necessities, but have kept *Tuesday* 4th p.m.—that is Evening. Will you dine with me & go to something as "low" as possible after? There is nothing at the theatres I can stand & I must wait for B[ernard]. S[haw]. till he comes on at night.[38] But I *could,* I think stand a Music Hall, & if I have a word from you—for which I fondly hope—that you *can* do these things (*here,* please, on Thursday a.m. if possible—or even kindly *wire* me) we will close on it. The sight of you is much desired by yours, my dear Jocelyn, always

Henry James.

ALS: Houghton bMS Am 1094.1

LAMB HOUSE, RYE, SUSSEX.

Dear dear Jocelyn. [22 January 1907]

Irresistible to me always any tug on your part at the fine & firm silver cord that stretches between us—as I think I never fail to show you: at any twitch of it by your hand, the machine, within me, enters into vibration & I respond ever so eagerly & amply! (My image sounds rather like the rattle of the telephone under the effect of a "call"; but I mean it well, & I mean it, above all, my dear Jocelyn, affectionately!) I sit here late this harshly-cold January night—very, very un-Roman, ah me!—& I read over your letter with a strange mixture of envy &—well, call it philosophy. I am glad you

---

37. Wife of a Tory MP and coal magnate, Mary Smyth (Mrs. Charles) Hunter (1857–1933) entertained HJ and other artists frequently at Hill Hall, her Essex estate. In 1906 the George Hotel, on the corner of Lion Street and High Street in Rye just two blocks from Lamb House, was over three hundred years old.

38. Shaw's 1906 play was *The Doctor's Dilemma.*

are seeing Rome as your age (which is delicious,) & your *siècle* [Fr.: century] (which is on the whole disgusting,) combine to offer it to you—"on toast" as they say; & on the india-rubber tyres of speed & opulence; but I will talk to you of the ancient paradise of *my* remote youth & of the time when the awful change wrought within the last 25 years (above all) was still to come. I rejoice at any rate that you are stuffing yourself with impressions & I propose to pick them out of you plum by plum. Therefore come back as gorged & replete as possible—you will fit the tighter into my embrace! Alas, I have never been to Subiaco—nor even to Viterbo:[39] few people have ever rushed about less. It is only just apparent to me, however, that I absolutely can't tread a little in your present steps next month—as I have been almost thinking I might. The dear good Henry Whites,[40] our American ambassadors, asked me some time to come & stay with them from the early part of next month to about the 20th (when they begin to break up for their move to Paris, to which he is appointed;) & I have been dallying with the idea. But it is quenched by impossibilities now, & it isn't very much the *way* I wanted to go [to] Rome; (an immense sacrifice of freedom—& all to *Society!*) But I definitely go to Paris, for some stay, by the ⟨a page or part of a page is missing here⟩ all the same, the days & weeks, are passing for me like the small stations seen from a tearing express. So much the better for their bringing you nearer again to yours, my dear Jocelyn, don't you see how tenderly?

Henry James
Jan. 22*d* 1907.

ALS: Houghton bMS Am 1094.1

58 RUE DE VARENNE. Paris

Dearest Jocelyn.   May. 4*th* 1907.

This is a small yearning word of appeal to you for some little news of your present state—let it break with a gentle crystal splash the black depths of our silence! I can rub along a certain time in that occasional darkness, but the day comes when I desire the sound of your voice, & then I thus invoke you. Besides which I "kind of" like to think that you feel a

---

39. Subiaco is an Italian town on the Anio River and Viterbo an Italian city not far from Rome.

40. An American diplomat, Henry White (1850–1927) was first secretary of the American Embassy in London and then American ambassador to Paris in 1908. His wife was Margaret Stuyvesant White (1854–1916), daughter of American astronomer Lewis Rutherfield.

little—even resent a little—my own long inaudibility. I came to Paris early in March for 2 or 3 weeks—to spend them with these excellent friends the Edward Whartons[41]—& then do a few more independent things—& lo I have staid *ten,* instead of my projected fortnight, & the end is not yet. It *is* to be, however, a week hence—when I dash down to Italy (at the empty, *ebbing* moment I love best,) to put in 30 days in Rome & Venice. I have had here a very interesting agreeable time—one of the most agreeable I have ever had in Paris; through living in singularly well-appointed privacy in this fine old Rive Gauche quarter, away from the horrible boulevards & hotels & cosmopolite crowd. My friends have simply stamped on me very hard when I've spoken of going—& je me suis laissé faire [Fr.: I have let myself go], philosophically—& come in for a great many social impressions of a sort I hadn't had for a long time—some of them of a more or less intimate French sort that I had *never* had: mixed, all, with a great deal of wondrous & beautiful motoring. We made some time since (the weather was then admirable) a tournée [Fr.: journey] of more than 3 weeks in the South (of France—Centre, Pyrenées & Provence & Burgundy,) during which I felt I was seeing the country in detail, & in an altogether thrilling & delightful manner. And here I have seen people & types & manners—to a tune that will give me plenty to tell you on some blest Sunday, after my return, when you come down & stroll with me in the *abutours* [Fr.: surroundings] of poor dear little russet Lamb House: which appears to me from here *so* russet & so humble & so modest & so British & so pervaded by boiled mutton & turnips; & yet withal so intensely precious & so calculated to rack me with homesickness—which it does even in the midst of this gilded bondage. Well, you, no doubt, have been having every day & all day, close at hand, according to your gallant custom, the thrill of life & the assault of impressions & the vision of types, that I have had to seek in foreign lands & at a considerable sacrifice of time & convenience—not to say of another precious element. (I calculate that when I leave this I shall have *seven* servants—including the wondrous American chauffeur—to tip handsomely!) Tell me at last, dear Jocelyn, something a little more cheerful of yourself than *that.* I wish you could have been here a little of this recent time. We could have taken you in very well—into our system!—& wd. have done so very heartily. My hostess is sympathetic, admirable,

---

41. See the biographical register for Edith Wharton. Her husband, Teddy (1850–1928), a Boston socialite, turned out to be emotionally unstable, and the couple divorced in 1913.

amazingly intelligent. Tell me you are *well,* solid, easy, brave, & that you sometimes think of your constant old friend

Henry James

ALS: Houghton bMS Am 1094.1

LAMB HOUSE, RYE, SUSSEX.

Dearest Jocelyn! *July 9th 1908.*

It was one thing to be greatly touched the other day by your gentle little telegram from passionate Peebles,[42] & quite another to snatch the right moment for responding to you as I desire. The whirlwind that is inevitably let loose on me at this Season—whirlwind of people & things, & calls to London, & necessities at home, & general tornado & conflict of complications, is just now rather at its maximum (I got back from a feverish further go at London but yesterday,)—so that the end is not yet. The foreground of my life is just now much occupied with near & numerous *relatives*— very delightful & interesting to me, but with the bump of visiting luggage frequent on my poor old staircase, & the attempted command of my time more or less futile & ridiculous.[43] Which I mention only to waggle my hand as out of the storm & stress—meaning it as a fond sign that we will make up these rather barren weeks (as far as our own blest contact is concerned,) at some more auspicious hour—which heaven speed! Yes, I just waggle at you a rather distracted head & fatigued hand—& I just hope passionate Peebles wasn't *too* hot for you. I remember how when I last saw you I wanted to breathe upon you an entirely *cooling* affection. I have vast chambers of *that* at your service—& through these you will wander again, in these you will sit again yet, with yours dearest Jocelyn, always & ever

Henry James

ALS: Houghton bMS Am 1094.1

LAMB HOUSE, RYE, SUSSEX.

My dearest Jocelyn. August *21st 1908.*

It is since last writing you that I have received, 1st: your gentle sign of written (à la Jocelyn!) remembrance from the unutterable place in Wales; & 2d a brace of grouse unidentified as to donor, but bearing the postmark

---

42. The small Scottish burgh of Peebles, where Jocelyn Persse hunted, is in the largely agricultural Peeblesshire not far from the English border.

43. The relatives would have included William and Alice James and three of their children, who visited HJ at various times during that summer.

of passionate *Peebles,* & which I thereby instinctively associate with you, & with the amiable people there was the question of our going over together to see from Edinburgh in the spring. I thank the amiable people very kindly & you very tenderly for the delectable game—very welcome at this very *peopled* & flushed little phase of the modest existence of Lamb House. I have had, & seem still likely to have, a considerable coming & going here, & the smallest contributions are thankfully accepted. Your Welsh letter gave me the particular joy & touched me as the particular way that any form of personal emanation from you, so to speak, never, dearest Jocelyn, fails of—& I should be sending you back this poor responsive token at this very hour, in all probability, even had the bloody birds not arrived. This hour is almost my first of solitude for a long time—& that only because a friend who *was* to have dined & spent the night here had to depart, by an ill-timed train, after dinner; whereby I sit here thus slightly disburdened at the evening's end. My brother left me but yesterday, to join his wife & daughter in Flanders, but they all presently return here together, & September too has the air to me of being destined to be rather interestingly— & at any rate continuously—agitated. But this splendid season & golden weather have made my modest scale of hospitality most easy & blessed— my little green garden has counted almost as another room—to turn amiable inmates into. And I have got on very well, with almost no *bad* interruption of cherished occupations, thank the Lord: though this now *generally* invaded & exploited & convulsed & disfigured little place—I mean the wretched Rye at large—has been bursting with damnable so-called sociabilities, curse their name! However, there I draw the line, & I crouch—crouch *and* crawl—behind my old red walls in proportion as the outer babble grows more furious. I've had two or three beautiful motor-afternoons—but they were peaceful enough, through quiet tracts of the wondrous Kent countryside, so much of it quite adorable. Meanwhile I read your Welsh note over & am confirmed in the belief that, your Irish visit performed, you *are* at P[assionate]. P[eebles].—or perhaps by this time further afield & the delight of another circle. Wherever you be I pray, dearest Jocelyn, it be very good & very salutary to you—& wherever you be I yearn & yearn over you. I shall probably myself cross the border for 3 or 4 days lateish in September—go to see the friend in Forfarshire whom I went to last year.[44] But when these agitations & others are spent (as I

---

44. See the biographical register for Mary Cadwalader Jones for his friend in Forfarshire.

suppose London will possess you a little before the end of that month,) you must come to me here for the two or three clear good days that we haven't had together for a desperate & dismal time. The watchful powers close round you all kindly till then. I am ever so tenderly faithful to you & addicted to the intimate vision & thought of you—which is to say that I am, dearest Jocelyn, your devoted & re-devoted old friend

H.J.

ALS: Houghton bMS Am 1094.1

My dearest Jocelyn.

LAMB HOUSE, RYE, SUSSEX.
[16 September 1908]

We communicate on unequal terms—you with the unerring gun, I with the scratchy stylograph; yet your sure aim brings me down, as it were, & you "miss" me, & my fond emotion at any sign from you, no more than you missed the excellent brace of grouse one member of which constituted the all-in-all of my refined repast this evening. Passionate Peebles has again its arms about you, I infer—& I can only congratulate & envy passionate Peebles! I have had only to-day to wriggle out of an engagement to go to Forfarshire that I had been more or less expecting to abide by—& for reasons (of wriggling) that are good & sufficient—& at all events imperative. The ebb & flow of my brother & *les siens* [Fr.: his people] through my humble home continues, & with more flow than ebb, & will till October 6th. But I enjoy it quite enough to wish to profit by *all* of it—& it's awkward for me to leave home. Later on—before next month rattles away—you must give me those promised two days here, remember—to make up for the starvation diet, as it were, on which the fates appear to have conspired for so many months to place us. There are charming days here still, in the midst of the general ruin of weather that I hear of elsewhere—& what is conveyed me of the considerable general beastliness in Scotland—though passionate Peebles has, I suppose, a tropic ardour peculiar to it—console me for not making that pilgrimage. Nothing, however, dearest Jocelyn, consoles me for not having you a little more in my existence—so I already hang all wistfully, as it were, about the gates by which heaven grant you may at no late day re-enter it. Continue meanwhile to adorn the lives of the more fortunate—& even a little to enjoy your own. Yours all constantly

Henry James
September 16*th* 1908.

P.S. I infer that you may *not* be present at your gifted Hamilton's première[45]—(the 21st I believe?) Forbes R[obertson]. behaves like[46]—well, *the* typical mountebank—over *my* little piece.

ALS: Houghton bMS Am 1094.1

LAMB HOUSE, RYE, SUSSEX.
[22 October 1908]

Dearest Jocelyn.

All thanks for your tender *petit mot* [Fr.: little word]—from which I am very sorry to gather you have been on your back with an ailment that I don't, I confess, wholly decipher. I trust that doesn't symbolise any untreatable—untractable—obscurity in it. I heartily pray that when this reaches you, you may be all your beautiful wholesome salubrious self again. As for me I have completely picked myself up from the temporary flatness into which I had been rather violently floored on Thursday a.m.—& as to which it was a positive comfort to me that you witnessed it!—and feel already like a giant refreshed. I mean I see things in their perspective & proportion, & see my own resources & conditions—& the sight, so far from being bad, is excellent. Most of all do I cherish the resource of this exquisite relation of ours, which gives a charm to life & in which I am always, dearest Jocelyn, more & more yours

Henry James
October: 22*d* 1908.

ALS: Houghton bMS Am 1094.1

[Reform Club, London]
July 4*th* 1909.

Dearest Jocelyn

It's a great interest & joy to hear from you. I had taken your absence for granted as inevitable &, as I hoped, beneficent & soothing to you—& this was confirmed to me by a couple of inquiries in Park Place. I have staid on here conveniently enough—but am now struggling homeward, in spite of

---

45. This might be Clayton Meeker Hamilton (1881–1946), American playwright, producer, and critic whose *Materials and Methods of Fiction* appeared in 1908.

46. Forbes R. was Sir Johnston Forbes-Robertson (1853–1937), London actor, manager, and producer for whom HJ converted his story "Covering End" into the play *The High Bid*. The play opened in Edinburgh in March 1908 and later had a very brief run in London. Persse saw the play's opening: "I went to Edinburgh as his guest to see the production of 'The High Bid' (a very beautiful and delicate work) but too delicate to be a popular success" (5 August 1937, Edel Archive, McGill University). Persse also suggested the actor Edward Sass for the role of the father (1 October 1927, McGill).

two or three complications that a little hinder & delay. I am not *certain* of being "in residence" till Saturday next, the 10th; but then I shall definitely be there, & alone, &, as I needn't say, delighted, dearest Jocelyn, to see you. Make me a sign therefore if I *may* expect you then. I am not in very famous "form"; but I look forward with yearning to these next months of quiet & complete rustication. I congratulate you all tenderly on having yourself enjoyed that boon in the high places & under that fine old Swiss protection—of the decency & serenity of which I have quite sacred memories—from of old; or rather from of young. You must tell me all about it, & we shall be happy & intimate again together. Take this as a sign of the all-faithful affection of yours, dearest Jocelyn, all constantly ever,

Henry James

P.S. This is a Sunday a.m. & your letter came last night. But I shall have wired you tomorrow, to the address you give me.

ALS: Houghton bMS Am 1094.1

LAMB HOUSE, RYE, SUSSEX.

Dearest Jocelyn. July 16*th* 1909.

I returned last night from a 3 days' motoring bout—which an amiable & imperative friend (Mrs. Wharton,) swooped down on me just after you left (last Monday) to whirl me off to. We were three, & the weather was admirable, & the fine old county of Sussex, which we did in detail, is wondrous; but my prized concentration has suffered & I've come back to a mountain of letters, amid which I find your sweet little cluster of hiero-glyphics. Burgess[47] assures me that no *coat* of yours whatever remained behind you—not a rag of your elegant drapery has come to light. So I'm not detaining anything as a fond or blest relic—though I shld. be almost capable of that. May the missing object suffer, at the worst, some other detention—in that spirit. May your present adventures be also otherwise blest to you. Our days together a week ago but confirmed for me (as such always do) the felt beauty of our Intercourse. We shall never fall below it— it is the dearest thing possible; & I am, as always, dearest Jocelyn, ever so tenderly yours

Henry James.

ALS: Houghton bMS Am 1094.1

---

47. Burgess Noakes (1887–1980) joined HJ's Lamb House staff in 1901. He took time off from his service there to join the British forces during World War I.

Dearest Jocelyn. [5 November 1909]

I have had, against my will, to wait a day or two to thank you for your note from the Raleigh Club—a new scene of activity for you, so far as my remembrance is concerned! May it prove a happy—as it is indeed perhaps an ancient—one! I am both sorry & glad to hear the pheasants weren't from you—I mean having Mrs. Black in the latter case to thank[48]—& shall write tonight to Mrs. Black to express my obligation to her. But, oh but, dearest Jocelyn, I can't go to Ockham on the 20th![49] It is impossible, & what makes it more so is that I have promised to go in a moment of accursed enfeeblement (for I don't find Ockham *very* interesting or amusing!) on the 27th. Can't you shift your visit till then—or come *again* on that day????? It's very sad, ah me, & all the more so that I'm really not in sorts for visits or social efforts at all. However I shall have to be in London for a few days at that time—& the die seems cast! And I am meanwhile delighted to hear of your being alleviated of your carnal superfluity—for I would give my most immediate jewel to be able to reduce myself to within a far cry of your bloatedest. I envy you thus more than ever your enchanted physique—though I would compromise on your beauty if I could only have your ease! We must meet somewhere & somehow about the month's end. I grieve at the Ockham perversity,—but rejoice you have renewed with the good old Monument & the Monumentals[50]—that 1st evening of ours under whose roof is a memory for all our days. Goodnight dearest Jocelyn. Ever your tout-dévoué [Fr.: all-devoted]

H.J.

Nov. *5th 1909.*

ALS: Houghton bMS Am 1094.1

---

48. See the introduction to the Persse letters for an account of his relationship with Mrs. Black.

49. Ockham was the home of Countess Mary Caroline Wortley Lovelace (1848–1941), wife of the second earl of Lovelace, Ralph Gordon Noel King (1839–1906), the grandson of Lord Byron. Countess Lovelace had asked HJ and John Buchan to read letters Byron had written to Lady Melbourne and deposit their written opinion of that correspondence in the British Museum.

50. The Monument and The Monumentals refers to the Sidney Colvins, who introduced HJ and Persse.

Hendrik Andersen. (Papers of Hendrik C. Andersen, Manuscripts Department, Library of Congress.)

Hendrik Andersen, 1930. (Papers of Hendrik C. Andersen, Manuscripts Department, Library of Congress.)

Hendrik Andersen's bust of Henry James, 1908. (Papers of Hendrik C. Andersen, Manuscripts Department, Library of Congress.)

Howard Sturgis and friend (possibly William Haynes Smith) at Queen's Acre, Windsor. (By permission of the Estate of Edith Wharton and the Watkins/ Loomis Agency, and the Beinecke Rare Book and Manuscript Library, Yale University.)

Henry James in 1907 on the steps of Cernitoio, near Vallambrosa, Italy. Howard Sturgis is on the left. (By permission of Bay James and the Houghton Library, Harvard University.)

Tilton portrait of Henry James, Venice, 1890. (By permission of Bay James and the Houghton Library, Harvard University.)

Pen-and-ink drawing by Howard Sturgis of Frederick Leighton's illustration for George Eliot's Romola, *"Father, I will be guided." (By permission of the Honorable Mrs. Crispin Gascoigne and the Bodleian Library, Oxford University.)*

3 May 1905 photograph of Henry James, by Katherine McClelland. (By permission of Bay James and the Houghton Library, Harvard University.)

Henry James in the garden house of Lamb House, Rye. (By permission of Bay James and the Houghton Library, Harvard University.)

Jocelyn Persse at his wedding to Mrs. Lorna Hutton Black, December 1938. (Photo courtesy of Yvonne Jarzebowska and Michael Jarzebowski.)

Hugh Walpole, 1940. (By permission of the Estate of Edith Wharton and the Watkins/Loomis Agency, and the Beinecke Rare Book and Manuscript Library, Yale University.)

95 Irving St. Cambridge Mass. U.S.A.

Dearest & most beloved Jocelyn. Oct: 27:1910.

If I have been hideously silent for so long it's because my troubles & griefs & hindrances have been so many & so absolute. I have been constantly & renewedly ill since coming to this country; though at first, for a short time after my beloved Brother's grievous death (which took place a week after our arrival,)[51] I bore up much better than I had feared. Then, however, began, under the effect of that blow, a series of relapses into the miserable conditions of my interminable illness of last winter & spring—conditions that still hung sadly over me when I caught you for that deplorably brief but intensely "dear" talk on the morning of July 15th. A dismal anxious pitiful time over my brother's state, with a retreat to Rye that made everything impossible till we sailed, swallowed me up after that—& I left England perforce without making you another sign. But it took my damnable situation so to hamper & haunt & preoccupy me, as it has taken the sad sequel since to work the same blight. My sister-in-law & I have been breasting, since my brother's death, a perfect flood of letters—as to the main mass of which however I have been able but to gape & sigh & postpone. By a blest dispensation, at any rate, I have just lately been enjoying an apparently serious respite from my evil tendency to drop down to black depths again—& I snatch a favouring moment to try & what is called put myself a little more right with you, my dear, dear old friend. I really believe I have taken a better turn that means something, & if that be true the spirit of our old felicity together will again (with a little more time & patience,) benignly visit us. It is true that I am expecting to spend the winter & spring in this country—but I am not less expecting to leave it then never again (D[eo].V[olente]. [Lt.: God willing]) to return to it; especially if I can get my dear sister-in-law & some of my so delightful nephews & niece (4 in all) to form the habit of coming regularly out to me (though such questions are of course complicated—they depend on so many things.)[52] We cling at any rate much together—closely & intimately

---

51. HJ's beloved brother William died on 26 August 1910, with his wife Alice and HJ in attendance. HJ and Alice had taken William from England back to his farm at Chocorua, New Hampshire, hoping that his health might improve there, but by that time his heart condition was too far advanced.

52. William and Alice James's children were Henry "Harry" (1879–1947), William "Billy" (1882–1961), Margaret Mary "Peggy" (Porter) (1887–1950), and Alexander "Aleck" (1890–1946). HJ became close to these four relatives after WJ's illness and subsequent death, and they visited him in England often.

so; & I can never be glad enough to have come over at our tragic crisis, or to be in this particular place now. I shall certainly stay here (on this spot) till January, & probably then go on to New York for a few weeks—or the rest of the winter; or even go for a little while to the South to meet the spring. (There is in this country the great boon that you can get into a great Pullman train & sit there comfortably enough for 3 days & 3 nights or so (from New York, say;) & then one morning wake up to find your carriage-window brushed more or less—in Florida or Georgia or Louisiana,—by the orange-bough & the passion-flower! It's not a question, alas, however, of your Monte-Carlo or your Villefranche or whatever.) In spite of these grim notes of absence, dearest Jocelyn, I want you to feel with what a rush, a passionate, yearning rush, I shall return. The time—this time—will pass—I find that even in darkness & pain it does insistently pass—& one shall recover something, as nearly as possible everything, of our beautiful *other* time. We shall make it live again. Before long will come round the anniversary of our rather odd & melancholy, but also exquisite, Sunday at Ockham—Nov. 27th–29th, 1909—in those fantastic contiguous apartments. When I think of such scenes & occasions from *this* point of view I grind my teeth for homesickness, I reach out to you with a sort of tender frenzy. I really converse about England with my small British Burgess, whom you will remember at Lamb House, & who is sturdily & faithfully useful & devoted; though, in general, in this country, one is divided between the impossibility of doing without some species of valet or doing *with* one. However, we are both much at our ease in this most pleasant & kind & commodious house—the mere flood of sunshine, the splendour of weather alone, makes up in these *parages* [Fr.: localities] for many things. And poor little Burgess is tasting of pure American freedom—after 9 years under the large British heel & indeed all the rest of the big authoritative foot—of Mrs. Paddington (with whom, by the way, before leaving England, I parted forever.)[53] But good-bye, beloved Jocelyn—though I have asked you nothing about your delightful old self. You will tell me all you can without that—you will make some faithful & generous sign to your fondest, tenderest old

Henry James.

P.S. You perhaps won't conceive where I *am,* exactly—unless I tell you that this place is just 3 miles from Boston (is practically continuous with it;) &

---

53. Mrs. Paddington was Joan Paddington, HJ's housekeeper at Lamb House. She retired prior to his move to Cheyne Walk in London.

that Harvard University, the seat of my brother's long & illustrious activity, makes us our goodly background.

ALS: Houghton bMS Am 1094.1

LAMB HOUSE, RYE, SUSSEX.

Dearest Jocelyn. October *4th 1911.*

I have been back in England since the mid-August, yet I have, all advisedly, made you no sign.[54] I've waited, on purpose, to do so in as fit & favouring a form only as should be worthy of both of us. You haven't been for a day out of my mind's, or my heart's, eye; but I returned, by a fatality, to a great many disconcerting & rather blighting influences & accidents— & I never want to approach you save when I'm as serene & steady as your poor old battered & tattered, though ever so fondly faithful, friend can nowadays ever again hope to convey to you the impressions of his being. Thank goodness the last fortnight has made a great difference for the better with me—& *now,* dearest Jocelyn, I let myself celebrate it. The biggest celebration I can think of is just at last again to get into relation with *you*— as a preliminary to never again getting out of it (so far as I have *been* out of it—save by more lapses of superficial sound) so long as I may go on for the rest of my earthly course near you. I fear I mayn't at this moment be so near you—or you at least so near me—as for you to be able to dine with me all blessedly alone on Tuesday evening the 10th at the R[eform]. C[lub]. (I shall have then to come up for 2 days.) Or if Tuesday is impossible to you would Wednesday be manageable?—I wd. in that case stay over for the loved sake of you. I darkly fear you may be on tour—that is out for sport— in Paris (or, more tremendously, Peebles;) but I greatly hope for you, as I shall all tenderly welcome. Then we shall be able to settle for your coming down to me here—as I shall particularly appeal to you to do. If you are at a distance on the days I speak of that is all the greater reason why I shld., on some slightly later day, have you here. That's all *now*—we shall jaw every-thing out so much better. Dear & beautiful to me is the prospect. Make me yourself some faithful even if undecipherable sign—& if I have to spend much "time over it," that will be nothing to the time I want now, & after this dark interregnum, to spend over *you*. Let me begin, at last, soon & well, & believe me, dearest Jocelyn, ever your all affectionate

Henry James

---

54. HJ has returned from his trip to America, where he spent almost a year after his brother William's death.

P.S. I told my Publisher (Methuen,) a few days since, to send you a small new book of mine, *The Outcry.*[55] May it safely have come.

ALS: Houghton bMS Am 1094.1

THE REFORM CLUB

My dear* Jocelyn. Dec. *2d 1911*

They have wired me that a box is reserved for me, & as the play is early beginning 7.30 we shall have to make a great effort. I shall at any rate await you there; but if you are late (*don't* be!) I shall leave word below that you be conducted thither—with . . . I hope it's Ms. Black.[56] I shall only have some tea—& reserve myself for your supper though even then scant fare must be my portion. The whole (turn of the) situation is charming, & I am more than ever, dearest Jocelyn, your fond

old H.J

* This poor substitute for the superlative is merely the effect of slightly harassed haste!

ALS: Houghton bMS Am 1094.1

REFORM CLUB, PALL MALL. S.W.

Dearest Jocelyn. May *31st 1912*

I have just (after considerable doubt & difficulty) accepted an invitation from Lady Lovelace for Saturday July 6th. There have been some reasons against it; mainly, I mean, that I have lately been by no means remarkably well & that that always makes me nervous & deprives me of confidence for performance of pledges of this order a good deal ahead. What has sustained me is the memory of our visit there together 3 years ago,[57] & the intense hope that you may be of the occasion this time. I count on that, & pray it may be given me to hear from you presently that you *have* been asked. *Be* asked, dearest boy; make sure of it somehow. It is probably just what she intends—but I shall be sold indeed if you're not there. I shall see you long

---

55. *The Outcry*, inspired by the public outcry when foreign money nearly took Hans Holbein the Younger's *The Duchess of Milan* out of England, began in 1909 as his last play. During his year spent in the United States he turned this play into a surprisingly successful novel.

56. A note in someone else's handwriting is pencilled in below "it's Mrs. Black," saying that "Jocelyn married Mrs. Black later after HJ was dead."

57. This visit, again, was HJ and Persse's visit to Lady Lovelace's Ockham on 27–29 November 1909. HJ had alluded to the visit before in loving and sentimental rhetoric.

before that, but this is a precaution taken. I have been keeping very still—have had to go very gently & live, generally, in the minor key; which has made me seem unsociable & even inhuman, doubtless. But I have difficulties—& it's sometimes all I can do—! Trust me, all the same, a little longer, & believe always all affectionately yours

Henry James

ALS: Houghton bMS Am 1094.1

Lamb House Rye

Dearest Jocelyn. Oct *28th 1912*

Lady C. has written me,[58] but it's hopelessly impossible. I am simply wretched—& had to go back to bed after your departure (at once!) & stay there till noon today. The end seems still far off, & my making an engagement for a London revel & riot in a few is an idea presented to me (by poor *urgent* Lady C.) as an almost cruel derision. I can't *write,* dearest J.; but I am none the less all so affectionately yours (seeing you, having you here, the other day, had so all the old charm again!)

Henry James

P.S. I have of course written—in adamantine terms, yet also honeyed, to Lady C.

ALS: Houghton bMS Am 1094.1

21, CARLYLE MANSIONS, CHEYNE WALK. S.W.

2417 KENSINGTON.

My dear dear Jocelyn!   May 18*th* 1913 (forgive smirches—*May 18th*)

I am sitting to Sargent for my portrait—that is I began to-day, & have the next sitting on Thursday next 22d.[59] He *likes* one to have a friend there to talk with & to be talked to by, while he works—for animation of the countenance &c; & I didn't have one today & we perhaps a trifle missed it.

---

58. This might be Lady Carnarvon, Elizabeth Catherine Howard (1858–1912), whom HJ met in 1878 and with whom he lunched in July 1912, or it could be Lady Crewe, with whom he dined in July 1912. He also corresponded with Lady Coleridge. He knew Lady Frances Sitwell Colvin (1839–1924), to whom he wrote on 25 October 1912. A final possibility is Lady Katherine Marble Conway (1856–1933).

59. Famous American painter John Singer Sargent (1856–1925) painted a portrait of HJ to commemorate his seventieth birthday. Friends had raised money to pay Sargent for his work, but he announced that he would not accept payment, and the subscription money went instead to sculptor Derwent Wood for HJ's bust. In his pocket diaries HJ noted that he had a sitting with Sargent on 18 May 1913.

Will you—can you, & should you care to, come for this helpful purpose the next time—on this coming Thursday aforesaid? Do if you can. The thing will then be to be at Tite St by 11.15, say,—*31* Tite St., Chelsea. I sit for about 2 hours—make it even *11.30* (I begin at 11.) Let me, kindly, hear by a word—I *may*, then, "apply elsewhere." Yours, dearest Jocelyn, all & always

Henry James.

ALS: Houghton bMS AM 1094.1

LAMB HOUSE, RYE, SUSSEX.

TELEPHONE 51 RYE

Dearest Jocelyn. [11 August 1914]

It was because I had come to imagine with some intensity that you might have been caught, held up & otherwise made to suffer, on the Continent—like so many unfortunates I still know there; & your wire is now an unspeakable relief. I rejoice with all my heart that you are so present here, & even so near. In normal conditions I should be saying, with urgency, "Can't you *come* here for a night or two & *won't* you, on the spot?"—but everything is so hideously dislocated that one doesn't take such possibilities, such pleasant & happy ones, quite for granted. I am *better*, much, in spite of the horrors going on, than I was 6 months ago, & I have my niece & my youngest nephew with me—he caught by the coat-tail just as he was skipping over to Germany on August 1st.[60] They cramp my other hospitality. They are good for me, & *to* me, & will remain till their going back to America can take place on some safe & convenient basis. *Then* you must indeed let me ask for you—as things may stand. But oh the appalling blackness of it all, & the horror of having lived to see it![61] We are all alike overwhelmed by that, aren't we? & we can only exchange execrations & dismays, all round—when we speak at all, & I think we never generally talked less. But it's a blessing, as I say, to know about you, & it *will* be a delight to see you as soon as the situation makes for our coming together with any ease. I hope you are well & that, wherever you are (I don't *place* you in the county,) you are some comfort to somebody—as how can you possibly help being? I myself even try to work—to escape turning too abjectly sick. But the thought, the lurid image, that while this

---

60. This is Margaret Mary "Peggy" James and Alexander "Aleck" James.
61. HJ speaks of the beginning of World War I, an event that caused him much sorrow.

loveliness of season & scene, here, prevails, such things are going on just là-bas [Fr.: over there] haunts unspeakably, dearest Jocelyn, your ever-affectionate old

Henry James
Aug. 11*th* 1914.

ALS: Houghton bMS Am 1094.1

21 CARLYLE MANSIONS CHEYNE WALK S. W
TELEPHONE 2417 KENSINGTON.

Dearest Jocelyn. Oct: 8*th 1914*

I rejoice to hear of your successful incorporation & hope with all my heart you may find your work interesting & sustaining.[62] I therefore give you all my blessing & backing on it. To feel yourself *doing* something must make our hideous tension more tolerable—all but impossible do *I* find it to bear in my aged & helpless inaction. My telephone *hasn't* been wrong—I'm sorry you had trouble: it was a bungle of the exchange. But I'm sorry to say I've been unwell & 2 or 3 days in bed since you were here; in spite of my "looks" alas I have occasional horrid collapses. But I am better & have been out today. *Do* come & see me again if you have a chance after you're at work—as to [*sic*] you intimate that you *may* have. I shall want greatly all your facts—& I pray they be salubrious ones. More than ever affectionately yours, dearest Jocelyn

Henry James

ALS: Houghton bMS Am 1094.1

21 CARLYLE MANSIONS CHEYNE WALK S.W.
TELEPHONE 2417 KENSINGTON.

Dearest Jocelyn. [4 November 1914?]

I have been greatly touched by your note, but the omens proved very unfavourable for my getting out early in the a.m. today to see you step forth. I am able in truth in these days to attempt nothing in the least active at all *betimes* in the day: the early hours are my worst & I have to trust them to get better, as they generally do, as the day goes on. On any possible opportunity I shall be so glad to come down & see you. How can one imagine anything more "right" than to do what you have done?—or that there should be any question of it?[63] Surely you will find it an immense

---

62. Persse had joined the Royal Welsh Fuseliers but came down with pneumonia while in camp at Essex and was sent home on sick leave.

63. This must refer to Persse's going to the regiment.

appeasement to your nerves & spirit, & you have my fondest blessing upon it. I intensely envy you the sense, & the fact, of *doing*—almost no matter what that directly helps, that sets the example and keeps up the pitch above all: to remain inactive at such a crisis, in your splendid prime, still, of manhood, would be a thing to make you eat your heart out. Therefore I heartily embrace you & applaud & back you. We shall *all*, it seems to me, have "very little to live on," but we shall live together in the honour & the adventure of it—& I will *always* share a crust with you. Yours, dearest Jocelyn, through everything all faithfully

Henry James
Nov. 4*th*.

ALS: Houghton bMS Am 1094.1

21 CARLYLE MANSIONS CHEYNE WALK S.W.
TELEPHONE 2417 KENSINGTON.

Dearest Jocelyn.   Nov: 15*th* 1914

That any word of mine should in the midst of this strange handling the Fates are treating us to have at all "cheered" you is a great comfort to me here. As I think of you this miserable morning under the lash of the elements I feel that you must need all the cheering you can get. Very interesting to me all the same your pencilled letter of 3 days ago, with its suggestion of the stern reality of your conditions & the picturesque variety of your associates. I greatly hope that among the latter you may find some sympathetic or understanding spirit or two. You will probably *live into* all the queerness & roughness of it & find your whole sense of proportion & even of propriety change—this seems to be what happens pretty quickly to most men—& when you *do* get a bath it will be to you such a heavenly balm as you had never dreamed it could be in the good old days—if any days can be called good that were so villainously leading up to these. Keep up your heart & hold up your head—you will infinitely rejoice in the eventual future to have had a hand in the Great Time. You'll be more interesting to yourself—& also more interesting, much, to your friends— even to those who, like me, had thought they had almost measured your interest. Most of the men one has had any observation of, moreover, have found themselves positively the *better* for camp, after once they had got the hang of it, & I am full of the fond fancy that this is the case with you. Burn your ships—don't look behind or beside (at the Club for instance;) do the thing itself for all it's worth, & it will yield you up secrets & values. I wish I had some rousing news to regale you with; but the public tidings (which are good, if not rousing) reach you freely, I take it, & private circumstances & occurrences seem simply not to exist. I go this evening to sup en famille [Fr.: at home] with the Sutros[64]—I usually don't sup at home Sundays; but there is no very high colour (though a pleasant friendly tint) in *that*. Is there anything you want or need or fancy (even like a lady on the way to be a mamma,) that I can send you? Try to think of something "rich & strange"—either in the way of tobacco, underclothing or literature. I will send you any underclothing but female—which I am told the Germans are often found uncannily wearing! I draw the line at *that*—even to make you even with them. Hullo, it's clearing up—the sun floods of a sudden my room & gilds your image & scene as gallantly presented to yours, dearest Jocelyn, more than ever

Henry James

ALS: Houghton bMS Am 1094.1

21 CARLYLE MANSIONS CHEYNE WALK S.W.

TELEPHONE 2417 KENSINGTON.

Dearest Jocelyn. *Nov. 16th 1914.*

When I came in lateish last evening it was a shock to me to find you had been here & I had missed you. If I only could have dreamed you might come!—for the sight of you would have greatly heartened me. I almost always dine at a club on Sunday p.m. to give the servants the evening to themselves. But I am glad you got your day off for your own relief, as I suppose I may call it. I wrote to you at some length a letter which I trust will have reached you on Monday a.m. *This* only renews my good hopes, all my affectionate old confidence for you. Do let me see you somehow *concertedly* after a bit. Again I groan at your having made your journey to no rewarding end yesterday. Well, believe in all the greater affection (while you stiffen your back & hold on to your soul) of yours always & ever

Henry James

ALS: Houghton bMS Am 1094.1

---

64. HJ socialized often with British couple Esther Isaacs Sutro (c. 1865–1934), artist, writer, and pianist; and Alfred Sutro (1863–1933), author and translator who wrote more than forty plays.

Howard Sturgis

During the first few years of the twentieth century it seems that Henry James fell briefly but passionately in love with Howard Sturgis, a love that Sturgis may have reciprocated. This was the love of a powerful older man for a younger socialite and writer who lacked James's own professional confidence and security, who sought from James support and reassurance regarding his writing.

On more than one occasion James told Howard that he could live with him.

> You *were*, historically, here and you will as substantially (without reflection on your figure,) be again. It's so much gained. We can arrange, always, with a view to you. You were a most conformable (don't read that by mistake comfortable—for who knows?) & delightful guest. I repeat, almost to indiscretion, that I could live with you. Meanwhile I can only try to live without you.[1]

But as much as James desired companionship and love at this time in his life, he was unable to prevent himself from criticizing Sturgis's work freely, criticism that must have been wounding. The relationship lessened in intensity after 1904, and though toward the end of his life James expressed deep affection for Sturgis, the two never achieved a long-lasting bond.

Howard Overing Sturgis (1855–1920) was a third beloved younger friend for Henry James. Although Sturgis had a lifelong companion, a distant cousin, William "The Babe" Haynes Smith, he had other intimate friendships with both men and women, including an affectionate relationship

---

1. HJ to Howard Sturgis, 25 February 1900.

with James. He came from a wealthy expatriate American family, his father a prominent banker with the firm of Baring Brothers. The Sturgises entertained frequently at their homes in Carlton Terrace and Walton-on Thames. After his schooling at Eton, Cambridge, and the Slade School, Sturgis returned home to care for his parents, both of whom were ailing. Russell Sturgis, after years of invalidism, died in 1887 and his wife, Julia, the subsequent year. Sturgis's own health suffered after his parents' death, and he may have developed some ambivalent feelings toward the authoritative parental figure and concomitant feelings of personal insecurity as a result of his family experiences, as witness his own pen-and-ink drawing in a letter to Sir Lewis Harcourt. This brief letter reproduces Leighton's illustration to George Eliot's novel *Romola* and shows a figure bowing in submission to the father saying, "Father, I will be guided." Later accounts of Sturgis suggest that he was indeed eager to please others.

Sturgis, only twelve years younger than James and the oldest of the four men represented in this edition, became both sociable and intellectual in his own right after recovering from the death of his parents. He entertained frequently and lavishly at his estate at Windsor, Queen's Acre (or Qu'acre), and often invited James for long weekend visits. Oblivious to nineteenth-century gender roles, he acted female parts at Eton and Cambridge and as an adult wore shawls and did needlework while the "Babe" played billiards. In his diary Arthur Benson noted, "I have had rows with Howard, but he is more feminine than most of my friends."[2] James's correspondence itself reveals an easy and joyous relinquishment of conventionally gendered rhetoric vis-à-vis Sturgis, as he salutes his friend as dearest "Miss Hurter" in one 1909 letter. Sturgis had many friends of both sexes, friends that he nourished both through his own correspondence and through his constant generous entertaining, friends who were tolerant of his differences:

> But most of all he was companionable, with a caress in his playfulness; people thought him original and odd, but also very domestic, very cosy, as he hooked at his woolwork or stitched at his silken embroideries; and sometimes you could see people begin by thinking him suspiciously exotic, with his pretty pastimes and his caressing ways, and then expand in confidence when they found him so amusing, so considerate and rational.[3]

---

2. *The Diary of Arthur Christopher Benson,* ed. Percy Lubbock (New York: Longmans, Green, 1926), 157.

3. Percy Lubbock, *Mary Cholmondeley; A Sketch from Memory* (London: Jonathan Cape, 1928), 58–59.

Sturgis, known as "Howdie" within his intimate circle, was continually mindful of his friends' needs, as his own unpublished correspondence attests. To Francis Jenkinson, University Librarian at Cambridge from 1889 to 1923, he wrote a series of supportive letters. One letter, dated 13 December 1885, reveals Sturgis's personal generosity in supporting a student, whom he calls "the young cuckoo I laid in your nest."[4] In the same letter he showed concern for another young Etonian named Simpson in humorous rhetoric: "He [Simpson] has a heart of gold, & curls of the same, but unfortunately a fair supply of other forms of the same metal, & though not without plenty of brains, he is not in the least intellectual."[5] He promoted his friends' causes, at one point trying to raise a purse for A. C. Ainger, clergyman and biographer.[6] He was interested in politics, both on a local and a national level, agitating for Ainger to become bursar, probably at Cambridge or at a church, and in another letter inveighing against Chamberlain and the Boer War:

The row of cherub faces with little high collars in the Daily papers day by day, & "Killed" or "died of wounds" underneath makes me sick. I don't wish Joseph [Chamberlain] anything so good as to be haunted by their pretty ghosts, but I hope ugly old Boer Generals with ghastly holes in their stomachs will surround his couch *nightly*.[7]

Several letters reveal his passionate love of books, as he asks Jenkinson to buy a number for him at an auction. He also had interests in both art (he studied at the Slade for a time) and theater, remarking to Sir William Harcourt, "I went with Lily & Mary to see your friend Mrs. Patrick Campbell as Ophelia last night, & was charmed with her: she is the first Ophelia I ever saw who was content to make the part what Shakespeare meant it to be, a poor weak girl, shattered by the events, in the midst of

4. Als, Howard Sturgis to Francis Jenkinson, Cambridge University Library, Add 6463/460, p. 3. This and subsequent citations to the Jenkinson papers are by permission of the Syndics of Cambridge University Library.

5. Ibid., 7.

6. Als, Howard Sturgis to Sir Lewis Harcourt, Bodleian Library, letter of 5 June 1901, Ms. Harcourt dep. 436, pp. 213–15. This and subsequent citations from the Harcourt papers are by permission of the Honorable Mrs. Crispin Gascoigne and the Bodleian Library at Oxford University.

7. Als, Howard Sturgis to Sir Lewis Harcourt, Bodleian Library, letter of 31 October 1899, Ms. Harcourt dep. 436, p. 61.

which her poor little lot was cast; & her mad scene was distressingly convincing."[8]

James's friendship with Sturgis was a long-standing one that varied in degrees of intensity. James had known Sturgis's father and thus Sturgis since he was a young man.[9] But in 1899 their relationship changed. The bright-eyed, prematurely gray and sturdy Sturgis became James's intimate, yet another beloved companion with whom James socialized and corresponded. In March 1900 James sent Howard a book to commemorate their "congress" (the dictionary gives "coitus" as one meaning for this word), beginning his love letter with diction scarcely reminiscent of the "Master" just beginning his major phase: "'Henry' quite basks & waggles his head to be scratched, in the pleasant warmth of it."[10] Sturgis in return sent James a gift for his bedside. James called Sturgis his nursing mother and commiserated with him about the back problems both experienced.

As a writer himself, Sturgis valued James's advice and appreciated the time James spent with him. Sturgis published a novel in 1891, *Tim: A Story of School Life*, a homoerotic and sentimental tale of a frail young boy who falls in love with an older stout lad, Carol Darley. The epigraph to the novel reads, "Thy love to me was wonderful, passing the love of women," and the text as a whole is a passionate defense of male-male love. While sentimental, its tone suggests that the love of Tim and Carol is pure and lofty, a noble thing.[11] Macmillan advertised it as one of its series of "Dollar Novels," without using Sturgis's name. Perhaps before the Wilde case, Sturgis (and Macmillan) had less reticence about promoting same-sex love narratives. His second novel, *All That Was Possible; Being the Record of a Summer in the Life of Mrs. Sibyl Crofts, Comedian* (1895), is written in epistolary form, as forty-six letters written by Sibyl Crofts, an actress abandoned by her longtime lover, the earl of Medmenham, who left her to marry Lady Florence Marlow. Although the plot itself is inherently didac-

---

8. Als, Howard Sturgis to Sir William Harcourt, Bodleian Library, letter of 20 November 1897, Ms. Harcourt dep. 436, p. 64–65.

9. See Kaplan, *Henry James*, 210.

10. Als, HJ to Howard Sturgis, 4 March 1900.

11. As Tim is dying, his friend Carol realizes how much the young man had loved him: "He forgot himself, Violet [his fiancée], his love for her, everything for the moment, in contemplation of this devotion, so single-hearted, so lofty, so pure and unselfish, which had been his, all his, and at which he had been so far from guessing." See *Tim* (London: Macmillan, 1891), 314.

tic, the protagonist herself is likable, honest, and somehow not stereotyped despite her stereotypical plight. The novel's old-fashioned flavor, though, old-fashioned even for 1895, keeps it from being a better book. It seems to take place in the eighteenth century rather than the nineteenth.

When he began his third novel, *Belchamber* (1904), he sought help from James, as he evidently struggled with writing it, telling Francis Jenkinson on 1 January 1902, ". . . I *must* stay at home & try & finish my wretched book."[12] Unfortunately, however, the help James offered with the "wretched book" may have contributed to a diminishing of their relationship. James was pointedly critical of this work in progress, and while Sturgis claimed these critiques strengthened the novel, it is hard to believe that James's blunt comments did not wound. In December 1903, when Sturgis evidently had decided to withdraw the novel from publication, James urged him not to do so, but nonetheless the professional took its toll on the personal and the intensity of the friendship waned. Sturgis continued to speak warmly of James's texts,[13] seemingly bearing no malice toward James, but James never encouraged Sturgis to continue his writing. More recent generations of readers have been kinder to *Belchamber* than James was. E. M. Forster said in a 1934 review of Edith Wharton's biography *A Backward Glance*, "[*Belchamber*] seems to me now, as it did then, brilliant, amusing, unsparing, poised, full of incidents and characters, indeed, well on the way to a masterpiece."[14] The novel was then revived in 1935, and it was reprinted as recently as 1986 by Oxford University Press.

After *Belchamber*, Sturgis published only two slight works, a short story, "On the Pottlecombe Cornice" (1908), and a memorial essay on Anne Thackeray Ritchie (1919).[15] Sturgis had in some ways internalized James's critical habits, as he later did much the same sort of thing to Theodora Bosanquet,[16] as she wrote her memoir of James. He told her that a stranger reading her description of her late and respected employer would see a

---

12. Cambridge University Library, Add 8596/142, p. 3.

13. In a letter written 4 December 1904, HJ thanks Sturgis for his earlier friendly remarks on the "Bowl" (HJ's novel *The Golden Bowl*).

14. "Good Society," *New Statesman and Nation*, 23 June 1934, 952.

15. See Elmer Borklund, "Howard Sturgis, Henry James, and *Belchamber*," *Modern Philology* 58 (May 1961): 255–69.

16. Theodora Bosanquet (1880–1961) was HJ's last secretary of three. He had a high regard for her abilities. Her book about him, *Henry James at Work* (1924), gives an account of their work together.

picture of a "grotesque quality, & I am sure that is not how you saw Henry or would wish to present him to those who had never seen him—a sort of cross between Chesterton & 2d Charles Beresford, & dressed like a clown."[17] He had warned her earlier that this style of criticism has become his own: "I have such an unfortunate trick of telling people just what I think of their work, and though many people have taken it in good part, a few have been annoyed."[18]

After James's hard lessons in literary criticism, however, the intensity of the relationship lessened and the two saw one another less frequently as the years went by. James's witty and warm letters, though, continued unabated. And even though James was unhappy with how the three Boits, who were Howard Sturgis's American cousins, behaved in Lamb House while he was on his 1904–5 American tour, James seems not to have blamed Sturgis in any way for their actions. In 1906 he was a boa constrictor, giving Howard an accolade, and on 15 April 1913 he said, "Better news than that you are facing homeward there couldn't possibly be. I long to see you with a great ache of longing—& poor affair as I myself am (or have quite preponderantly been) we will each on our side work for it."[19] Sometimes James seemed to put off Howard's visits, telling him in the fall of 1908 that there was nowhere appropriate for Sturgis and the Babe to stay in Rye—whereas in the early 1900s James urged Sturgis to visit him at Lamb House, alone. James and Wharton motored to see Howard at Queen's Acre together often, but visits from Howard to James in Rye seemed far less frequent. Sturgis mourned when his friend died, telling Theodora Bosanquet, "I suppose one ought to be thankful that he has been spared what might have been & what was too hideous to think of. But all I seem to feel is that the friend of all those years is gone, & that I never can see him again."[20]

Sturgis himself had developed stomach problems in 1914, later diagnosed as cancer.[21] He had surgery at that time, which seemed successful,

17. Als, Howard Sturgis to Theodora Bosanquet, 10 November 1916, Houghton bMS Eng1213.3 (196). This and subsequent quotes from Sturgis's letters to Theodora Bosanquet are by permission of the Houghton Library, Harvard University.

18. Als, Howard Sturgis to Theodora Bosanquet, 18 June 1916, Houghton bMS Eng1213.3 (195).

19. HJ to Howard Sturgis, 15 April 1913.

20. Als, Howard Sturgis to Theodora Bosanquet, 29 February 1916, Houghton bMS Eng1213.3 (192).

21. Shari Benstock, *No Gifts from Chance: A Biography of Edith Wharton* (New York: Charles Scribner's Sons, 1994), 293.

but he finally died of this disease in January 1920, Edith Wharton noting, "In Howard Sturgis's case a fatal illness had declared itself, and much suffering was inevitable; so that his best friends could only pray for the end to come quickly. Happily it did, and he faced it with lucid serenity."[22] The Babe stayed with him until the end.

22. *A Backward Glance* (New York: Charles Scribner's Sons, 1964), 365.

Hotel d'Europe *Rome*

My dear Howard.   May 19. 1899.

It's a great pleasure to hear from you in this far country—though I greatly wish it weren't from the bed of anguish—or at any rate of delicacy: if delicacy may be connected, that is, with anything so indelicate as a bed! But I'm very glad to gather that it's the couch of convalescence—only, if you have a Back, for heaven's sake take care of it.[23] When I was about your age—in 1862!—I did a bad damage (by a strain subsequently—through crazy juvenility—neglected,) to mine; the consequence of which is that, in spite of retarded attention, & years, really, of recumbency, later, I've been saddled with it for life, & that even now, my dear Howard, I verily write you *with* it. I even wrote *The Awkward Age* with it:[24] therefore look sharp!—I wanted especially to send you that volume—as an "acknowledgment" of princely hospitalities received, & formed the intention of so doing even in the too scant moments we stood face to face among the Rembrandts. That's right—*be* one of the Few! I greatly applaud the tact with which you tell me that scarce a human being will understand a word, or an intention, or an artistic element or glimmer of any sort, of my book. I tell *myself*—& the "reviews" tell me—such truths in much cruder fashion. But it's an old, old story—& if I "minded" now as much as I once did, I should be well beneath the sod. Face to face I shld. be able to say a bit how I saw—& why I *so* saw—my subject. But that will keep.——I've been in a warmish quietish, emptyish, pleasantish (but not maddeningly so,) altered & cocknefied & scraped & all but annihilated Rome. I return to England some time next month (to the country—Lamb House, Rye—now my constant address—only.) I see of course considerably Waldo & Mrs. W.[25] He is not at all well, & should take 3 months'—imperatively—rest &

---

23. Throughout his life HJ suffered from back problems, deriving (at least in part) from an injury sustained while fighting a fire in Newport, Rhode Island, on 28 October 1861. He refers to this injury in his second autobiographical volume, *Notes of a Son and Brother*, as a "horrid even if obscure hurt" that he suffered at the same hour as the Civil War began (although his dating here is incorrect). Some later commentators interpreted this hurt as a sexual injury or castration, but there is no concrete evidence for such a view. This letter corroborates the idea that "the obscure hurt" was indeed a back injury.

24. *The Awkward Age* (1899) concerns adults carrying on drawing room conversation before adolescent daughters. He composed it as a sort of drama cast in novel form. HJ was himself pleased with the novel, but the public did not rush to buy copies.

25. Waldo and Mrs. Waldo refer to sculptor Thomas Waldo Story (1855–1915) and his wife Maud Broadwood Story (c. 1860–1932). They lived in the Barberini Palace in Rome. They separated in 1898 and later divorced.

regimen. But his vast marble-shop! However, this is only to greet & warn you—& to be, my dear Howard, your affectionate old friend

Henry James

ALS: Houghton bMS Am 1094 (1184)

LAMB HOUSE, RYE.
February 2d. 1900.

My dear Howard.

Comme cela se trouve! [Fr.: how things turn out]—it is delightful. Everything is delightful save that you won't give me a name—not even, as if I were a dog, a bad one. Call me Henry James & have done with it. Begin (if we may talk of beginning after more than 20 years!) with that, at any rate—& we will then work on to something better. Your letter is very charming to me; I rejoice extremely that you name a decently near date, & you shall be made as welcome as my poor house knows how. The fatted chicken shall be sacrificed to you; the house swept & garnished; the retinue feebly drilled. Admirable of you to bring the literary egg which you are so commendably hatching toward a book.[26] This quiet nook is an excellent incubator. You shall have organized privacy—a receptacle in which to "set," as they say here—& I shall take the greatest interest. I give you all my thanks & my full promise in respect to your condition of the unmitigated or unmodified Morning. Yes, that has to be my own daily piety too. I shut myself up from 10 clock [*sic*] to luncheon (with an amanuensis & a type-writer!) but after that I am genial & diffuse. I can be with nobody more so than with you. What a life you are leading, & what a wealth of anecdote & illustration you will come prepared to pour out! This thatched village will rarely have listened to such echoes. Rye is a *petite demi-heure* [Fr.: a short half-hour] from Hastings. There are several trains hither in the day: a very convenient one at 4.28 (from H.;) another (equally so) at 4.50.

---

26. The "literary egg" was Sturgis's third novel, *Belchamber.* James's criticism of the novel formed one of the main topics of his letters to Sturgis during subsequent months. "Sainty" or Baron St. Edmunds and Chambers, the hero of *Belchamber,* lame from a childhood riding accident, is always unfavorably compared to his younger brother, Arthur, who is active and athletic. Sainty is happiest while a student at Cambridge, but he is called from his studies to be head of his family's estates when he turns twenty-one. Friends and family alike betray him, and he marries a woman, Cissy Eccleston, who detests him. Cissy will not sleep with Sainty on their wedding night. In fact, the marriage is never consummated, but she soon becomes pregnant with another man's child. Nonetheless, Sainty loves and cares for this baby, but the infant becomes ill and dies. Cissy then leaves him to live with his cousin Arthur.

Only *specify*, in time, & I will meet you, of course at this station, which is but 3 or 4 minutes' walk from my house. Will you recall me very kindly to the memory of the venerable Miss Perry?[27] I knew her in old Hans Place days & imagined her now gathered to her fathers. I know not why—only through long silence over her name. When I shall have got your address from her, I shall ask her leave to make an easy pilgrimage over to see her. Good-bye—à bientôt [Fr.: until then]. Only make me (the day before if possible) a sign as to the definite day * & hour; & believe me always, my dear Howard, your affectionate old friend

Henry James

* something like Wednesday 14th, I gather.

ALS: Houghton bMS Am 1094 (1186)

LAMB HOUSE, RYE.

My dear Howard.   February 25*th* 1900.

Your good letter is the last wave, stirred by the genial breeze of your presence here—the last to break, with a certain melancholy softness, on my lonely strand. It prolongs a little the pleasure of that presence— peoples, in a ghostly manner, my solitude—&, above all, gives me a kind of document to hold on by when the future too blankly stares. It's not the baseless fabric of a vision. You *were*, historically, here and you will as substantially (without reflection on your figure,) be again. It's so much gained. We can arrange, always, with a view to you. You were a most conformable (don't read that by mistake comfortable—for who knows?) & delightful guest. I repeat, almost to indiscretion, that I could live with you. Meanwhile I can only try to live without you. It has been going quite hard till now. No one to listen to my lucubrations—no one to forgive my ⟨poulterer?⟩—no one to admire my Timothy.[28] (Tim is practising the nocturnal wail, even as I write, at the door of his chambre à coucher [Fr.: bedroom]. But it dies away sooner each night.) Your allusion to your sacrificed "parts" & your fleecing friends stirs in me afresh the fount of tears. I see it all even more intensely than you—& the drama moves to its dark climax with a grim greek fatalism. You're a conscious, irrecoverable Victim. It *is* tragic. There's nothing so tragic in life as to be generous & to have let it be discovered. It's not for our Vices we pay, but for our Virtues. Il

---

27. The "venerable Miss Perry" may be related to Thomas Sergeant Perry (1845–1928) and family. HJ knew the Perrys since his Newport days; he met Perry there when they attended school together in 1858.

28. Timothy was probably one of HJ's dogs.

faut en avoir le moins possible [Fr.: one should have the fewest possible]—
& you go & have lots. I know of but one thing that will save you: your
sticking to the Subject you told me, & partly—too tinily—read me of.[29] It
is full of stuff—admirable; cling to its neck, its nose, its' [*sic*] anything—
only cling tight; & you will ride it into port. The only salvation for you
(given your deplorable merits,) is to clutch some work in the light of which
babies & nurses pale. Your Anglo-Belge is beautiful:[30] the translation most
neat. But the young person who makes the answer is painfully like *you*. I, as
the other young person, the questioner—who was probably, however, as
old as me, am moved to cry: 'De peur qu'il ne pleure? [Fr.: what fear keeps
him from crying]' Damn him, my dear—*let* him blubber!: Good night!—
among your Jekylls![31] always, dear Howard, yours

                                                            Henry James.
ALS: Houghton bMS Am 1094 (1188)

My dear Howard.   March 4*th* *1900.*
    "Henry" quite basks & waggles his head to be scratched, in the pleasant
warmth of it. He sends you moreover the tattered record of aristocratic
crime to keep as your very own, particularly desiring as he does that you
should, that you *shall,* not escape the adhesion or infiltration of some
material memento of our so happy little congress of two[32]—a real peace-
conference, & highly superior, it would surely seem, so far as effects, or
non-effects, go, to those lately held. Usually, I believe, a medal is struck or a
picture painted; but for the congress of Rye an extremely dilapidated
(though most interesting,) volume, only, is given. I ought to have it, first,
bound for you—& by heaven, after all, I will! Save that I believe you won't
read it then—& I *want* you to read it (the Brinvilliers chapters, & the
Montespan ones, especially, for the envers [Fr.: reverse or backside] of the
age of Louis 14.)[33] So here goes, without the present delay of binding. Send

---

29. His "Subject" is his book-in-progress, *Belchamber.*
30. "Your Anglo-Belge" probably refers to Sainty, the main character in Sturgis's
Belchamber, although Sainty is in fact three-quarters English and one-quarter French.
31. "Your Jekylls" may refer to Herbert Jekyll, private secretary to Lord Houghton and
his wife. HJ knew them through the Wolseleys.
32. One dictionary definition of this word is "coitus."
33. Francoise de Montespan was a royal favorite and mistress of Louis XIV's. De
Montespan, along with Jean-Baptiste Colbert, had financial control over literary and
architectural projects. Her husband was thrown into the Bastille, and their marriage was
annulled. She bore the king seven children. Marie Madeleine, marquise de Brinvilliers, was

it back for that process later. I find one reads things in the dear old French lemon-coloured covers more freely than after the trail of Bain & Hatchiard (who get my binding done for me.)[34] Good-night, then, cher collègue & confrère [Fr.: dear colleague and comrade]—till our prochaine séance [Fr.: next meeting]. All thanks for your warnings against Sneyd & her kind[35]— or rather against undue exposure of my own affability. But the whole point is that I *don't* tell ces dames [Fr.: these ladies] that I could live with *them;* I hadn't passed the remark, as our crapy friend would say, for a long, long time to anyone till I passed it to you. And I daresay I shall pass it to you again before I pass it to any one else. I'm right glad you let Arthur B[enson]. know that things were not all ill with us;[36] for he had really had to do with my mustering courage to signal to you. I sounded him as to your accessibility & he encouraged me. He deserved therefore to smile benevolently on his work. Yours always

Henry James

ALS: Houghton bMS Am 1094 (1189)

My dear boy Howard.   April 10*th 1900.*

How horribly I have delayed to thank you! I have been (at the Dentist's, all,) three days in town & came back on Saturday to arrears, to abysses. Deep in the gulf of prostrate admiration I have indeed, ever since, practically lain. I must tenderly thank you for the exquisite object, a new feature in my life, a positive accelerator of bed time, a refinement of luxury—springing, truly from a still more charming refinement of friendship, & resulting, above all, in a refinement of gratitude. It will stick to me for life, & will hold its nice little firm listening cheek close to the final register of the ebb of that fever. Meanwhile it will in its inveterate intimacy,

---

the wife of the marquis of Brinvilliers. She and her lover, Sainte Croix, poisoned her father, brother, and sisters. Sainte Croix then accidentally poisoned himself, and she fled but was caught and executed in Paris.

34. James Stoddart Bain (b. 1872) was a London bookseller who frequently supplied HJ and his friends with books. The "lemon-coloured" volumes have not been identified, although French publishers of that period had a particular cover style and color. Buyers purchased them bound in soft covers and then sometimes had the books leather-bound to their own specifications.

35. Sneyd could refer to Emma Whitley Sneyd, wife of Major General Thomas William Sneyd. The Sneyds lived in Cheshire.

36. See the biographical register for Arthur Christopher Benson. Benson and Sturgis had been close friends since the 1880s.

remind me as repeatedly of your elegant hand & generous heart. I delight to hear—by what you hint—that you are already counting the "volumes" of your great chronicle.[37] What could look like progress if not that? Well, count them—but also hatch them: catch them, patch them, thatch them. They will cover in, I seemed to see, a very vivid picture. I too am ticking away, but I don't get, alas, even to the apprehension of volumes.[38] The little watch-bed is a royal mattress, but remember that I shall some day claim another—I decline to take this as putting me to coucher à la porte [Fr.: sleep at the door]. I shall knock there at no distant day & am meanwhile yours in extreme elegance & fidelity

Henry James.

ALS: Houghton bMS Am 1094 (1190)

LAMB HOUSE, RYE, SUSSEX.

Sept: 18: 1902

Why, atonement, dearest Howard, for all sorts of silence & stupidity—or rather, quite, for one sort in especial: my having found nothing to reply to an extraordinarily kind letter received from you long, long ago—quite at the beginning of the summer. (I had left London unwell, flying to *this* asylum, & had written you as much; whereupon you had written to me as how *your* house was my natural asylum, & as how it stood open to me in every emergency.) The tears came into my eyes & fell into my ink—but I never "took up" that too generous remark. I left you with the last word, & I have been conscious all summer of having more to say to you than was getting itself (thanks to waves of obscuration,) uttered. Therefore contrition was full upon me when I (to add injury to insult,) strove to wipe you out of existence, as a reminder of my fault, by that crushing literary missile. There you are, in spite of me—you simply rejoice like an angel. Very interesting your magnanimous letter—poor victim of a golfing age, or rage. I see you at St. Andrews', amid the wild waving of clubs & hiss of projectiles, dodging and ducking for your life—& "trying to write"![39] It's a devotion to letters that shld. be commemorated in immortal verse. But I too have been trying to write, & that, with the shock of the social battle

---

37. "'Volumes' of your great chronicle" refers to *Belchamber.*

38. James had begun work on *The Sense of the Past* in the spring of 1900 and then put it aside for fifteen years. The novel was never completed.

39. Sturgis's distant cousin and companion William Haynes-Smith was a golfer, and he must have accompanied "The Babe" to the famous course at St. Andrews, working on his book while Haynes-Smith golfed.

round me, has been of the reasons I haven't been to see you. I will come, my dear Howard, with great joy, the first time I'm in town long enough to come, advisedly, on that basis. Coming straight up from here makes, I fear, rather an ambitious flight (requiring a far spread of wing,) of a country visit. I come up on Jan. 1st, or about, to stay for several months—but I don't, heaven knows, cold-bloodedly put it off till then. Only can't you, won't you, before that, come to *me* for a couple of days? I have the most genial recollection of the one or two visits you *have* been so good as to pay me, & I shall have a lovely autumn, & your presence will be singularly welcome. Let me make you a sign later on—an elegant, a pleading, a pressing one. May you, as the centre of the most complex combinations, not meanwhile be ground to powder, reduced to that mere gold-dust which is the logical residuum of your nature. I am glad to know that poor Ned Boit is to be with you & would send him some message if I knew of any that could fit his tragic case.[40] But I'm not surprised that you didn't get to Vallombrosa in August &c—it is, with all respect to it, a terrific summer pilgrimage. Good night: it's as usual for me, over my poor letters, the witching & midnight, the more than midnight, hour. And I'm to be called at 6.30 in the a.m.—for a purpose that sounds mysterious, but it's only a purpose worthy of you, a kind of errand of mercy. I am the more prepared for it by the ½ hour spent with you. Yours, my dear Howard, always & ever

Henry James

ALS: Houghton bMS Am 1094 (1202)

LAMB HOUSE, RYE, SUSSEX.

My dear Howard. September 30*th* 1903.

All thanks for your lucid exposition of your so interesting case. I shall rejoice to see you on Saturday 10th & shall immensely applaud your arrival. We shall be able to talk the lurid past well over—for the agitated (though, thank God, less agitated than hitherto,) present will then belong to it, & a community in our fate—to compare my small with your great (it drives me into delirious rhyme!)—will render us eloquent. Let me remind you that the *4.28* from Charing Cross, changing at Ashford, will be your best train, & that I shall embrace you, tenderly, at the Station at *6.40.* Heaven speed the day! I will keep everything till then. Bring your Novel (if

---

40. The Boston-born artist Edward Darley Boit (1840–1915) was somehow related to Sturgis. His vallombrosa villa, Cernitoio, was just outside of Florence, Italy. An earlier letter from HJ to Sturgis of 4 May 1902 indicates that Boit's wife had just died (Houghton bMS Am 1094 [1201]).

you have a 2d copy) & Read it Aloud! Apropos of which I wrote to Bain last night to send you mine (the deadly last, "The Ambassadors,")[41] & am preferring tonight a similar request in respect to "W. W. Story & his Friends,"[42] "out" today. Forgive this avalanche & believe me, my dear Howard, yearningly yours

Henry James.

ALS: Houghton bMS Am 1094 (1207)

LAMB HOUSE, RYE, SUSSEX.

My dear Howard.   October *3d 1903*

I greatly grieve to hear of your disabled state & of its possible effect on your coming here, & I am moved to say that if you are not straightened out a week hence, & quite easy of wind & limb, you must frankly put off your visit till the end of the month—literally the 31st (unless you have some embroilment at home for that date.) It appears not impossible (what I didn't tell you in writing the other day,) that we shall not be alone—that is that *I*, so to speak shan't!—about the 10th, owing to the coincidence of a visit (from Hendrik Christian Andersen of Rome, if you know whom I mean,) that I have agreed to for either that Saturday or that Monday & that I had agreed to 3 or 4 weeks ago. (He is in England but for a few days & I fear is not moveable.) I confess that, with much *brooding* on it, the idea of not having you alone & thereby intimate & free-talking, has struck me so unfavourably that if I *may* shift the sight of you on without losing it, I take refuge in that improvement with a certain relief. On the 17th I go for 2 days to the Henry Whites'[43] (a thing I do regularly & traditionally once a year;) & on the 23d a friend & his wife come for such time as may seem to them good (only, in all probability, however, for 3 days.) But on the 31st the coast is clear, absolutely, & I shall be able to enjoy you with a free mind, & detain you, if you will let me, with a free hand—the shadow of other

---

41. He wrote to James S. Bain to send his novel *The Ambassadors,* published in 1903. Referring to it here may well be an allusion to James's mastery of the genre and a reminder to Sturgis of his own inferior abilities as a novelist.

42. *W. W. Story and His Friends* was James's biography of sculptor William Wetmore Story (1819–1895), published in two volumes in 1903 by Blackwood. Story's family had persuaded James to write this biography. HJ's comments on Story himself are minimal, but the book paints a fine picture of the American expatriate group in Rome during the late nineteenth century and quotes from some remarkable letters written to Story.

43. The Henry Whites were Henry White (1850–1927), American diplomat and secretary of the American Embassy in London and later American ambassador to Paris, and his wife, Margaret Stuyvesant White (1854–1916), a woman of beauty, taste, and ambition.

presences not then hanging over the scene at all. If you can definitely *engage* to come then I shall rejoice that you make it your date instead of the 11th, & this in spite of my ungracious appearance of thrusting you off to a distance. The distance will near itself with no great slowness, & your compromised state had time to fall from you. Only you must, I beseech you, *nail* & fix the day, & defend it against all comers. If you can do this I shall greatly rejoice. Meanwhile, for goodness' sake, make the acquaintance of the blessed new remedy *Aspirin*—a specific against rheumatic & gouty affections [*sic*] which—unless you *have* tried it & found it wanting—you will thank me, if I mistake not, for making known to you. I am myself just steering clear of a lumbago *and* gout crisis (I think,) by its aid—*absit omen!* [Lt.: all bad omens absent]—& I have heard no one (of several I have heard) speak of its virtues without calling it blessed. It was mentioned to me last spring as a new & striking French thing—Aspérine, the quintessence of Asparagus; but since then it has made its way here & all good (the best) chemists have it in their own white pillules, or in Burroughs & Welcome's.[44] Ask your Doctor, if you don't want to ask your chemist straight—& if I am not fatuously & ridiculously preaching one of the converted & informed. Let me add—at the risk of further superfluity— that the thing must be taken with caution in respect to its action on the heart—but that *with* that discretion this action is not to be feared. I am taking 2 pillules a day at the present time (these 4 or 5 days,) & they have all the appearance of nipping a catastrophe in the bud with the same quiet firmness that I attributed to them, with confidence, several months ago.— —Beyond this, don't think me odious & insidious if I ask whether, in respect to its influence on lumbago & sciatica you have sounded the depths of *Diet.* Forgive the unpleasant word & the offensive imputation—the suggestion, I mean, that your ailment is the blowsy Daughter of Excess; but after years of intolerable liability to the foul fiend I learned, à n'en pas douter [Fr.: without doubt], that a joyless abstinence has more to say to keeping him at bay than any other precautions—& I allude here to lumbago quite as much as to gout. But enough of this shameless long-windedness. Get better as you can, but for God's sake get better. I am glad the volumes safely reached you. Not a sound has come yet from any Story lips—in reference to *that* production; which in your reading of it, however,

---

44. There was a nineteenth-century pharmaceutical firm, founded by two American pharmacists, called Burroughs & Wellcome. Today the firm has merged with another drug company to become Glaxo Wellcome.

may explain to you their reserves.[45] And yet why, either—? You will see for yourself to what my material reduced itself—with the most artful stretching & amplifying & embellishing; [the *editing* I lavished on all the poor little (Story) documents being such as they could ill enough have spared.] However, it all doesn't matter—ouf! Let me hear that my amendment in respect to your coming *does* fall in with your possibilities—& yet not only because you are all afflicted & thereby believe that you considerably comfort yours, my dear Howard, always

Henry James

ALS: Houghton bMS Am 1094 (1208)

LAMB HOUSE, RYE, SUSSEX.

My dear Howard. November 8*th* *1903.*

I send you back the blooming proofs with many thanks & with no marks or comments at all.[46] In the first place there are none, of the marginal kind, to make, & in the second place it is too late to make them if there were. The thing goes on very solidly & smoothly, interesting & amusing as it moves, very well written, well felt, well composed, well written perhaps in particular. I am a bad person, really, to expose "fictitious work" to—I, as a battered producer & "technician" myself, have long since inevitably ceased to read with *naïveté;* I can only read critically, constructively, *re*-constructively, writing the thing over (if I can swallow it at all) *my* way, & looking at it, so to speak, from within. But even thus I "pass" your book very—tenderly! There is only one thing that, as a matter of detail, I am moved to say—which is that I feel you have a good deal increased your difficulty by screwing up the "social position" of all your people so very high. When a man is an English Marquis, even a lame one, there are whole masses of Marquisate things & items, a multitude of inherent detail in his existence, which it isn't open to the painter *de gaieté de coeur* [Fr.: of the happiness of the heart] not to make some picture of. And yet if I mention this because it is *the* place where people will challenge you, & to suggest to you therefore to expect it—if I do so I am probably after all quite wrong. No one notices or understands *anything*, & no one will make a single intelligent or intelligible observation about your work. They will make plenty of others. What I applaud is your sticking to the real

---

45. Here HJ refers to W. W. Story's family and their response to his recently published biography. Story's son was Thomas Waldo Story (1855–1915).

46. The proofs are of Howard Sturgis's *Belchamber.*

131

line & centre of your theme—the consciousness & view of Sainty himself, & your dealing with things, with the whole fantasmagoria, as presented to him only, not otherwise going behind them.[47]———And I also applaud, dearest Howard, your expression of attachment to him who holds this pen (& passes it at this moment over very dirty paper;) for he is extremely accessible to such demonstrations & touched by them—more than ever in his lonely (more than) maturity. Keep it up as hard as possible; continue to pass your hand into my arm & believe that I always like greatly to feel it. We are two who can communicate freely.———I send you back also Temple Bar,[48] in which I have found your paper a moving & charming thing, waking up the pathetic ghost only too effectually. The ancient years & images that I too more or less remember swarm up & vaguely moan round about one like Banshees or other mystic & melancholy presences. It's *all* a little mystic & melancholy to me here when I am quite alone, as I more particularly am after "grand" company has come & gone. You are essentially grand company, & felt as such—& the subsidence is proportionally flat. But I took a long walk with Max this grey still Sabbath afternoon— have indeed taken one each day, & am possessed of means, thank goodness, to make the desert (of being quite to myself) blossom like the rose.[49] Goodnight—it's 12.30, the clock ticks loud & Max snoozes audibly in the armchair I lately vacated. I needn't assure you I will bury 10 fathoms deep the little sentimental secret (of another,) that you gave me a glimpse of. Yours, my dear Howard, always & ever

Henry James.

ALS: Houghton bMS Am 1094 (1211)

LAMB HOUSE, RYE, SUSSEX.

My dear Howard.   *Thursday* night [12 November 1903?]

The two enclosed have come for you & I blush you shld. see that I rudely tore open the *envelope* of one of them, finding it on the table with some of my own. But the sheet within was not removed before I saw my

---

47. Here HJ acknowledges that although the novel tends toward the sentimental and while Sturgis lacks HJ's own subtle skills in developing character, the reader is allowed to see more and more of Sainty's internal drama as events unfold.

48. *Temple Bar* was a popular nineteenth-century British magazine published in London by Richard Bentley and Son. The magazine, which serialized novels, was named after a historic site in England at the junction of the present Strand and Fleet streets, over against the law courts. Sturgis's article was "A Sketch from Memory [of Margaret Oliphant]." *Temple Bar* 118 (October 1899): 233–48.

49. Max was HJ's dachshund.

mistake, & the contents are strictly inviolate.[50] I hope you carried out your graceful programme yesterday & that your halls & bowers have again greeted you as they should. I am very lonely & so proofless as to feel almost roofless. Yes—I *could* have lived with you. That is you might with me! Yours all & always

Henry James.

Houghton bMS Am 1094 (1212)

LAMB HOUSE, RYE, SUSSEX.

My dear Howard. November 18*th 1903.*

I have too much delayed—partly because I've been up to town for four or five days & that has made a hole in my time. But I have had your last good letter, as well as your copious last proofs (161–224) which I gratefully return—just as I do full justice to your (amiably superfluous) explanations of grounds, logic &c, in respect to your hero's social position &c. I think that as that thing goes on, these grounds, this logic &c, speak more for themselves—so that the reader will see your wherefore & your concatenations. You *keep up* the whole thing bravely—& I recognise the great difficulty involved in giving conceivability to your young man's marriage. I am not sure you have taken *all* the precautions necessary—but one feels, in general, that Sainty's physiology, as it were, ought to be definitely & authoritatively established & focussed: one wants in it a *positive* side,—all his own—so that he shall not be at *all* passivity & nullity. The thing is at any rate always interesting, observed, felt, ironised—copious & various. Send along the rest—I won't again delay so long.——I went up to town for 24 hours & staied [*sic*] eighty or ninety or whatever, caught in the *engrenage* [Fr.: gears]. All that was wanted to make the whirl complete was that I should have gyrated to Windsor. But this I only want, ever, to do, with the necessary protocols & solemnities—after preliminary gloatings. Now I'm very much back here in deep *recueillement* [Fr.: meditation]— modified by an elegant brochure of Arthur Benson's which he has sent me & for which I mean to thank—I mean his official announcement of departure.——Let me add that you will see that I have *marked* nothing at all in your proofs—not because I haven't here & there made my observation, but because it's late for any such interposition—& only & vainly worrying to you—& also not urgent. Vôtre siège est fait [Fr.: your game is

---

50. HJ was always very particular about the privacy of his—and others'— correspondence.

made]—& will take the town. But morning dawns, & I am yours, my dear Howard, always & ever

Henry James

ALS: Houghton bMS Am 1094 (1213)

LAMB HOUSE, RYE, SUSSEX.
Nov. 23*d 1903*

My dear Howard.

I return, not in silence, the unedited text—for I must at least break my silence with thanks. Beyond this, however, it is difficult to write—comment & criticism would take me too far, & it is clumsy work (I mean c. & c. are;) so that we must wait & *jaw,* & then I shall try & be—all proportions kept—as interesting to you as you are to me. Suffice it for the present that I am perhaps just a wee bit disappointed in the breadth of the celebrated nuptial night scene—though I don't think, I confess, that Miss Cholmondeley will find it "adorable."[51] Then I see, on reflection, that what keeps the scene, after all, decent, is that with the key in which you keep Sainty it can't not be. Resistance, pressure, the turn of the trodden worm—these things would have brought the crude fact to the surface, & only these *could.* It's kept under by his not pulling, not stirring it up. I re-wish immensely that I might have talked with you while the book was a-writing; in the interest of a Sainty with a constituted & intense imaginative life of his own, which would have been to be given (given more than anything else,) out of which all relations with people would have come as baffled & tragic *excursions*—mangled & bewildering days (or nights,) "out." But see already how clumsy it is to try to talk! We will make it up later. Start next year *another* book & let me anonymously collaborate. I *will* come down with joy for a night or two as soon as I am in town on a basis. And you will be—you *are* daily—avenged, meanwhile, for my coarse invocations of what *might* have been by the humiliating difficulty I am having here over my own stuff—in which I've come nearer to sticking fast than ever in anything. Continue at any rate to remit—& to *permit*—& believe yours always

Henry James

ALS: Houghton bMS Am 1094 (1214)

---

51. Mary Cholmondeley (1859–1925) was an English novelist and short-story writer who socialized with Percy Lubbock, Sturgis, and HJ in the 1910s.

134

My dear Howard.

I am again, in returning you the enclosed, but too aware of how little "comments" have their place, in any suggestive or supervisory sense, in regard to a finished & accomplished thing. I think then the thing continues very interesting & animated & *soutenu* [Fr.: sustained], very vivid & clear, never for a moment dull or flat. It suffers (as I have already said this it may not—or may it just the more? aggravate you that I shld say it again?)—it suffers from Sainty's *having no state of his own* as the field & stage of the vision & drama—so that the whole thing doesn't seem to be happening *to* him: but happening at the most round him; & one says: "To whom *is* it happening?" This is particularly sensible in the matter of his life, on the essentially *bafoué* [Fr.: scoffing] terms, under the same roof, day by day, with his wife—which would be really for him an experience of *some* kind of Intensity. There was something in him (at the worst!) to wh: this was to be *shown as happening*—horribly, tormentedly, strangely—in some way or *other*—happening; & "the abysses with her which was the beginning of dislike"—on p. 284—strikes me as a phrase of an almost giving-away (of *him*) inadequacy. "Beginning of dislike?"—*end,* rather of something-or-other-else! *What* was for you to find. *And* I wish his failure to conjoin with her about 2 am. that night on the drawingroom sofa, could for his sake have been a stand-off *determined* by some particular interposing, disconcerting, *adequate* positive fact—of impression, suspicion, alarm: something not so merely *negative* for him. He couldn't afford there (for interest,) to fail without a reason—& the reason était à trouver [Fr.: was to be discovered]. I don't undertake now to find it for you—but I *could* before! I repeat all the same that nothing of this—all this will be missed by the B.P.,[52] who will degustate much that you have given & find the sense of ⟨temptation?⟩ quite delightfully ⟨*reabruse?*⟩. But enough—save that I want more, & am always too hurryingly (through this one day in town,) yours

Henry James

ALS: Houghton bMS Am 1094 (1215)

My dear Howard.

I came back last night from a small complicated absence—the "week's end" the other side of London & a night in London thrown in—to find

---

52. "B. P." refers to the "British Public," about whom HJ was frequently satirical.

your too lamentable letter, in which you speak of "withdrawing" your novel—too miserably, horribly, impossibly, for me to listen to you for a moment. If you *think* of anything so insane you will break my heart & bring my grey hairs, the few left me, in sorrow & shame to the grave. Why should you have an inspiration so perverse & so criminal?[53] If it springs from anything I have said to you I must have expressed myself with strange & deplorable clumsiness. Your book will be the joy of thousands of people, who will, very justly, find it interesting & vivid, & pronounce it, though "painful" &, probably cynical, even "disagreeable" &c, vivid & lively, curious & witty & *real*. My esoteric reflections over the subject will occur to nobody else at all, & the whole thing will excite marked attention. So if you love me let your adventure take care of itself to the end. Forgive, otherwise, this scrawl—I find a pile of letters awaiting me here. Send on *la suite* prochainement [Fr.: the sequel soon] & believe me yours my dear Howard always & ever

Henry James

ALS: Houghton bMS Am 1094 (1216)

LAMB HOUSE, RYE, SUSSEX.

My dear Howard. Dec: 16*th* *1903*

I was very sorry about yesterday, but I had absolutely to dash the cup from my lips. I came up to town for a rigorous 24 hours only, & it was of vital importance (it has proved so on the spot,) that I shld. be back here this a.m. Have a little patience with me, & I promise you, & myself, a visitation the reverse of mean. I learned from Mrs. Wharton, after wiring to you, that I should have found Mrs. Sheridan with you,[54] which I didn't know & which increased much my regret. Your note of 3 or 4 days ago repeats a word of hers about something in The Ambassadors which I greatly value. And you tell me in that note of your impending journey to Paris. I envy you it really—I mean in such conditions of welcome as you'll have. I wish I could work myself into it—but nothing could be more impossible. Speak well of me to dear Etta Barrace[55]—to whom, indeed, I

---

53. After all the negative criticism HJ has given Sturgis concerning *Belchamber*, he is now surprised that HS is considering not publishing it.

54. She may have been the mother of Captain Wilfred Sheridan (c. 1879–1915), husband of Clare Frewen Sheridan (1885–1970). Wilfred and Clare Sheridan were HJ's friends in Rye.

55. Etta Barrace may possibly be HJ's friend Henrietta Reubell (c. 1839–1924), who was probably the model for Miss Barrace in *The Ambassadors*. Henrietta Reubell's nickname was "Etta." She was a Parisian hostess to artists and writers.

shall write, tenderly, for Xmas. Be, all the same, kindly nice about me to her. If she is nice about me to you she will be very generous, for I have long & horridly failed to go near her. You have never told me when Belchamber comes out, but I shall see by the posters & sandwichmen. Yours all & always

Henry James

ALS: Houghton bMS Am 1094 (1218)

LAMB HOUSE, RYE, SUSSEX.

My dear Howard. Jan: 22*d 1904.*

I go up to town on Thursday p.m. next, & I am wondering if the following Saturday 30th would suit you for my coming out for the Sunday? If so I shall be ravished (I mean as to my inner being.) I postpone all further overflow till then, & ask meanwhile but for the favour of *one* kind word. Yours always

Henry James

ALS: Houghton bMS Am 1094 (1219)

LAMB HOUSE, RYE, SUSSEX.

My dear Howard. [25 July 1904]

I feel this to be very sad news of yours, though I was more than half prepared for it. I was afraid you were late for finding a berth, & that the prospect, or the possibility, of our being together would shine before our eyes a moment only to leave them the more darkened afterwards. It is really very miserable that we should be sailing within a short time of each other & yet so helplessly & coldly separate. But how well I understand that you shouldn't dream of paying £85 for a berth—or anything d'approchant [Fr.: approaching it]! I am appalled, when it comes to the point, at what I myself am paying, & yet it's far enough from *that,* as you may imagine. May you be "suited," presently, on a big & serene & robust Boston steamer—for this I earnestly pray. That was quite what I was planning for myself, but there interposed some time ago a tiresome complication, too special & uninteresting to relate to you, & booked me, inconsistently, for New York. I even yet have a sneaking hope, or fear, that something, at the last, will prevent me from going—but something won't![56]——As for the possibility of my being able to come to you this week, my dear Howard, it

---

56. HJ prepares for his grand American tour, sailing from Southampton on the *Kaiser Wilhelm II* on 24 August 1904. Sturgis also went to America that summer but was unable to accompany HJ on his voyage.

is deplorably small, & the fact that Mrs. Julian is about to be with you fills me with regret for my impeded state.[57] Very particularly & intensely should I have liked to seize this opportunity of seeing her—for I fear indeed that, pressed & positively ridden & haunted—with things to be done & work, above all, to be finished before I sail, I shall not be able to grasp at any other occasions. For my not being able to be in London these days there are really more reasons, & more imperious ones, than I can burden or bore you with. I *have* had to be, in a longish, & shortish, snatch or two lately, & the heat & the crawl & the treacherous depths of the whirlpool made me ill & almost deprived me of reason. The torrid air of town, in such visitations, almost by itself gives me brain fever. So you see what a poor subject I am. Will you give the assurance of my very affectionate constancy to Mrs. Julian, & ask her to continue to me, out of her charity, the beautiful patience she has always shown? I rejoice greatly that she has come to you for a little. Good night, dearest Howard, I feel the liveliest interest in your keeping up your courage & your faith—in a general way, as it were. Make our Young Friend find you prompt & easy transportation & we will meet somehow & somewhere in Tonic New England air. I give you meanwhile an affectionate accolade & am yours always

Henry James
July 25*th* 1904.

ALS: Houghton bMS Am 1094 (1226)

Chocorua N. H.
Sept. 5*th 1904*

My dear Howard.

This is but a fond, vague *gesture*—& the sketchiest symbol of an embrace! I can't stand an hour longer on this strange soil without doing something, however slight, that shall make for a renewed relation with you: wherefore let this mere wild "waggle" serve. We must meet, we must mingle, we must talk—& I hope, dearly, that next month will allow us a margin for some indulgence of that kind. I remain here, with my brother & his wife, till one of the last days of Sept., but Mrs. Wharton has held you out to me as a bait at Lenox and I have opened my month wide to the prospect of the same for 2 or 3 days.[58] Besides which, fortune may otherwise favour us. (I spend October mainly at Cambridge Mass.—still with

---

57. See the biographical register for Mary Maud Beresford Sturgis (Mrs. Julian).

58. "Lenox" was Lenox, Massachusetts, where Edith Wharton had her county estate, The Mount.

my brother.) I hope with all my heart that your so pious pilgrimage is being "blessed" to you. There wd. otherwise be no reason or truth in the universe. I am bearing up a little bewilderedly, but on the whole beautifully, & even to the pitch of extreme enjoyment. This place is both sunny & lovely. I take the liberty of greeting very kindly Mrs. Codman[59] & am yours, dearest Howard, always & ever

Henry James

ALS: Houghton bMS Am 1094 (1227)

Chocorua N. H.

My dear Howard.   *Thursday* [15 September 1904?]

Delightful both your new letters, & I desire greatly to thank Mrs. Codman for the cordiality of hers. Your information about trains & ways is perfect & precious, & I rejoice in every word of it. I *revel* in the thought of a dear old slow, stopping, American concatenation of cars, with boys shying packets of popcorn at one's head—I gloat over it in advance. Therefore I will, most devoutly take the 1.38, & replete with my upstairs luncheon (no Downstairs for *me!*) give myself up to the study of scenery, manners & linguistics. And what you so charmingly tell me of Cotuit further enchants me. It is just the sort of thing I yearn to see—I shall enjoy every minute of it. I shall fling myself on "Mr. Irwin's man's" at W. Barnstable,—on the arrival of train at 3.34—& surrender myself to my sensations—& then, dearest Howard, to yours! All kind regards. Yours evermore

Henry James

P.S. I spend Monday night at 95 Irving St., Cambridge, Mass.

ALS: Houghton bMS Am 1094 (1229)

HOTEL PONCE DE LEON ST. AUGUSTINE, FLA.

Dearest Howard.   Feb. 20*th* *1905.*

Ah, but I *must* write you, though the sense of a preposterously long story to tell warns me off as by the white (or is it the red?) flag of danger in advance. And I shan't, I can't, really "handle" my queer tale (or tail)—so that it doesn't matter. I am "on tour," & my queer tale, (or tail,) elongates even while I write. I am in Florida, on my way *up* (from Palm Beach, its

---

59. Mrs. Codman was Lucy Lyman Paine Sturgis, Howard Sturgis's oldest half-sister. She was the daughter of his father, Russell Sturgis, by his first wife. In 1856 she married American lawyer Charles Russell Codman (1829–1918); they spent their summers at Cotuit on Cape Cod.

southern point) having spent 4 or 5 really quite amused days (pardon the *blasé* sound) at the latter place, & 3 very much more colourless ones (by which I don't mean in flirting less with ladies of colour) in this inferior, this disappointing locality—"the oldest city in the U.S," founded by P[once]. de L[eon].,[60] early in 1500, yet with nothing at all (to speak of,) to show for it. The 2 or 3 more extremely subtropical spots, of which P[alm]. B[each]. is easily best, have a certain simplified Southern intensity—in spite of the abnormal ferocity, the down-reaching polar wave, of this winter, felt here in the fatal "freeze," as they call it, of a single night, a month ago, when the pine-apple crop all went (with ruin to cultivators,) & the admirable green palms & flaming hibiscus (such a wealth of the latter) were turned to misery where they stood. In spite of this I have had in a manner a revelation of the possible blandness & munificence of nature in these latitudes (I had never had it anywhere else;) the air, on the best days, is a liquid blast, & the little golden fruit-ranches (the oranges, strangely enough, have *not* gone, nor the dense-hanging huge grapefruit either) seem verily small gardens of Eden, or 3 acres & a cow on bosky blue-rimmed isles of the Blest. The true revelation, however, perhaps, is that of the huge American people taking its ease in its huge American hotels (these quite extraordinarily good of their kind, with a wondrous liberality of appointment, finish of system & pervasion of spotless neatness,) & letting one see it mapped out as in one of its own flat city charts: decent, gregarious & moneyed, but overwhelmingly monotonous & on the whole pretty ugly: likewise unacquainted with the rudiments of tone, or indeed with any human utterances. But I am there handling my tail—Forgive this stupid skip! [on an otherwise blank page] & the coils thereof are too multiplex— & I must steer clear. I refer you to future volumes—oh, but volumes. I have likewise "done" more or less New York, Washington, Philadelphia & a slice, before this, of the middle South—notably this last by spending a week with George Vanderbilt at his colossal chateau of Biltmore[61]—the château de Blois enlarged & glorified—2500 feet in the icy air & on the North Carolina Mountains. Roll three or four Rothschild houses into one,

---

60. Juan Ponce de León (1460–1521) was a Spanish explorer born in San Servas. He was governor of Puerto Rico. In search of a fountain of perpetual youth, he discovered Florida in March 1512 and was made its governor.

61. George Vanderbilt owned a 130,000-acre North Carolina estate, the Biltmore, which included Mount Pisgah. He spent a total of three million dollars planning the construction and design of the chateau and landscaping the grounds. He married an American socialite, Edith Stuyvesant Dresser.

surround them with a principality of mountain, lake & forest, 200,000 acres, surround *that* with vast states of niggery desolation, & make it impossible, through distance & time, to get almost any one to stay with you, & you have the bloated Biltmore. I fled from N. Y. after 3 weeks, by reason of its awful midwinter conditions of life (I am to go back for 3 weeks more in May,) but I divided my breathless period between Mary Cadwalder [*sic*] J[ones]. & our Lady of Lenox. Mrs. Wharton housed me in a *bonbonniere* [Fr.: snug little house] of the last daintiness, naturally—but we were more compressed than at L[enox]., & Teddy more sandwiched between, & we gave a little more on each other's nerves, I think, & there was less of the sweet Lenox looseness. Still, she was charmingly kind & ingenious, & taste & tone & the finest discriminations, ironies & draperies mantled us about. I go hence *straight* back to Boston (that is with a night—only one—in New York,) for my Dentist of Damnation—3 days of him only, he promises: there is a wonderful train from here to N.Y. in some 36 hours. Then I go straight to Chicago, St. Louis, &c.—the West & California, to be back east about May 1st. I've taken my passage on the *Saxonia* for July 4th. I tell you all these things so that you may see I am really trying to work out my Salvation. I couldn't have staid on for the mere beaux yeux [Fr.: beautiful eyes] (even when reinforced by the winter red nose) of Boston the Funny. But *bear* with my agitated absence—I shall be *more* worth your while (for the clearest of my conversation [)]—when I reappear to you. I am eternally homesick—but I live with it as one travels with a cinder in one's eye—the country, the "social spectacle," is disagreeably interesting—but it isn't the least little bit thrilling. Now Windsor, e. g., thrills me to the marrow—"every time." To which you will say "Oh well—!"—fortified by a perverse conviction that that's all they ever *do* say of Windsor. I've been delighted to see that *Belchamber is* to flaunt its rich veridities in the white American light. May they not too much darken the same. I rejoiced, dearest Howard, in your so handsome & charming Malwood letter.[62] You *do* seem to come in with the undertaker's men—but you stay, beguilingly, after them & cause them to be forgotten. Poor Lady H. *must* breathe freer;—she will become another Mme Waddington[63] &

---

62. There were two streets in Victorian London named Malwood: Malwood Road, Balham, and Malwood Road, Streatham, Wordsworth.

63. This may refer to Mary Alsop King Waddington (d. 1923), whose book *Letters of a Diplomat's Wife* (1883–1900) was published in a number of editions.

write about her court frocks & "handsome" dinners. With which cynical sentiment I am yours dearest H., always & ever

Henry James

ALS: Houghton bMS Am 1094 (1236)

LAMB HOUSE, RYE, SUSSEX.

My dear dear Howard! August 24*th* *1905.*

It has been adorable to hear from you, & I almost hysterically thank you for your letter, but I wasn't "standing," heaven help you, on any question of anything "unanswered from Florida" (heaven help *it!*)—or "standing" at all in fact, or doing anything but sit, or lie, very flat, under the rich but inane & ponderous consciousness of all the *arrears,* here at home, by which I have been paying for my year's absence, & must still pay; though I have reached out of them, in spirit, yearningly, again & again, toward your more or less recaptured presence, & again & again appointed, to myself, the fond moment for binding it once more to me by a few free pen-strokes. That moment has kept missing the appointment—I've had so many (more enslaved) other penstrokes to make; but I snatch this midnight hour & I greet you with clasping arms. I must be brief—there would be so much to say if I wasn't! The essence really is that I want awfully to come to you for a Sunday, or that sort of thing—partly as a sort of attestation to myself of my having recovered root, as it were, in this good old soil. It will be too good to be true till I have been for 24 hours at Quacre [Queen's Acre]; when it will be just good enough. I'm spoiling for a "good long talk" with you—there is no one else here—I mean in all the land—with whom I can have it (in respect to everything of là bas [Fr.: over there].) But the pity is that I can't propose myself for a good many days yet—that is before the last week, say, in September. Then—about then—I should hugely like to put in that blessed palaver. Let us, my dear Howard, cherish the prospect, &, as they say, work toward it with a grim concentration. I came back with unprecedented engagements to *produce* & I have had to get into the shafts & pull the cart hard—& must pull, without stopping, from now through most of September. *Then* the poor animal will draw up at the Quacre trough to water. Likewise I returned to domestic desolation—have but one servant in the house (my "let" worked ravage,)—yet *like* that, too, & wish to goodness that the peace & ease of it could go on always.[64] (I mention it

---

64. HJ rented Lamb House to American newlyweds Louisa Horstmann and John Boit, and Louisa's sister, Ethel Dallas Horstmann. Although Louisa Boit later wrote glowingly of

because having had, in consequence, almost to "do" the doorstep myself, I have had the less margin for a clutch of you.) Walter Berry came down here in plaster for 2 days & is now,[65] very madly, to my sense, on his way to Italy, the country of plaster-figures, the very Newcastle of such coals—&, seriously, a crazy place for him, at this season, battered & broken as he is, (pathetically so, it seemed to me,) in the service of ces demoiselles [Fr.: these women]. I know a little ces demoiselles & see them flutter & flounce, all rustling wings & vocal sounds, through your *so* exposed vicinage. Quel temps, quelles moeurs [Fr.: What an age, what customs]! O tempora, o mores [Lt.: What an age, what customs!]! Nous causerons de tout cela [Fr.: We will speak of all this]. I shall "keep" for you—only keep for *me*, & believe me, my dear Howard your fidelissimo [It.: most faithful]

Henry James

ALS: Houghton bMS Am 1094 (1237)

LAMB HOUSE, RYE, SUSSEX.

Dearest Howard.   [27 February 1907]

No, no—not another hour shall pass without my doing my poor precarious best, at least, to make up for not having lately written to you! I have just had a note from Teddy (!!) Wharton (I am supposed to be presently going to stay with them a little,) in which he speaks of their having lately had a very *abbattu* [Fr.: dejected] letter from you (though he doesn't say from where) & it brings home to me that about a fortnight ago,—or a little more—on my getting in a kind letter from Percy Lubbock[66] a mention (the first that had reached me,) of Mrs. Codman's death, I had vowed not to let that day, or evening, pass without making you, dearest Howard, the tenderest of signs. But in view of my going abroad (on the 6th or 7th) I have been intensely occupied with the desire to polish off an urgent and arduous job or two here, & that anxiety has played the deuce with others, even with so great & real a one as my vivid sense of your felt bereavement & my realization of your inevitable pang. I take all the bearings of the event & of its impression on you, as if they were matters, almost, of my own personal history, & I lay my hands on you now, all affectionately, with the wish to communicate that deep & lucid com-

---

this experience in 1946 in "Henry James as Landlord," *Atlantic Monthly,* vol. 178, no. 2, 118–21, James felt that the group had disturbed his servants.

65. Walter Van Rensselaer Berry (1859–1927) was an American lawyer and diplomat. He and Edith Wharton were very close friends.

66. See the biographical register for Percy Lubbock.

prehension. You have the finest genius I have ever encountered for wincing under this particular periodical turn of the screw of fate—& I'm not one who could wish for you, ever, any crisis of sensibility less. One sees plenty, all round one, of that "less"—& of remonstrance offered in the name of it; but I like absolutely to share with you the *more*—& I pretend even to know where & how these wounds most ache. It's in fact almost as if I now knew just *why* I made that unforgettable little pilgrimage to Cotuit nearly three years ago: so that I can speak to you tonight *all* as I should like to. Therefore take it from me as I give it—the intimate participation & vision. How good it must be to you that you went then—& how justified that you didn't go again last summer—when in the shadow of what was coming there would have been no felicity. So—there it is; I pat you "intimately" as I say, on the back. If you had been nearer I wd. have gone straight to see you, or tried to get you to come here; but even now who knows if I mayn't have some chance of our meeting. Vague & mixed to me are your probable adventures up to this time, yours & your niece's—& only rather distinct, I fear, that wherever you've been you've not come in (by what one generally hears) for much basking in the southern sun or nibbling of the southern lotus. I am destined to spend probably 4 or 5 weeks in Paris—after which there's a possibility of my making a dash into Italy. But at what point of your Wanderjahr [Ger.: year of travel]—"Jahr!" I hear you groan!—will you then be? However, this may be yet for you very much in the vague— even as I consider my own small adventure—as to its later developments—to be; only if you were to turn up in Paris before I depart thence we might make something not wholly lugubrious of that. I feel you wondering with me what I meanwhile shall make of our always more or less palatial friends, & I shall doubtless have plenty to tell you about that when we do meet. Trust me at least to cull for you every sweet flower of incoherency that blooms in the table-talk—or stable-talk—of my host! After my visit to them I am desirous to give myself a little to my very sympathetic nephew[67]—one of those you saw at Cambridge Mass.—who is working in much good faith at the Jullian *atelier* [Fr.: studio]—or rather to give myself as much to him as possible. That may keep me on & on a little. I have even half promised to go with him to Madrid—if he is free to go (or I am) for the right days (i.e. that suit us both.) But I want to go for a little to Italy, & the two things conflict. I don't speak to you of dear

---

67. HJ's nephew was William "Billy" James II (1882–1961). He studied at Julien's, an art school on the Rue St. Denis, for a period of time.

144

demolished Robert Cushing, because there is really too much to say in that connection.[68] His family—*les siens* [Fr.: his own]—appear to have shed him even as water is shed by a duck's back, & Louisa's serenity is particularly—impenetrably—fine & gay & high. (Yet she too bore—without turning a becoming grey hair—the brunt of the whole tragedy.) [(]Olivia came up from Rome for the afterpiece.) My little nephew Edward, who came out for the same, was with me, very genially, for a couple of days; but he requires special treatment.[69] Nous en causerons [Fr.: We will speak of this]—I mean of the totality. I, at least, shld. have liked so to see the dear man—& I didn't. Percy L[ubbock], writing me most beautifully about my American book (lately out,) tells me that your niece has profited in nerves & healths—& I send her my friendliest old benediction. What history you two must have been making—or undergoing! Should *you* care for the heavy bulky luggage-augmenting American book? If so I'll send it you—but I really recommend you to wait till you can spread it out on a big square solid English table. I'll put it on one for you then. I shall be from the 7th at 58 rue de Varenne—for at least a week.[70] I embrace you, my dear Howard, violently, & am yours all & always

> *Henry James*
> Feb: 27: 1907.

ALS: Houghton bMS Am 1094 (1245)

[58 rue de Varenne, Paris]

My dear Howard. [20 March 1907]

In a calmer life I should have found means to thank you sooner for your beautiful letter of so many days ago, but I have in these conditions few pretensions to calm, few even to coherency. I snatch nevertheless these fleeting moments, before being whirled off tomorrow on indiarubber wings (or wheels—cela revient au même [Fr.: they seem the same]) to the Pyrenean frontier, just to tell you I am with you, yearningly, in remembrance & sympathy, but that alas I fear I have no prospect of getting to Sicily, with or without you, this blessed time. I come back to Paris

---

68. Robert Maynard Cushing was married to Olivia Donaldson Dulany. Their daughter Louisa married Edward Holton (Ned) James (1873–1954), son of HJ's brother Robertson James (1846–1910) and his wife Mary Holton (1847–1922).

69. Nephew Edward was one of the most eccentric of James's nephews. James later cut him out of his will because Ned wrote a pamphlet critical of King George V.

70. In March 1907 HJ went to Rue de Varenne to visit the Whartons, with whom he stayed for weeks.

(D[eo].V[olente]. [Lt.: God willing]) with our friends at—or a little after—the end of the month—but I shall then have but a scrap of my times abroad left;—& though I *may* get down to Rome for 10 days, this will be the most.[71] I have been here a fortnight & it has been very interesting & social & Parisian & funny & indescribable until we meet. Our friend is a great & graceful lioness, & I have come in for many odd bones & other odd leavings of the Christians (if Christians they can be called) who have been offered to her maw in this extraordinary circus. In fact I have an indigestion of chères Madames [Fr.: dear madames] & other like phenomena. Mrs. Wharton has been exquisitely kind—she is a dear of dears, & Edward [Wharton] has exceeded my fondest hopes.[72] It has really been lovely—& you shall *have* it all from me under English June boughs— for which same fine features of British density I am already as homesick as I could wish. I rejoice heartily that the brave Babe comes to you.[73] Lift up your heart & walk straight—il n'y a que ça [Fr.: there is nothing but that]. I greet again ever so kindly your so sympathetic companion. À bientot [Fr.: Until I see you] then, after all, dearest Howard. Je vous embrace bien [Fr.: I embrace you tightly] & am yours all & always

Henry James
58 rue de Varenne
March 20*th* 1907.

ALS: Houghton bMS Am 1094 (1246)

Gd. Hotel de Turin. *Torino.*

Dearest Howard.   *May 12th* 1907

It hasn't been that I haven't appreciated your happy & delightful news about your staying on in Rome that I've been brutally dumb—but just for the joy of making you with small delay this definite & eager sign from firm (I trust!) Italian soil. I got here last night & shall have to stay 4 or 5 days absolutely to do some urgent & imperative proof-reading (of a revised & altered book) for which the New York publisher clamours,[74] & which being a work of needful concentration & difficulty, suffered inordinate

---

71. After two weeks in Paris, the Whartons took HJ for a three-week motor tour to the south of France.

72. Edel transcribes "exquisitely kind" as "exceedingly kind" in *Henry James, 1901–1916: The Master* (Philadelphia: Lippincott, 1972), 342.

73. See the biographical register for William Haynes Smith.

74. He was revising parts of *The Princess Casamassima.*

obstruction amid the Saturnalia of Paris[75] & the dire enchantments of Circe.[76] (My classical references are muddled, but they mean that my *convenience* & health went to pieces through Circean wiles—& only my bliss—without those adjuncts—survived.) At all events I beg [you] to be gentle with me for the greater part of this week, while I ply the pen in this oh so favourable desert (excellent hotel & room,) & to expect me toward the end of the week. I will then write again. I go to Hotel de Russie for old acquaintance & association's sake. Tanté saluti [It.: good health] all round. Your devotissimo

Henry James

ALS: Houghton bMS Am 1094 (1249)

Gd. Hotel de Turin

Dearest Howard.   *Wednesday* a.m. [15 May 1907?]

Your letter wrings my heart—I received it just after scribbling my own poor note in answer to your telegram. I *fly* to you, *donque* [Fr?: then]; if you will charitably consider it flying for me to leave for Rome tomorrow Thursday p.m. at 8, & reach that place at about 10 a.m. of the morrow. I am vulgarly going in for the night-journey by reason of a gruesome recollection of the day run from this—by the Genoa & Pisa way I mean: a thing of the stuffiest tunnels alternating perpetually with the glaringest summer-heat. And I gain my day for my work—which has not been all a matter of proofs, but a much tougher & as yet unfinished job.[77] It *must* have seemed to you that I was staying my southward steps overmuch—so that you must let me breathe to you how (in addition to my particular necessity here,) there has been operating with me a force that always intensely works after I have been steeped up to my chin (as I was in Paris) in the human & social imbroglio: the constitutional deep need for a few—even if very few—days of receuillement [Fr.: rest] & solitude. Well, I shall have got them à peu près [Fr.: a little]—& Richard's himself again![78] I shall have several

---

75. Saturnalia was the festival of Saturn, held on 17 December. For several days in Rome work stopped and gifts were exchanged.

76. According to Greek legend this celebrated enchantress was the daughter of Helias and the sister of Aeïtis and Pasiphaë. She changed the companions of Odysseus into swine, but he forced her to break the spell.

77. The "tougher & as yet unfinished job" might be pages he later added to his *Italian Hours* (1909) memorializing his journey, a section he called "A Few Other Roman Neighborhoods."

78. "Richard" was HJ, evidently.

good—*archi*-good—Roman days with you; & I shall minister (or endeavour to) to your mind diseased—all so needlessly—by every art of tenderness & sympathy, & subtlety & sagesse [Fr.: wisdom] that I can bring into play. I only lament that you've been—Mildred lapsing too[79]—bodily *piano* [Fr.: soft]. Never mind, I'll tune you both up with the silver key of irresistible speech—or, if you prefer, with the golden one of silence (while I sit holding a hand of each.) Don't *dream* of coming to the Stazione [It.: station]—if any such fell impulse shld. take you—I shall arrive dirty-faced & dishevelled (even if by a tangle of so few threads,) & will wait upon you (from the H. de Russie) almost immediately after. May I come to déjeuner [Fr.: lunch] (at 12.45 say?)—do let me! I shall assume your leave. *Vale* [Lt.: Greetings]—as far as possible & believe me ever so validly (as yours)

Henry James

P.S. Will you *repeat* my love to the noble Maud S. (if you see the chance)?[80] I shall immediately go to see her. Edith's another affair, & ⟨*me?*⟩ fait peur [Fr.: is frightening] to me too.

ALS: Houghton bMS Am 1094 (1251)

Dearest Howard!   October 17*th 1907*

It isn't very plain that I can "write" to you—write to you "plain," that it is; but it is at least clear that I can embrace you, so I hereby confer on you the very handsomest of accolades & the most affectionate of hugs! (That looks a good deal like *hags,* & I suppose an "affectionate" hag is less to be welcomed than any other—but I *am* not dispatching you an hysterical harridan.) I have hovered about you "all the time", in fond memory, in rosy hope, in brooding wonder, in searching surmise—nursing the vision that you still clung, all summer, to your so perfectly padded eyrie—in which even I theorised that you were renewing your youth, & Mildred's as well, like the eagle. I think it a very wonderful thing of you, & a very enviable & memorable, to have come in for a long Tuscan summer in such exquisite conditions, a romantic passage, after all, which all the Shepherds & all the flocks can scarce have prosed the charm quite away from. But oh

---

79. "Mildred" was Howard Sturgis's niece Mildred Seymour, daughter of his sister Mary and her husband, Colonel Hamilton Seymour.

80. Maud S. (c. 1860–1932) was probably Maud Broadwood Story, who married Thomas Waldo Story (1855–1915), sculptor and son of sculptor William Wetmore Story. Maud and Waldo Story separated around 1898.

how it makes me want to see you & to hear you, with the scent of Arcadia still hanging about you & the lingua Toscana still bubbling from your lips. I am at the present time very urgently & intensely *busy,* working for dear life—otherwise I would break away at once & rattle in my favourite station fly straight up to your door. This must *wait,* but I cherish the chance, I am really quite sick with impatience for it. Believe, my dear Howard, in the absolute & affectionate sincerity of this & that I shall manage it at the very 1st slight clearing of my *selva oscura* [It.: dark wood],[81] my just now exceptionally dark & thick wood, a perfect tangle of occupation. Just as I liked to figure you on those sublime terraces, so I now fondly tuck you into the cosy corners that express in durable upholstery the genius of Britain, & so insist on feeling at sudden ease about you till I come & experiment on your true inwardness. I send "best love" to William & Mildred [Seymour]—& delight in what you tell me of the precious Percy [Lubbock]. Keep a-wanting of me all you can, you won't exceed the responsive desire of yours, dearest Howard, ever so constantly

Henry James

ALS: Houghton bMS Am 1094 (1253)

Reform Club S.W.

Dearest Howard. April *23d 1908.*

This doesn't even begin to be so much as an apology for a letter. It is only a frenzied incoherent irrelevant *geste* [Fr.: sign] made you as I pass through town tonight on my way to Paris—or rather to Amiens—tomorrow. At Amiens the most gracious of ladies & kindest of friends & most accomplished & *remuante* [Fr.: restless] of women is to meet me in her chariot of fire & take me a little turn about of 2 or 3 days through "that part" of France—that is through some goodly bit of Normandy (& eke perhaps Brittany!.) I remain là-bas [Fr.: there] till about the 7th & hope to be in London from about the 10th (May to the 10th June—or à peu près [Fr.: thereabouts].) As soon as I come back I will come down to you & dine (& not sleep.) I yearn over you, I love your letter, I love your person & I bless your name. There, dearest Howard, I can't say fairer than that. The little Plaything is to flourish its few times—to go *on* flourishing them, that is, apparently, in the provinces but a week or two more, & is trying hard to effect a footing in London—that is to secure a good *small* theatre here—

81. Here HJ refers to the opening lines in Dante's *Inferno.*

for next month & June & even July &c.[82] But alas they are all fatally pre-empted, *accaparés* [Fr.: monopolized]—& short of some unexpected turn (as by the collapse of something else) the prospect looks dark. In that case there can be no London production till the autumn. But Forbes R. *may* be able to work some miracle on the spot[83]—when he comes up in person on May 4th (after a week at Liverpool;) his "spring-tour" being then over. However, when I come down to you we will talk of better & less Crummles-&-Nickleby things—as well (a little) as of that.[84] Miss Snivelièce has made a great little personal success of her chance.[85] Good night, dearest Howard—I have had a long toothbrush-buying London day & it has spent—by *his* fatal spendings—& bowed down with a midnight imbecility of fatigue yours always & ever

Henry James

P.S. Tanté saluti [It.: Good health] to the Babe & the Niece.

ALS: Houghton bMS Am 1094 (1255)

LAMB HOUSE, RYE, SUSSEX.

Dearest Howard.   *November 2d 1908.*

Most characteristically kind & generous your letter to which I gratefully respond. Yes, I have been hearing from Edith Wharton of late & she is at the present time afloat, I trust, in the *Provence,* due at Havre I imagine about the 4th—at any rate she apparently expects to motor thence on to Dover on the 5th (these whirling Princesses!) & I go on there—to Dover—on that a.m. or afternoon to attend her (these obedient admirers!) She rather likes, I gather, the idea of spending some little time in England—& I have asked her to come down *here* for a jabbering *week* (!)—j'ai été capable de ça [Fr.: I was capable of that]! But I am sure she would also be glad to come to you for a little—no art that I could employ would avail to dissimulate to you, on my part, that conviction. Do be kind to her then (I

---

82. "The little Plaything" was *The High Bid,* which premiered in Edinburgh on 26 March 1908, with HJ and friends present. It enjoyed a good run there, but it only had a few London matinee performances in February 1909.

83. See the biographical register for Sir Johnston Forbes-Robertson.

84. Crummles and Nickleby are characters in Charles Dickens's 1838–39 novel *Nicholas Nickleby.* Nicholas Nickleby supports himself for a time as an actor in the provincial company of Vincent Crummles.

85. In *Nicholas Nickleby,* there is a family (Mr., Mrs., and Miss) Snevellicci who are actors in Crummles' company.

needn't say it—for you'll be l'ange de l'hospitalité [Fr.: the angel of hospi-
tality] full-feathered & with an aureole that it would take all the gilt paper
in the kingdom to represent or imitate.) If you *can* entertain her for a little
I *might* be able to look in then—though my time in town (for a bit at first,
near her) will have to terminate after a few days. I am obliged to go up
there (on another matter) on Wednesday 4th, & if I go to Dover I shall
have to go from London (which is far) rather than from here which is near;
also I have an old old engagement to a visit (*from* the Metropolis) for the
7th–9th. But I shall be probably three or four more days in town from the
9th on. It is *after* those that I have thought of proposing to her to come
here—but that is easily arrangeable. She will however give me her own
idea when she arrives. *What* an incoherent life! It makes me crouch more
dodderingly than ever over my hearthstone. And she has asked me to take
rooms for her in London at the Berkeley. Thus in one way & another I feel
I may sort of see you soon—&, frankly, I like to feel you there! À bientôt
[Fr.: until then] then. Love to the Man of Affairs & the Man of Letters!
Yours, dearest Howard, plus que jamais [Fr.: more than ever],

Henry James.

ALS: Houghton bMS Am 1094 (1257)

LAMB HOUSE, RYE, SUSSEX.

[5 May 1909]

Dearest Howard. For a Hurter you extraordinarily little even *want* to
Hurt—which was indeed only what She at *first* did; & you seem to be the
prey of more Weeks, or even Months, Wimbushes than any Lion of them
all—which is, however, after all, only natural from your being so un-
mistakeably & notoriously a Tiger. But the moral of it all is, you see, that I
am *not* in London this week, as it turns out—I have been unable to free
myself for going till next Monday 10th. Then, however, I do really go. I fear
I can't make any tryst quite yet, but I will play the telegraph straight at you
as soon as I arrive, & will then take gratefully what your Wimbushes (such
a dense *shrubbery* of whims!) scrappily leave me. You will chuck that refuse
to yours

H. J. (over)

P.S. Stay, dearest H.,—I could come on Saturday of *next* week (15*th;*) but
this is too soon for you [to] be sure of that yourself. So don't—& *have it!*

May 5*th* 1909.

ALS: Houghton bMS Am 1094 (1261)

Dearest Howard.   *July 11th 1909.*

It was almost as beautiful of you to write me on the occasion of Percy's admirable & exquisite article[86]—which I have written to thank him for & express my emotion (not half-copiously) enough in presence of as it was for that gentlest of our friends himself to build (& as with a wave of his so very fine young wand,) the shapely monument. It is a very superior & a charmingly distinguished thing, the lovely paper, & I intensely & gratefully & almost tearfully appreciate it. If he is with you at this moment, dear creature, please repeat to him that I have assured you thus of the high & rare pleasure he has given me—from which I can't help feeling that appreciable benefits & glories will flow to both of us.——As for our aquiline Edith, *elle plâne* [Fr.: she hovers], for the hour, just over this province—& the matutinal telegram from her, supplementary to the nocturnal (of last evening,) leads me to hope for her séjour [Fr.: stay] with me for at least tomorrow to Tuesday. I daresay it is written in the book of fate that I shall even motor with her to Folkestone & wait upon her departure there. But these things are in the lap of the goddess herself. The iridescent track of her Devastation—the phosphorescent lights of her wake—suffer, I suppose, at Quacre, gradual extinction, & I can only hope your rest-cure flourishes & that the dose is proportionate to the disorder! So much only, dearest Howard, for this crowded hour. I have a friend staying with me[87]—a simple scene enough after your cave of the winds of friendship, but the burden, again, is to be measured by the beast! The sense of your splendid gallantry for the past month or two abides with me,—on that sense my affection for you feeds & "battens." I must renew our contact before too long again; my spirit has acquired, as it were, the fatal habit of you. Also of the firm, free William—to whom I beg you kindly to commend me. Yours, dearest Howard, all constantly

                                          Henry James

ALS: Houghton bMS Am 1094 (1263)

                                          [Lamb House, Rye]
Dearest Howard.   [1 February 1910]

I get on a little—but slowly, & with setbacks. Yesterday a very good day—today a poor one & this lame note. But I have sat up both days for 5

---

86. This was Percy Lubbock's 11 July 1909 laudatory article on James in the *Times Literary Supplement.* HJ told several friends that he was very pleased with the article.

87. According to the *Notebooks,* the guest was Jocelyn Persse.

hours, & I shall worry through. It is only so woefully lonesome—without Babes or Kith or Kin of any kind, & no company but doctor & nurse & Thoughts—*these* such bad company. But this isn't a wail, dearest H.—it's only a patient little weary sigh. I hear somewhat from E[dith].W[harton].—but bear you lightly on her in thought: she has had & is having great anxieties inconveniences & complications about Teddy (who has had no "melancholia" but on the contrary excess quasi-demented excess of levity & gaiety which has translated itself into incongruous & extravagant forms & consequences.) I can't say more—& *don't know this from me please:* I can't speak of it—mustn't yet. What a nightmare the Paris history—but the wondrous firebird doesn't indeed seem to have feared the water very much.[88] She's prodigious, & I am *not!* But I am your only retarded & all devoted H. J.

Feb. 1st.

ALS: Houghton bMS Am 1094 (1269)

[Lamb House, Rye]

Dearest Howard. [6 February 1910?]

Your visits have indeed about them every attribute of the angels' save that of fewness or far-betweenness. You're angelic *and* abundant—& I think it simply must be because you're an Archangel, rather, & that *they,* the supreme seraphs, are allowed longer hours "off," which they employ after your celestial fashion. I thank you almost with tears for your adorability—& want you to know that I am really picking up. I wish only that you were as fast—which it doesn't at all (your acct. of yourself) sound like. *Of course,* however, you can't say that "nobody kneads you"—so essentially known to your friends as you are as "bon comme du bon pain" [Fr.: good as good bread]. You see I *am* on the mend; sitting up more & more each day, feeding again at last without positive loathing (even though still not with reckless passion) & taken out this a.m. for an hour & ½ by my good doctor in his motor-car; a beautiful soft grey morning here, & a most restorative process. I am a little tired, & have written 3 or 4 letters of this slouchy kind (I can't sling ink yet;) but gradually I revive.[89] You shall

---

88. This refers to the severe flooding that occurred in Paris in January 1910, just after Edith Wharton moved into her 53 Rue de Varenne quarters.

89. HJ had a number of health problems, starting in late 1910. He had no appetite, his hands were stiff, and he finally crawled into bed. Rye doctor Ernest Skinner could find no physical cause for his illness, although he suspected he was severely depressed. HJ himself thought the cause was Fletcherism (chewing one's food many times before swallowing, a

have more of me yet.——Yes, that's right; be very gentle, though vague, with Poor Edith. She has been having in every way a hell of a time—& there's more to come. I make out that Teddy, after great "gay" pranks in the U.S., is about to be returned on her hands as finally demented (now only more or less, but increasingly & beyond appeal) & this *soin* [Fr.: care] is what she has now to look forward to.[90] I hope there may be some help in the fact that his Sister (wholly free by the Mother's death) is now in Europe[91]—& also that E[dith]. has Miss Bahlmann with her.[92] But ça ne sera guère folichon [Fr.: but that will not be very exciting]. If you write her, however, only feel your way—with your perfect native tact! My nurse, impatient, calls me to bed—but don't give this statement a larger application than justly consorts with the still conservable langour of yours dearest Howard, all loyally even in limpness,

Henry James
L[amb].H[ouse]. Feb. *6th*

ALS: Houghton bMS Am 1094 (1270)

HILL HALL THEYDON BOIS EPPING.

Dearest Howard. [May 1910?]

I have been hideously silent, but it has been inevitable—I couldn't till now write except *blackly*, & that with immense effort, & with such *an inflection* & such a demonstration I didn't wish to afflict you. But I at last feel a little definitely better—& believe it will increase—& this I owe it all affectionately to your boundless benevolence to let you know. It would be complicated to tell you how it was that 15 days ago, a good & gentle & hospitable friend pressing hard, & my "advisers," medical & other including my own intimate sense of things, prescribed on me so urgently the breaking of the spell of my long imprisonment at Lamb House, that my yearning to do something for change at any cost sustaining me, I allowed

---

practice advocated by American doctor Horace Fletcher). His nephew, Harry James, WJ's oldest, sailed from New York in mid-February to help his uncle. London specialist Dr. William Osler declared James in good physical condition for a sixty-seven-year-old, and by April, when William and Alice arrived at Lamb House, he began to improve.

90. Teddy Wharton's problems grew more pronounced around this time. Dr. Sturgis Bigelow, who first had a promising career in medicine and later lectured at Harvard on Buddhism, spent time with Teddy early in 1910 and diagnosed him as having what we now call manic-depressive bipolar disorder.

91. Teddy's younger sister was Nancy Wharton, who had traveled to Europe with him.

92. Miss Bahlmann was Anna Catherine Bahlmann (1849–1915), Edith Wharton's governess and later secretary after 1904. She was fiercely loyal to Edith Wharton.

myself to be conveyed hither (to the Charles Hunters',)[93] where that same change, of air, diet ("cuisine") & every condition has really done my miserable nervous state much good. I was in grievous need of it, & I have, I believe, crossed the Rubicon toward gradual recovery. My brother is at Nauheim (the "Cure") in Germany[94]—&, leaving this on Tuesday, we go in as few days as possible, to join him—& go, so far as we can, afterwards, to some tonic & sanitary air (& quiet place if there *be* such,) in Switzerland. These things, I kind of feel, will if I can do them, help me not a little. My enemy now is *all* my liability to nervous distress & trepidation, but the time has blessedly come when (as I feed better—almost normally,) *movement* on my legs, is good for it & tends to dissipate it. It is almost as if I could *walk* myself well. Meanwhile I have wondered & yearned over your great adventure. May it all have proceeded happily & healthily. May it in short have been thoroughly "blest" to you. L[amb].H[ouse]. of course always finds me. Could you kindly send this to *Edith* to read? My arrears of letters are like a millstone round the neck of your fondest old

Henry James.

ALS: Houghton bMS Am 1094 (1274)

REFORM CLUB, PALL MALL. S.W.

My dear, dear Howard.   July 16*th* 1910.

If I have left your beautiful letter from Paris so horribly unanswered I can only ask you to forgive me with your usual generosity. Things have been & still are intensely, & at times insurmountably, difficult for me—& the end is still not yet. We got back from "abroad" on Tuesday night, & though I had, in spite of the whole considerable nightmare of *that* (my dear brother much less well being a very anxious part of it,) been gaining ground a good deal, I am now having a succession of evil days (3 very bad ones in a row—& it's an immense effort to write this;) so that I am sadly afraid I can form no plan for coming down to you in the beautiful way you adorably propose.[95] I can form & entertain *no* plan, alas; & can fight my battle (of unspeakable nervous agitation & depression) but from hour to

---

93. The Charles Hunters were Sir Charles Hunter, Tory MP and coal magnate, and his wife Mary Smyth Hunter (1857–1933). She was a socialite who frequently entertained HJ and many other artists at her estate in Essex.

94. Nauheim is Bad-Nauheim, a German health spa in whose warm mineral baths William James found temporary respite from his heart disease.

95. William, Alice, and Henry James had been at Bad-Nauheim in Germany, HJ since 8 June. HJ's condition improved there, but William's did not. Here, though, HJ's condition has worsened since returning from the spa.

hour & with inordinate difficulty. I sail for the U.S. with my blest companions on the 12th August—& am here, for & from various necessities, for
the next few days.[96] (They—my companions—are at 34 Brook St. W.) We
go down to Rye for 10 days before we sail—& I dread that nest of
associations of illness—but in truth I dread everything. See what black
things I write when I *do* write, & don't want more of them. I'm afraid our
meeting isn't arrangeable just now—unless this coming week I have some
relief from my present condition—which makes every thing precarious.
Forgive, above all, this dismal showing & believe me your none the less—
your all the more—fond & faithful

Henry James

ALS: Houghton bMS Am 1094 (1275)

Salisbury, Connecticut.

Dearest of dear Howards.   [May 1911?]

Your letter of the 18th of this month is simply divine, & my response to
it in the first place is that I am now ever so much better & on more firm &
fixed a basis than when I wrote you in that very stricken and baffled sense
from New York.[97] I could *then* express myself in no other, from the
moment I expressed myself at all, for I had pretty inevitably given way, for
the hour, under the effect of a rather cruelly & mystifyingly bad month—
& I had a beautiful bountiful word from you before me which I didn't wish
to put off acknowledging. I told you to *wait,* yes—& you have as admirably broken that injunction, at the end, as you at first admirably obeyed it;
for I see how much too long I was keeping you in in [*sic*] the dark, as the
weeks went by, & giving the noble appetite of your generosity & your
tenderness nothing to feed on. Well, the reason was, in a manner, that as
soon as I left the bedevilling City (not that *it,* however, had, in its total lack
of any insidious art, much to do with my bedevilment) I began to come
round, & have since then gradually risen to a level much higher & much
more steadily kept than any at which I have hitherto moved, so that the
way before me has more & more been looking bright & straight & simple.
The change is great & real, evidently, the relief immense, & your sympathy

---

96. HJ would return to America with William and Alice James to help them as best he
could during their trip. HJ and Alice planned to take William to his farm, Chocorua, in
New Hampshire, in the hopes his health would improve there. It did not, however, and he
died in August 1910.

97. HJ had been in New York staying with Mary Cadwalader Jones, where he went
almost daily to Dr. Joseph Collins at the Neurological Institute.

& gratulation as beautifully assured as they will, dearest Howard, be devotedly rewarded. This improved & in fact transformed condition (really the dawn of the adage, following the darkest hour,) has been very much the reason why I have postponed my sailing for England from the 14th June to the 2d August—the latter *absolutely* now my date. Urgent & intimate family reasons have conspired to prescribe the wait—entaché [Fr.: blemished] as it is with the gross defect that it will keep me from seeing you till some 6 weeks later than I had been planning. But then our nearness will be, D[eo].V[olente]. [Lt.: God willing], for so beautifully long again. I hope to be with E[dith]. W[harton]. during a part of July at Lenox—as you probably now know that she sails for this country (from Cherbourg,) on the 17th, Teddy having preceded her by several weeks, in order to go to the Virginia Hot Springs while she went to Salso.[98] (So many cures for so many troubles—& yet the troubles surviving them all. If other hot water would get them out of *theirs!* Teddy, I gather, seems rather *plausibly* & yet not conveniently nor genuinely nor intimately better.) I am staying here with some very amiable & hospitable Emmet cousins[99]— mainly young, & all dear—who motor me profusely through this really beautiful & vast Connecticut Arcadia. New England at its best is nobly idyllic; & save only that the summer is too much of a summer, the mountains & vales & woods & waters & the huge overarching umbrage (such mighty & ubiquitous & embowering elms & maples) only want to be a little more sophisticated & interesting—as Nature, with the least encouragement, *can* so gladly be—to give one the highest satisfaction. I shall probably spend a good portion of next month at Nahant the sup- posedly cool (there are already torrid days in the land, & the drought & fine weather unprecedented—the general bigness & muchness & violence of everything, especially of everything one doesn't want, makes such fos- tered little nests of civilization & proportion as Quacre & L[amb].H[ouse]. appear verily small particles of paradise.) July I shall divide—unequally!—between the Mount & my dear Sister's much- appealing roof in New Hampshire, & then I shall embark on the Mauritania almost *for* Quacre. I ought to be in London by the 8th or 9th of August. Altogether adorable & ineffable the spirit of your invitation to come for a stay. Thank heaven I expect by that time to feel that I go home

---

98. Salso, short for Salsomaggiore, a town in Parma, Italy, was a popular watering-place.

99. His Emmet cousins were Ellen "Elly" Temple Emmet (1850–1900), Minny Temple's sister, and her daughters, Edith Leslie Emmet (b. 1887), Ellen Gertrude "Bay" Emmet (Mrs. William Blanchard Rand (1876–1941), and Rosina Hubley Emmet (b. 1873).

with confidence, & I already, for that matter, miss the occupation & concentration that L. H. will promote. Your picture of the bloom of your garden & sweetness of your scene is none the less like the kindest of all hands put forth to pull me, & I can't tell you how my fond imagination lets itself go. The only shade on the vision is that you are on your back in it. However you were on the upward incline & are doubtless now erect & alert. The gracious gods keep you so—I number our William [Haynes Smith], for the occasion, among those. But this must go off to the post. Should you make me another brave sign the Cambridge address always serves. I have just read the very touchingest dying scrawl from dear subli-mated Augusta Freshfield—whose state must play wonderfully on Mrs. Cornish's fine chords.[100] But good-bye, dearest Howard. Ever your faithfully fond old

Henry James

ALS: Houghton bMS Am 1094 (1281)

LAMB HOUSE, RYE, SUSSEX.

Beloved creature!   August 17th 1911.

As if I hadn't mainly spent my time since my return here (a week ago yesterday) in writhing & squirming for very shame at having left your several, or at least your generously two or three last, exquisite outpourings unanswered. But I had long before sailing from là-bas [Fr.: there], dearest Howard, & especially during the final throes of exhaustion, been utterly overturned by the savage heat & drought of a summer that had set in furiously the very 1st of May, going crescendo all that time—& of which I am finding here (so far as the sky of brass & the earth of cinders is concerned,) so admirable an imitation. I have shown you often enough, I think, how much more I have in me of the polar bear than of the salamander—& in fine at the time I last heard from you pen, ink & paper had dropped from my perspiring grasp (though while *in* the grasp they had never felt more adhesively sticky,) & I had become a mere prostrate, panting, liquefying mass, wailing to be removed. I *was* removed—at the date I mention—pressing your supreme benediction (in the form of eight sheets of lovely "stamped paper," as they say in the U.S.) to my heaving bosom; but only to less sustaining & refreshing conditions than I had

---

100. Augusta Charlotte Ritchie Freshfield (d. 1911) was the wife of Douglas William Freshfield (b. 1845) and the eldest daughter of late Hon. W. Ritchie. Mr. Freshfield was educated at Eton and was an editor for *Alpine Journal*. Mrs. Cornish has not been identified.

hoped for here. You will understand how some of these—in this seamed & cracked & blasted & distracted country—strike me; & perhaps even a little how I seem to myself to [have] been transferred simply from one sizzling gridiron to another—at a time when my further toleration of gridirons had reached its lowest ebb. *Such* a pile of waiting letters greeted me here—most of them pushing in with an indecency of clamour before *your* dear delicate signal. But it is always of you, dear & delicate & supremely interesting, that I have been thinking, & here is just a poor palpitating stopgap of a reply. Don't take it amiss of my wide affections if I tell you that I am heartily glad you are going to Scotland. Go, *go,* & stay as long as you ever can—it's the sort of thing exactly that will do you a world of good. I am to go there, I believe, next month, to stay 4 or 5 days with John Cadwalader—& eke with "Minnie" of that ilk (or more or less;) in Forfarshire—but that will probably be lateish in the month; & before I go you will have come back from the Eshers & I have returned from a visit of a few days which I expect to embark upon on Saturday next.[101] Then, when we are gathered in, no power on earth will prevent me from throwing myself on your bosom. Forgive meanwhile the vulgar sufficiency & banality of my advice, above, as to what will "do you good"—loathsome expression! But one grasps in one's haste the cheapest current coin. I command myself strongly to the gentlest (no, that's not the word—say the firmest even while the fairest) of Williams, & am yours, dearest Howard, ever so yearningly,

Henry James.

P.S. I don't know of course in the least what Esher's "operation" may have been—but I hope not very grave & that he is coming round from it. I shld. like to be very kindly remembered to *her*—who shines to me, from far back, in so amiable a light.————————I left our great Edith in very deep waters—but it's all too long & too sad a story. She will *probably,* before she comes back, in September or so, have done 2 things: 1° definitely sold the Mount, its full contents & all, for a lump sum down (but nothing *like* its'[*sic*] value—for now, in its richer maturity & fuller extension, it's a really splendid little place—English "little," American big!) & 2d have

---

101. See the biographical register for Mary Cadwalader Jones. John Cadwalader, her cousin, was a lawyer in New York and the son of a former assistant secretary of state. Late each summer he rented a hunting camp in Forfarshire, Scotland, and Minnie Jones went with him as his hostess and housekeeper. The Eshers were Reginald Baliol Brett (1852–1930) and his Belgian wife Eleanor Van de Weyer, Viscount and Viscountess Esher. He was later the governor of Windsor Castle. Sturgis had been in Scotland with them.

formally & "legally" separated from Teddy—who is perfectly sane & in the stoutest, toughest physical health, but utterly quarrelsome, abusive, perpetual-scene-making & impossible. He simply & absolutely, otherwise, will do her to death, & then where should we be?
ALS: Houghton bMS Am 1094 (1282)

LAMB HOUSE, RYE, SUSSEX.

Dearest Howard.   October 10*th 1911.*

It's delightful to hear from you so beautifully & kindly—with that ideal generosity that is the very essence of your nature! I shall see you before long, because I *did* bite at Clare Sheridan's artful bait[102]—such a large, sweet, substantial one—& am to "meet" you there—whenever it may be (I have the date—toward end of Oct.—somewhere.) Meanwhile I keep turning over—but never "spewing out"—the hook in my jaws. Besides which I am "leaving for London" an hour or two hence, & I shall be there this autumn & winter as much as I possibly can. I came back here 18 days ago with hopes of "settling in" with impunity—but hopes much turgid with skepticism, & alas the scepticism is what has been justified. I say "alas," but there is a good side to it. I have had, suddenly,—a week ago—a bad, a damnable collapse into a condition of unwellness that I believed (or hoped) I had really left behind & that is but too clearly the effect of my again being thrown wholly on my so compromised self here, in complete solitude &, now that the autumn & winter rains & shortening days have set in (as they very percepibly [*sic*] have,) not so much as a walk, in all the circumjacent mire & marsh, to help myself to. The visitation has been damnable. I have had far too much of it all in the past years, and that it gives horribly on my nerves is what is the matter with me now—largely at least, I feel sure. I can't stand it, & practically I am bolting, at short notice, with a great desire to keep away from these wrong conditions as consistently as I may & a sad consciousness that dear old L[amb]. H[ouse]. (the *possession* of which I still cling to) is practically rather an incubus & a millstone. Also with a devout sense of gratitude for the luck of my still having my little Pall Mall perch to work, under stress—like a safe haven in a storm. At all events I think the prospect is that I shall be in a posture to see you more easily henceforth, as it were—"henceforth" is a big word, but

---

102. Clare Frewen Sheridan (1885–1970) was a British artist and writer. HJ knew Clare and her husband, Wilfred Sheridan (c. 1879–1915), who was killed in World War I.

I risk it: at any rate I can but put it to the proof. And on *Friday 27th* I make out that it really is—at all events. I don't in the least know where that couple are—I mean their address; but I suppose she will inform me. We might meet (as I suppose you will have to come by town,)—meet at the station & proceed together, mightn't we? I didn't know the Babe had really gone—brave, but on the whole unenviable & I trust fortunate Babe. How much he will have to regale us withal! Ever dearest Howard your af-fetuosissimo [It.: very affectionate]

Henry James.

P.S. From Edith a recent summons—very confident & expectant apparently—to join her at Salsomaggiore & go a 5 weeks motor-tour through Italy with her! It's Walter B[erry], who *has* gone. The Mount *is* sold & Teddy, described as "much better" is at Western gout-waters *French Lick* (*lick,* not sick) Arkansas[103]—while she is at Italian Lick Lombardy! What a dividing abyss!

ALS: Houghton bMS Am 1094 (1285)

105, PALL MALL, S.W.

Dearest Howard. Feb: *20th 1912.*

You have the art of writing letters which make those who already adore you to the verge of dementia slide over the dizzy edge & fairly sit raving their passion. One doesn't "thank" for such pages as I just receive from you—but one is prouder than ever of having always *entertained* a passion for the exquisite spirit capable of them. Yes, I *have* been unwell to rather a wretched degree, & have had a couple of times over to scramble down to Lamb House & put myself to bed. I came back thence last 5 days ago & have within the last two felt very distinctly better. When I *am* at all better London is best for me—I could weep tears over the thought of starting on your premises a new infirmary ward. What an angel of bounty you are, & what handsome advantage is taken of it! I shall not add by a touch, dearest Howard, to that handsomeness—the scene at Quacre strikes me as rich & rounded, to the ideal point, as it is. I have an impression that I am really now crawling out of my hole—& also one that I *needn't* so absolutely, some 5 weeks ago, have tumbled into it. I slipped & lost my footing, as it were, & then a series of mistakes, which I might very well have left unmade,

---

103. The town where Teddy Wharton traveled was French Lick, Indiana, not French Lick, Arkansas.

precipitated the rest of my descent. I really don't think it need so *stupidly* occur again. But it's dire to have to recognise that one *could* still be so stupid, after all one has paid for a grain of wit. I have to buy it, you see— that article; while to you it comes nat'ral—like every other grace & generosity.——Yes, but I can't *think* of Teddy's Victim when I'm myself down & *affaiblé* [Fr.: weakened]. I need *all* my resources—physical, moral & financial—to look the situation in the face at all, & even then I don't stare at it very hard, but give it every chance to cut me if it will. I can neither *do* anything, write to her or be written to, about it—& ask myself why therefore cultivate, in the commotion, a mere platonic horror— which permits me neither to hold her hand nor to kick his tail. I have got back to work here again—at my little Chelsea *trou* [Fr.: hole]—within 3 or 4 days; & that, when I can really do it, does me far more good than anything. Did any echo come to you of my having gone down to Wancote for the week end on Saturday Jan. 27th & having had to ask to be allowed to go to bed the hour after I arrived?—where I remained till the Monday a.m., when Mrs. Julian very kindly sent me home (to town) in her motor-car.[104] Your Sister May was to have come—that had been the grand occasion of *my* going; but she failed at the 11th hour & so precipitated—by the shock of not finding her—my collapse. And the cold was zeroic—as my resistance was *not!* To my Nephew Bill & his brave new Bride I have lent Lamb House for as long as they will stay[105]—& their being there is a great joy & pacification to me.——Yes, I *had* heard (from Galliard Lapsley)[106] that dear Arthur is lecturing on Symonds "with the disagreeable side left out!"[107] But it supremely characterizes Symonds that that was just the side that *he* found most supremely agreeable—& that to ignore it is therefore to offer to our yearning curiosity a Symonds exactly *un*characterized. However, Arthur is clearly doing him in the Key of Pink. But if a

---

104. Mrs. Julian was Mary Maud Bereford Sturgis, Howard's sister-in-law. Sister May was the wife of Colonel Hamilton Seymour. HJ must have been visiting the Julian Sturgises, who lived at Wancote in Guildford.

105. Nephew Bill and his bride were William and Alice's son William James II (1882–1961) and his wife Alice Runnells James (d. 1957). They spent their honeymoon at Lamb House.

106. See the biographical register for Gaillard Thomas Lapsley (1871–1949).

107. John Addington Symonds (1840–1893) was a Victorian writer and known homosexual whose books included two privately printed autobiographical volumes discussing his homosexuality: *A Problem in Greek Ethics* (1883) and *A Problem in Modern Ethics* (1891). HJ's remarks on Arthur Benson's lecturing on Symonds indicate he knew well the problems inherent in discussing Symonds's ideas on same-sex relationships.

course of lectures, generally, might be made of all the things, disagreeable *and* agreeable, he "leaves out," it might stretch almost to the length of his whole *oeuvre*—so far as at present perpetrated. But, dearest Howard, *here* is perpetration enough; so good-night; it's a joy to be told you're *sound*. Ever your fond old

H.J.

ALS: Houghton bMS Am 1094 (1288)

LAMB HOUSE, RYE, SUSSEX.

Dearest Howard.   August *5th 1912.*

You should have had sooner a report of my continued & intensified sense of all I particularly & generally owe you, had not my earnest care been since we parted on Friday afternoon to keep quite superstitiously *still*—so still that even the scratching of my awkward pen shouldn't break the salutary charm. This I have succeeded in doing, I think—in fact in perhaps overdoing; having spent most of my time between the sheets of recuperation. I flung them off this a.m.—& this afternoon I shall—an hour hence & in spite of much bluster of the sky & swagger of the "glass"—crawl out all gently & singly; attended neither by a confident firebird nor by a skeptical domestic dove.* I have returned here to an almost grimly simplified social scene & feel myself a very lone & tentatively-scraping & feebly-crowing fowl indeed. The glitter of my recent past is quite in eclipse, & I can scarcely believe I so lately led the great life & kept the great company. But I am trying to be good & keep tidy— though feeling I am rather whistling in the dark all the same. What most abides with me & hangs about me is the fragrance of your heavenly hospitality, at once the most profuse & the most exquisite that ever was in the world. When that article is so lavish it's mostly not so nobly & soothingly personal & divinatory, & when it has this tender & attentive note it's more or less measured &, so to speak, calculated. But the sign of your hotel might be "Abraham's Bosom"—unless indeed a still better one is simply Howard's Lap. I see at this moment Mrs. Maquay & George seated together in the softest centre of the same[108]—while the Firebird, perched fondly on your shoulder, pecks sociably at their heads—& your heart—& the Babe, astride of your back like an indulged Piccaninny, rounds off the picture.——*Later.* I was interrupted an hour—2 hours— ago; & shortly afterwards had, alas, another "anginal" access—very much

---

108. Mrs. Maquay and George have not been identified.

like the one (& in the same conditions, rather, as) at Cliveden—which rather disconcerts yours & Edith's all the more tenderly

Henry James

P.S. I don't go "out" of course—but further in—to bed; & have sent [for] my good, quite dear, local doctor.

* Not dose, which it looks like, but *dove!*

ALS: Houghton bMS Am 1094 (1296)

[*Dictated.*]

LAMB HOUSE, RYE, SUSSEX.

Dearest and best Howard! October 23*rd.*, 1912.

I can respond to your kindest of notes after a fashion (that is after a legible one) if you don't mind my resorting to this blest mechanical aid; which, all this month nearly that I have been ill, has truly helped me not to feel as shipwrecked, as utterly so, as everything else would make for. I can deal with my good friends to this tinkling tune *when* I can—and I can give it up, helplessly, when the power fails; which this morning, however, has absolutely *got* to see me through. I did have, nearly a month ago, to put Logan Smith off[109] (he was coming for two nights) by reason of a sudden, a violent and a most vicious attack of "Shingles";[110] which has necessitated, since then, my putting everyone and everything off—save so far as the present machinery has eked me out a bit. It has been really a horrid time, and the end, alas, is not yet; the nature of the beast being to persist and revive and recur and press one hard again (and how he *can* press is almost beyond all saying) after it has really seemed that one's reprieve is more than due. It has been a weird and woeful realisation of an ailment that one had but vaguely heard of and never had under one's eyes (have *you* ever?) and which one left loosely robed in the mantle of comparative innocence. It is really, however, quite a dreadful visitation, for pain and black inconvenience; and nothing is worse about it than that there seems nothing at all to be done for it—save, I mean, let it take its odious course and decline to be hustled or hurried or beguiled or entreated; to do anything in fine but torment one quite in the grand manner of time and space and exactly as the humour takes it. Such is my sorry tale—but I don't

---

109. Logan Pearsall Smith (1865–1946) was a British man of letters and society figure who often entertained HJ.

110. Shingles, or herpes zoster, is a viral infection of the nerves that usually affects one side of the body, usually on the lower thorax and upper abdomen. It is a painful condition that blisters the skin.

want to drench *you* with it. I've been, here, perfectly placed for the épreuve [Fr.: ordeal], since it was to come; this amiable house is really an ideal infirmary, and my good domestics have been simply ministering angels. There *will* be some end—even though a fresh relay of poor days and horrid bad nights has quite lately been dumped on me; and then I shall rebound, battered nonagenarian though I be, as I had before this wretched renewal of woe begun to rebound quite decently from a brutally bad July and August. I was facing to work, and some reassertion of even senile powers blighted, when I was thus again floored. Let me repeat all the same that, though bruised, I am not beaten; and should be just now, were you more within hail, and were your too imminent (and eminent) convives not less so, much more interested in your own adventures and impressions than in so sourly regaling you from *my* too rusty pot. What you give me a glimpse of has the rich glamour of all your backgrounds; you emerge as from purple lights, lime-lights almost in *that* milieu; and it all rubs off, even as I fondly gaze, on the ensconced Fairchildren,[111] and the presently-to-be-encushioned Percy and Gilliard.[112] Tell Percy from me, kindly, that I have greatly *goûté* [Fr.: relished] his article of the October Quarterly,[113] but that oh I should like to take him so wisely and tenderly and artfully and odiously in hand! See (or invite him to) what my laid-up state here saves him! Don't, at the same time, scare him, for I am moved to deal as I should like with him only in those cases in which I irresistibly admire and love! Gilliard I greet, please, as he will intimately know that he ever unbrokenly incurs my doing; but I can't hang over the charming circle you evoke and not too bitterly re-tumble to my pillow. Rich, my dear Howard, radiant and rare beyond all measure, your vision of my invasion of your premises with my complicated griefs, or of my fatuous conception of this concentrated little sick-room as shareable by the brilliant guest. I scarce know which of these brave suggestions does most honour to your large charity and sovereign fancy. I can for the time but unsociably crouch, but there will be other times, and better ones; and I am yours meanwhile all gratefully and unabatedly

Henry James.

TLS: Houghton bMS Am 1094 (1301)

---

111. "The Fairchildren" probably refers to Sturgis's cousin Edith, Mrs. Blair Fairchild, and her husband. They lived in Paris.

112. Percy is Percy Lubbock, and "Gilliard" is probably Gaillard Lapsley.

113. The Percy Lubbock article was "Review of the Centenary Edition of Robert Browning," *Quarterly Review*, October 1912, 437–57.

[*Dictated.*]

Dearest Howard.   December 10th., 1912.

Very lucid and liberal and, as we say, (or rather don't when we can possibly help it) lovely, your letter this morning received in our dear Firebird's interest, and which I have deeply digested. As a mere warning or red flag earnestly waggled on the line, I hadn't strictly been requiring it; with rockets from poor mad T[eddy]. himself lately much streaking my darkness; though not in a way that I couldn't more or less successfully deal with. My darkness has all these weeks been deep and is but a dreary dimness still; yet I didn't want it, if lighted at all, flushed with the particular lurid rays emitted by such a visitor. Edith has written me a little—and had moreover prepared me for your letter; so that I feel in full possession of the horribly depressing facts. If indeed the ground *could* only be taken for him by les siens [Fr.: his own] that he is a pearl of sanity and sense, the case in favour of his wife's divorcing him would seem to be simple and manageable. His great physical salubrity and activity give the matter at the least a different colour from what it appeared to have a couple of years ago. He writes me from Paris with the last and the crudest extravagance—but just that, however, argues in a manner against one's willingness merely to throw him upon the world. It's a peculiarly damnable case—that he's so impossible for intercourse and yet so possible for circulation (or at least would be were there only people, victims, subjects of devastation, enough, to go round.) I think she is very wonderful—to have been able to write the exquisite "Reef" (for I hold what is finest in The Reef to be really exquisite, and haven't scrupled to try inordinately to encourage her by putting that faith in the most emphatic way) with that amount of harum-scarum banging about her ears.[114] Your expression of the involved alternatives of the preposterous Wharton affects me, at any rate, as absolutely just.

I have given you no news for a long time, because I've had none but the dismalest to give. I have really been all these weeks (and I am now in the 11th.) down in hell, at the very bottom of the pit, gnashing my teeth and howling in perpetual pain. I did let you know, at the beginning, I think,

---

114. Edith Wharton called *The Reef* a "vast" novel. She finished it at the end of August 1912, and when it was published two and a half months later, she decided she didn't like it. Some commentators have called it the most autobiographical of all her novels. Reviewers praised the character of Sophie as well as Wharton's style, but otherwise it was neither a critical nor a financial success.

that I had been taken with an ominous, a really sinister-looking, attack of Shingles—and that ill appearance has been all this time keeping its promise up to the hilt. I have really had an atrocious ordeal, the end of which is not yet; since these last few weeks have been in particular, and in the most abnormal or even, so to speak, monstrous way, but a crescendo of aggravation. An eminent specialist, *the* great Authority, has been down from London to see me; but he left me, now three weeks ago, only more crucified & more helpless than he found me. It is really a damnable ill, for the infliction of suffering that no mitigation appears able to reach; and I feel that unless it now soon breaks (and no ray of dawn yet glimmers) the mere grim struggle with it will have added ten years to my life. Strange and sad to reflect that during all one's long past this gaunt spectre was stalking about the world and finding his victims without its at all (to speak of) having come home to one that the black work was proceeding. It's as if it had gone on in secret and under strange connivances (like the nightwork of other evil deeds)—so that the face of day, or one's own fatuous face, didn't really know it. Which means, in other words, that the beastly thing is of comparatively rare occurrence, and half the time is slight and fleeting. But *'tother* half—oh my dear Howard! It keeps me in no condition for accepting, toward Christmastide, your ever angelic hospitality. And yet, paradoxical though it may seem, I am, under the lash of my Doctors and at any hazard and cost, to make an heroic push up to town, in the interest of sovereign "change", at as early a day as possible; even if I have to be dragged howling from my bed and goaded on in my bedclothes. The celebrated "change" dear to all bored physicians is a recognised specific in this case when every other tattered trick has at last failed. I shall go to an hotel (my already quite familiar Garlant's)[115]—my Club being impossible in illness. With which forgive, dearest Howard, this mechanical, impersonal scrabble. By getting up from 11 to 1, my best hours of the day, I can thus to some degree keep abreast of the postal tides; I can't sit up and drive the jibbing pen. And the hell of it is that if the black blight only *could* be broken I feel that I should shine forth, and even be able to rise to the level of Quacre. And this *shall* eventually be!—as sure as I am yours and Babe's all constantly

Henry James

TLS: Houghton bMS Am 1094 (1302)

---

115. Garlant's is a hotel where HJ sometimes stayed while in London, on Suffolk Street, Pall Mall S.W.

2417 KENSINGTON.

Darling, darling Howard!   April 15*th* 1913

How can I tell you how touched—how verily *melted*—I am by the generous beauty & the so vivid pathos of your letter? I must just try to a little, though I've had, on this grim anniversary, a day almost as terrible as it has been beautiful.[116] It has left me not a little spent & voided—yet fairly cleaned out "emotionally" though I thus be I feel within me undiminished by a scrap of a scrap the precious stored treasure of my long & so rewarded affection for you. Undiminished, I absurdly say?—when what I really feel is how all your recent so distressful history has but fed & fortified my tenderness with every visiting image of your ordeal & your resistance. I have presumed really to know what they both, in their respective rigours (the cruel & the beautiful) were, all the while, & there hasn't been a day that I haven't spent pretty well the best hour of in tenderly tiptoeing (I allude to my spiritual toes, which I back against the herald Mercury's equipped ones) about your couch of patience. And now I have together from you both the sense of the tortured & the sense of the triumphant man—your dear ghostly pencilling; so brave in its weakness, speaks so of what was, for all too long, & what shall now differently be. Admirable & unforgettable your bringing it so generously off—I mean your achieving the blest little pages. Better news than that you are facing homeward there couldn't possibly be. I long to see you with a great ache of longing—& poor affair as I myself am (or have quite preponderently been) we will each on our side work for it. I have seen Percy today for a blest half-hour; he is an angel of goodness & silver-tonguedness. The beauty of his running of the show on which the night now descends!— (10.30 p.m.) However—how we will talk! Goodnight; but I hang about you, I stay round, I cherish you & bless you & all more devotedly than ever yours

Henry James

ALS: Houghton bMS Am 1094 (1305)

Dearest Howard.   [8 September 1913]

Don't groan at the sight of my awkward hand again: you perhaps will characteristically ululate the *less* when I tell you at once that the design of

---

116. "Grim anniversary" refers to the date, 15 April, HJ's birthday.

this is materially, & in respect to an article of your property, to prey upon you. I was on the point of proceeding to that extremity in my note of a day or two ago, but my courage failed, oozed out, & now this is, more brazenly, a reparatory postscript. To be brief I think you have on your groaning shelves (now is the time for *them*, like yourself, to groan,) the two green upstanding vols. of the *Harvard Memorial* biographies—which I know not how on earth to be able to look into unless I may pushingly prevail upon you to lend them—or as *we* say, to *loan* them—to me for a few days. I am, as I think I have told you, doing a still more fatuous sequel to the fatuous Small Boy, &, in relation to the impressions of the War-time, it befalls that I want to *verify* a few small facts about 3 or 4 of the young men, the falling in battle &c, of the Harvard Connection.[117] The book will blessedly *help* me, & if you *can*, without gross trouble, cause it to be conveyed to me by parcel's post my ever-grateful affection for you will even transcend the idolatry to which it constantly tends. I have an admirable parcel-putting-up parlourmaid whom I will send on to Quacre to prepare the treasure for transmission if you make me the sign; but perhaps the little Saint & Angel who ministers to yourself can somehow cause the process to be effected without that invasion. I shall at any rate bless you for the service, & the beautiful books shall be oh so tenderly handled, guarded & restored! Yours, dearest Howard, ever so spongingly,

Henry James
Sept. 8*th* '13.

ALS: Houghton bMS Am 1094 (1310)

21 CARLYLE MANSIONS CHEYNE WALK S. W.

TELEPHONE 2417 KENSINGTON.

Dearest Howard.   [27 December 1913]

It's a relief at last to have a pretext for writing to you that hasn't the sad banality of these Xmastide pretexts. I found it as soon as I spied on Rhoda B.'s[118] mantelshelf this afternoon the beautiful little photograph that you had lately sent her & that (small blame to you,) you hadn't sent *me*. I found it as soon as I seized the happy thought of escaping seasonal banality by crudely asking for a present instead of giving one—& thereby showing I too honour the time. So I *do* crudely ask—that you will kindly send me one of the admirable little portraits—& for no better reason than I deeply

---

117. HJ needed these volumes to help him write his second autobiography, *Notes of a Son and Brother*.

118. See the biographical register for Rhoda Broughton.

desire it. I *have* none of you, dearest Howard, & I can stand it—the privation—no longer. This one seems to me to do you the happiest justice—expressing both your physical & your moral beauty, both your delightful intelligence & your outward grace. It has something of the light of your exquisite soul. Surely it's a very triumphant little thing. Let me not languish longer without it. It shall be set even like the jewel it is. Strange a little, as the fruit of time, I admit, this intercourse by photograph, instead of intercourse by the—what shall I call it?—accolade, & vivid speech & consumed cutlet, as we used to have it (I to consume, & you to supply the cutlet;) but let us pipe in the minor key if the major is beyond us, & let us find everything that ever was still in these restricted but insistent symbols. I am doing very decently here, & some afternoon I will come down to you to tea. Write me a small word with the blest image, & let it speak of you handsomely. I wd. even come before very long if you can stand an hour of me. I would arrive about 4 & leave you about 6, & William wd. take me a little of the time. Yours & his all & always

Henry James
Dec: 27*th* 1913.

ALS: Houghton bMS Am 1094 (1312)

21 CARLYLE MANSIONS CHEYNE WALK S.W.
TELEPHONE 2417 KENSINGTON.

Dearest Howard.   [12 January 1914]

Your poor old Harry learns with joy from you that he may perhaps secure you for the 19th or the 20th—today or tomorrow week. Choose the 19th, please, if equally agreeable to you, as the nearer of the two—& you will delight the soul of Harry; especially if you can stay your proud Quacreised stomach (for *such* a drop from the Quacre standard,) to *1.45;* which will give me time to bundle out my Amanuensis & compose the disorder of toilet (virtually—even though virtuously—disordered, yes, *by* the Amanuensis,)[119] & be wreathed in smiles to receive you. Take it that I *expect* you Monday, if I hear nothing. If William is *disponible* [Fr.: available] of course I shall welcome him—but I figure him at that hour in the City; & frankly too, I should so like *all* of you: by whom I don't mean Robinson,[120] Mrs. Luce &c,[121] but the blest totality (or what the

---

119. His "Amanuensis" at this time was Theodora Bosanquet.

120. Robinson may be Moncure Robinson, who illustrated some of Edith Wharton's work.

121. Mrs. Luce has not been identified.

⟨surgeons⟩ have left of it, of your admirable Self. I have it there in your exquisite oval on—over—my bedroom chimneypiece; but I want it at my board & in my best armchair, & I am, dearest Howdie, your devotedest old

Harry.

P.S. *Isn't* Laura Wagnière a dear?[122] We talked so sweetly of you.

Jan: 12*th* 1914.

P.P.S. I mean that I should be jealous of your attentions to William in my presence & during that snatched & precarious *hour.*

ALS: Houghton bMS AM 1094 (1313)

LAMB HOUSE RYE SUSSEX.

Dearest Howard.   [11 August 1914]

How gorgeously generous & bounteous your letter, & how blest it is to be again in articulate communication with your heavenly understanding! But all I can do at this hour is to tell you of news of Edith given me by [Harry] White, whose excellent letter I, after answering it, too precipitately tore up, & by the enclosed from Mary Cadwalader (Jones) which I strain a point to send you, & which I beg you very kindly not to return me, but to destroy with your own hand. It's so interesting & gallant, & I'm sure she won't mind, seeing it's *you;* only, alas, up to this late Monday p.m.—or Tuesday a.m.!—hour, there's no sign of *her* having been able to get over. They missed doing so, at the end of week before last, but by a few hours— & greatly, on the whole, must they rue it. White is at Stocks with footmen & housemaids—the chef called back to grim service là-bas [Fr.: there]; & with expenses going on to his extreme dismay.[123] He went over to meet Edith on her return from Barcelona (!!) on the 30th, & bring her over, but she lost 24, or 48, hours & it was then too impossible for them to move. She sent *him* back then to take over her responsibilities to Stocks & servants &c here—& he speaks of his journey hither (he arrived Aug. 4th) in terms of mysterious luridity. He groans over the financial abyss—& so do *I*—& he's a very brave homme [Fr.: man]. Mary Cadwal's letter will tell you much of the rest. I do on the whole rather expect them. Will you *partager* [Fr.: share] this & its contents with dear admirable Percy, from

---

122. Laura Huntington Wagniere (b. 1849) was the daughter of Ellen Greenough Huntington, who owned the Villa Castellani, which figures in *Roderick Hudson* and *Portrait of a Lady.* Laura married a Swiss-Italian banker.

123. Stocks was an English house near Tring in Buckinghamshire that Edith Wharton had rented for the summer. It belonged to the famous British sentimental novelist, Mary Augusta Arnold (Mrs. Humphrey) Ward (1851–1920).

whom I have had a letter exquisite as always—in case of my failing for the hour to scrawl something even inadequate back to him? I grieve over your news of Ned Boit—which means, I suppose, the collapse of Cernitoio;[124] but how *can't* you not be sure you don't want him, after an all but achieved happy escape, dragged ruthlessly back to a life in which such abominations are possible as those at which we are assisting? Requiescat, requiescat [Lt.: Peace, peace]! How little I should thank *my* doctors & Hamilton Curtises[125]—if I had any! Even a Fanny Febridge[126]—that there should be any of *her* left, like the mutton-bone!—wouldn't be good enough! I'm glad to know you *did* get to Scotland—for any good that sort of thing does us, however, now! I don't think anything can do us any good, you & me, simply darlingest Howard, but the fact of our being so intimately united in affection, in execration, in prostration, & in the wish that we too had only done with so atrocious a world. Still, I never was on better terms, or on quite so good, with poor dear old England herself. And how wonderful & awful must be France! I am glad I'm old, old—and your all-devotedest

Henry James
Aug. 11*th* 1914.

ALS: Houghton bMS Am 1094 (1315)

21 CARLYLE MANSIONS CHEYNE WALK S. W.
TELEPHONE 2417 KENSINGTON.

Dearest of dear Howards. April *1st 1915*

Your letter is exquisite, entrancing, & it's only because life at this time & in this place is so much less so that I haven't been able to bless you for it with an even shorter delay. The lift out of the nightmare of the actual is an unutterable relief even when [one] can but enjoy but ½ an hour of it, & I plunged into the one you opened to me & drew out my half-hour quite to ecstasy. Above all have I felt a joy in the sweet hazard of having created for yourself the illusion of something other than the hideous present for a little—& that even, strangely enough, by all the badnesses of various kinds (those of dear Hortense seem to have been *so* various!)[127] in which the

---

124. Cernitois (spelled "Cernitoio" in some sources) was Ned Boit's summer villa near Vallombrosa in Tuscany, Italy.

125. The Hamilton Curtises have not been identified.

126. Fanny Febridge has not been identified.

127. The French writer Hortense Allart de Méretens (1801–79) was the mistress of Chateaubriand and Sainte-Beuve. HJ and Sturgis were apparently reading her *Lettres inédites à Sainte-Beuve (1841–1848)*, ed. Léon Séché (Paris: Societé de Mercure de France, 1908).

volumes invite one to wallow. What an hour, n'est-ce-pas [Fr.: no]? that in which poor little Mme Dacquet becomes of a soothing & refreshing commerce,[128] & the "intercourse," of whatever sort, of Hortense & Sainte-Beuve takes on a fine sweetness![129] That lady strikes me as one of the most wondrous salads that even the "mixing" genius of her great country has ever produced, though I am not sure that the vinegar in it doesn't rather predominate over the oil. No, she was not (or is not, to me,) sympathetic—I find her even repulsive through her having so much to *say* over her copulations; but there is something splendid in her freedom & ease—& she was far from *bête* [Fr.: stupid] as those votaresses mostly are. I must indeed truly read over "All that Was Possible,"[130] stamped clearly by you with the most genial divinations—I mean like the prevision of (the revelation of) Rhoda [Broughton]'s inky "Cocotte"!!![131] Dear R., who, alas, is to bring her stay in town in a few days to a close, delivers her appreciation & discriminations as straight from the shoulder as ever, & when one remarks that a certain person (a very fat & nice little person, frequently seen there,) seems to tend still further to expand, replies that she likes the individual extremely & supposed one did one's self. However, she's a very good reader & saw the point of Mme. De Combray as well as you did & as apparently Balzac didn't[132]—who shouldn't indeed have divested her of a single one of her psychological bristles. What *characters* people were in those days, & how much figure they contrived to have— also for what bloated mediocrities of princes they insisted on doing & being it all! No, even little bedraggled Mme. Coquet was scarcely a cocotte.[133] I prefer her much to Mr. Lyttelton![134]—a remark that will perhaps bewilder you till I explain it. It partly explains it that I find the

128. Madame Dacquet has not been identified.

129. The reference is to Charles Augustine Sainte-Beuve (1804–69), the great French literary historian and critic whose weekly reviews were collected in fifteen volumes as *Causeries du lundi* (1851–62).

130. Sturgis's second publication was an epistolary novel *All That Was Possible: Being the Record of a Summer in the Life of Mrs. Sibyl Crofts, Comedian* (1895).

131. Rhoda Broughton's "Cocotte" might refer to a character in her latest novel, *Concerning a Vow* (1914). All of her sentimental domestic fiction contained a variety of stereotypical heroines. HJ liked her but disliked her novels, so he may have been satirizing her in this remark.

132. Madame De Combray has not been identified; she may be a Balzac character.

133. Madame Coquet has not been identified, though again she may be a Balzac character.

134. Mr. Lyttelton is probably Alfred P. Lyttelton (1857–1913), British politician and once colonial secretary.

colossal "Fool" side of so much of the show that we seem to be making in this country just now more than I feel at times I can bear—& yet I don't see that I can do anything else but *have* to. The further, too, one gets—or *we* get—into the whole vast horror the bigger & blacker—or redder—it looms. And yet I had occasion to go into Harrod's today[135]—& there behold people buying Easter eggs, of the most fantastic embellishment, by the thousand, to all appearance—though perhaps of course for the Trenches, where their shells will be of such use. Forgive the desperate refuge of the gibe to yours, dearest Howard, ever

H.J.

ALS: Houghton bMS Am 1094 (1318)

---

135. Harrod's was, and remains, a London department store.

Hugh Walpole

In December 1908 the sixty-five-year-old Henry James received an unsolicited letter from a twenty-four-year-old erstwhile Epsom College schoolmaster who, with the acceptance of his first novel imminent, was standing "on the threshold of fictive art." The letter that James later described as "gentle," "gratifying," and "charming" does not survive,[1] but subsequent events suggest that Hugh Walpole's letter was more than another instance of his confirmed habit of "Writing to Authors." Inscribed alongside its admiration for James and its aspiration for fame must have been intimations of what Rupert Hart-Davis has identified as one of Walpole's recurring concerns, the search for the ideal friend, for what Walpole himself termed "the real right man."[2]

If the letter was a presumptuous act, James did not treat it as such. Instead he responded warmly to a young man who at the very least offered him another "link" in his long-standing relation with the Cantabrigian A. C. Benson.[3] Yet the increasingly self-reflective James had to have recognized salient features of his own youth in Walpole's early history: the son of an Anglican clergyman born abroad; a child shuttled from New Zealand, to England, to America, and back to England before he was ten; a diffident

---

1. For HJ's description, see his letter of 13 December 1908 to Arthur Christopher Benson, in Henry James, *Letters to A. C. Benson and Auguste Monod,* ed. E. F. Benson (London: Elkin Mathews and Marot, 1930), 66.

2. Rupert Hart-Davis, *Hugh Walpole: A Biography* (New York: Macmillan, 1952), 32. Walpole's occasionally extravagant language on "ideal friendship" prompts Hart-Davis to be either cautionary or evasive: "As the quest for the 'real right man' was intensified, the words 'friend' and 'friendship' occurred more and more frequently in everything he wrote, acquiring a special significance of his invention."

3. See the biographical register for Arthur Christopher Benson.

scholar, with no real sense of "home"; a recent Cambridge graduate with many acquaintances but no close friends; an aspiring writer about to descend on London; and a young man "to some extent afraid of women" and "always easier in the company of his own sex."[4] And the aging James surely found much to envy and to admire in the younger man's vitality, in his literary ambitions, and in his apparent zest for experience. In any case the result was a correspondence that quickly progressed to terms of endearment and a friendship that was soon marked with the tokens of intimacy.

Not until February 1909, however, did the two men first meet, in London, and Walpole's diary entry for the occasion also suggests that he looked to James for more than just his imprimatur:

> Dined with Henry James alone at the Reform Club. He was perfectly wonderful. By far the greatest man I have ever met—and yet amazingly humble and affectionate—absolutely delightful. He talked about himself and his books a great deal and said some interesting things. It was a wonderful evening.[5]

The relationship that began so delightfully, however, was to be comparatively short-lived. Only six years later, in September 1914, the weak-sighted Walpole, unfit for active military service, traveled to Russia as a correspondent and did not see James again before his death in February 1916. His diary entry for 13 March 1916 contrasts starkly with the ebullient passage quoted above: "Thirty two to-day! Should have been a happy day but was completely clouded for me by reading in the papers of Henry James' death. This was a terrible shock to me."[6] Not until after another sixteen years did the younger writer offer a fuller commentary on what James termed "our admirable, our incomparable relation": "I loved him, was frightened of him, was bored by him, was staggered by his wisdom and stupefied by his intricacies, altogether enslaved by his kindness, generosity, child-like purity of his affections, his unswerving loyalties, his sly and Puck-like sense of humour."[7]

How did James describe their brief but intense relationship? In his letter of 5 June 1909 to A. C. Benson he thanked him for "the gift that you lately

---

4. Hart-Davis, *Hugh Walpole,* 12–35.
5. Harry Ransom Humanities, Research Center, University of Texas at Austin (hereafter HRC), Walpole, H., Works—Diaries, 1908 [1909], 2 March 1909.
6. Walpole, H., Works—Diaries, 13 March 1916, HRC.
7. Walpole, *The Apple Trees,* 52–53.

made me in the form of the acquaintance of delightful and interesting young Hugh Walpole."[8] Within another six weeks he was speaking of them as "fast friends."[9] By mid-October Walpole was writing to his mother from Lamb House to say that James wished him to stay "more or less indefinitely."[10] Although occasional visits rather than an indefinite stay had to suffice, Walpole's successive letters touched, charmed, moved, quickened, interested, amused, cheered, comforted, inspired, pleasured, and dazzled James. Yet a candid James surely would have added that this "almost unbearably enviable youth" posed for him an epistolary challenge.

A letter could never be more for James than "the little outward and visible sign" of all the accumulating feelings that he struggled to express, a "poor small sign of gratitude & affection," "a small tangible token of my unspeakable sentiments," "the merest sketchiest stopgap—a fond, free, futile gesture of affection," "a poor expressional stopgap." The trope in his 15 April 1911 letter to a hospitalized Walpole is representative: "Let me then get at you a little this way—I mean all *but* as intimately as if I were bringing you jelly or grapes or the Strand Magazine or even Arnold Bennett's last up to that hour." For James always envisioned his letters to Walpole as bearing something more nourishing and sustaining than news and information. Their purpose was to establish a link, to feed a flame, to soothe, to sustain, to reassure, to "ease off." But that figurative something consistently defied any more literal or original definition.

After four decades of writing, and despite his preexisting intimacy with the equally young Hendrik Andersen, James still struggled to express his feelings toward Walpole. "Form alone takes, & holds & preserves substance—saves it from the welter of helpless verbiage," he wrote to Walpole on 19 May 1912, defending his low estimation of the Russian novelists. But the truth of the observation had already been borne out for James in a very different medium. For the form of the love letter escaped him, at least early in his correspondence with Walpole, reducing him to clichés, banalities, and amplification by repetition if not exactly to "helpless verbiage":

So for the moment enough said—even though so much less said than felt. It goes very deep—deep, deep, deep.

8. *Henry James Letters*, 4:522.
9. Letter of 24 July 1909 to Benson, in James, *Letters to Benson and Monod*, 69.
10. Qtd. in Hart-Davis, *Hugh Walpole*, 72.

Of course I shall deeply rejoice in any sign of affectionate remembrance
from you—"affectionate remembrance"!—forgive the deadly conventional phrase, but you know what I mean!
I am your, yours, yours, dearest Hugh, yours.
I take no end of affectionate pleasure (forgive my *banal* terms!) in this
impression of your blooming, bursting, bounding vitality!
I don't know how to tell you vividly enough how yearningly I pat you on
the back or in fact take you to the heart. But feel it, know it, like it.

In short, James's "powers of execution" were not adequate to his "inward
yearnings and dreams," which is perhaps only to say that there could be no
bridging of the divide between private feeling and public expression. If
there were limits to what James was willing to commit to paper, there were
limits as well to what he was capable of committing to paper. "The Elephant paws you oh so benevolently," he wrote to Walpole in an image,
more comic than erotic, that recurs in a handful of the letters.[11] On many
occasions in these letters one senses the essential rightness of the image,
that the elephant is indeed guiding the pen as best it can.

This lack of precision was not merely epistolary convention, the pre-
tense that mere words cannot convey the sincerity of true emotions, nor
some anticipation of the postmodern mantra that language cannot ade-
quately convey meaning or reality. Neither was the cause simply reticence
or discretion, although Walpole later ascribed to James no small measure of
the first trait.[12] In the handwritten postscript to his dictated and typed
letter of 30 January 1913 James professed to entertain "sentiments for you
which he can't flaunt, you see, in the bewildered face of Remington"; but
he also found that his sentiments for Walpole could not be flaunted even
from behind the midnight pen. The written language of love and affection
apparently did not come easily or naturally to James. The salutation from
one letter—"from Friend (putting it mildly) to Friend & Maître to
Elève"—bespeaks the recurring problem: if he was not simply being coy,
James was at a loss for how to designate his affectionate relationship with

---

11. For a somewhat tortured reading of HJ's elephant imagery as a link to one of
Walpole's novels, see Leon Edel, "Hugh Walpole and Henry James: The Fantasy of the
'Killer and the Slain,'" *American Imago* 8 (1951): 363–64.

12. "There was no crudity of which he was unaware but he did not wish that crudity to
be named. It must be there so that he might apprehend it, but it must not be named"
(Walpole, *The Apple Trees,* 53).

the younger Hugh, recognizing how poorly served they both were by the mild "friend." And while he may have been more definitive in the final formulation, James nonetheless felt the need to resort to the French "maître" and "élève," perhaps believing that in the foreignness of the terms resided the grain of difference to distinguish and ennoble the relationship. In another letter James tried to ascribe his verbal failure to the uninspiring atmosphere of Rye; "tokens don't grow, in any form worth speaking or thinking of, in the rude soil of our poor little tawdrified High Street," he complained. But in truth it was the geography of the heart more than the geography of Rye that constrained him.[13]

Visits and talks, the chances to meet "cheek by jowl" to "jaw for a little," were of course always preferable. When they did meet, there was apparently no lack of mutual understanding. Walpole's diary entry for 6 July 1909 records a "ripping dinner with Henry James" and comments on the occasion in language reminiscent of Hendrik Andersen's own early appreciation of James: "That is a quite perfect affair in its own way and one begins to feel that the *one* thing that one really demands of the friend is perfect comprehension. Of course that is perhaps a 'council of perfection' but H.J. has got it."[14]

But there was as well no small measure of what Walpole highlights as "bewilderment" in the relationship. He emphasizes how James "was also a sick man during a great part of the time that I knew him, and I was then extremely healthy and as filled with vitality as a merry-go-round at a fair. It was this vitality that attracted & bewildered him."[15] As a consequence, while the perfectly comprehending James was just as often bewildered by Walpole, the fumbling James who was unsure of and tentative with the language of love became the fulsome James when he spoke of Walpole's comparatively adventurous and energetic life. James's language typically reinforced an image of the younger man that was either melodramatically or sentimentally *de trop*.

---

13. Perhaps herein lies the explanation for HJ's recurring exchange and discussion of photographs in these and other letters to his young admirers: the lover can look upon the beloved "with a really quite beautiful direct recognition & intelligence," the attempt to describe which lands James in lexical confusion: "So there you are—by which I mean *here*, so intimately, you are; & here *we* are—if it isn't 'there,' rather. I should say I am myself—by which I mean, again, (pardon these alembications,) at 20 Glebe Place, in a neat little box & frame."

14. Walpole, H., Works—Diaries, 1908 [1909], HRC.

15. Walpole, *The Apple Trees*, 53.

These letters reveal the degree to which Walpole existed for James as a "gallant youth," yet anything but a "Baby." He was a "child of light," a "universal youth," a "mighty youth," indeed the very "Prodigal Son." Walpole possessed an "almost unbearably enviable youth" and frolicsomeness; he was a "white lambkin on the vast epistolary green." Life was not all frolic, though, and James apostrophized "the gallant & intelligent young" about to "hurl" himself into "the deep sea of journalism." But neither was life all work, and James imagined the "young Hugh on the threshold of fictive art" ready to step off the train at Rye and into the "open arms" of James, with "a love-scene or something" to read. He was a companion with whom to enjoy an "Arcadian scene," a figure of vitality always "athletically" employed, and a figure leading a "multitudinous life" constantly "bounding through the hoops" of a "perpetual circus." This "wonder-working Hugh!" pushed his "merciless ravage" through the social round. The sheer "magnificence" of his life and the "splendour & prowess" of his youth—"breasting" the waves of society and "shiningly" swimming and diving, like a "peerless pearl-diver"—were dazzling and charming to a James who was as content to observe the personal spectacle as he was earnest to shape the professional career.

Confronted with these disparate responses, the contemporary reader can hardly be so certain that, as James declared, between the two men "there is no obscurity or ambiguity." To borrow a periphrastic passage from one of James's letters to A. C. Benson, the correspondence to Walpole "leaves one's appetite for ultimate definition a little unsatisfied."[16] But figurative description if not ultimate definition remains possible. The various motifs limned here—the loneliness and isolation of a life distant from London, the years spent in what might seem to others to be complete and utter self-sufficiency, the prolonged solitude relieved at last by a youthful companion, the difficulties of communication, the great divide between youth and age, the perceived responsibility of the tutored for the untutored, and most importantly the devotion to a "Master" of a youth who "lov'd me more than it was possible for him ever to love any Thing

---

16. See the letter of [31 May 1906], in *Henry James: A Life in Letters,* ed. Philip Horne (London: Penguin, 1999), 433. Hence the willingness to limn the friendship with hearsay. According to Leon Edel, "In his later years Hugh told the young Stephen Spender that he had offered himself to the Master and that James had said, 'I can't, I can't'" (*Henry James, 1901–1916: The Master,* 407). Yet, as Fred Kaplan points out, the anecdote is questionable because Walpole never defined himself as a homosexual (*Henry James,* 453).

before,"[17]—these features of his relationship with Hugh Walpole were all summed up by James in a single choice image: "I dream of the golden islands," he wrote to Walpole on 23 October 1909, "with you there, along with me, for my man Friday."

17. See Daniel Defoe, *Robinson Crusoe,* ed. Michael Shinagel (New York: Norton, 1975), 166.

My dear young friend Hugh Walpole.   December 13*th 1908*.

I had from you some days ago a very kind & touching letter, which greatly charmed me, but which now that I wish to read it over again before belatedly thanking you for it I find I have stupidly & inexplicably mislaid—at any rate I can't tonight put my hand on it.[18] But the extremely pleasant & interesting impression of it abides with me; I rejoice that you were moved to write it & that you didn't resist the generous movement— since I always find myself (when the rare & blest revelation—once in a blue moon—takes place) the happier for the thought that I enjoy the sympathy of the gallant & intelligent young. I shall send this to Arthur Benson with the request that he will kindly transmit it to you—since I fail thus, provokingly, of having your address before me.[19] I gather that you are about to hurl yourself into the deep sea of journalism—the more treach- erous currents of which (& they strike me as numerous) I hope you may safely breast.[20] Give me more news of this at some convenient hour, & let me believe that at some propitious one I may have the pleasure of seeing you. I never see A[rthur]. C[hristopher]. B[enson]. in these days, to my loss & sorrow—& if this continues I shall have to depend on you consider- ably to give me tidings of him. However, my appeal to him (my only resource) to put you in possession of this will perhaps strike a welcome spark—so you see you are already something of a link. Believe me very truly yours

Henry James

ALS: Walpole Collection (Recipient)

Harry Ransom Humanities Research Center, University of Texas at Austin

My dear Hugh Walpole.   December 19*th 1908*.

You were in so little danger, the other day, of "never hearing" from me, that this present will ⟨pass?⟩ before the even too prompt penalty, perhaps, normally incurred by those correspondents who truly move me! Your letter of yesterday just comes in to me, & behold I am catching the post of a

---

18. Walpole wrote to HJ in late November or early December 1908.

19. See the biographical register for Arthur Christopher Benson. HJ enclosed the letter to Walpole in his letter of the same day to Benson (*Letters to Benson and Monod*, 66–67).

20. In November 1909 Walpole resigned his teaching post in the Lower School at Epsom College to work with the London Literary Agency. In February 1909 he began reviewing novels for the *Standard*.

quarter of an hour hence with this little sign of thoroughly responsive interest. I have heard from A[rthur]. C[hristopher]. B[enson].[21] since writing to me [sic], & he has sympathetically suggested to me, dear man, that I shall not make a mistake in attempting, within my compass of the safely combustible, to feed your flame. I should only be glad to, didn't it strike me as so dancing & aspiring a one as really scarce to require more care than you yourself can give it; but, stretching a point, figure me chucking at you even now the very biggest handful I can scrape together of such stuff as will make it—at Tremans[22] especially—burn a beautiful blue & a lovely pink & a most promising fiery red. While your circle there admiringly considers it let them therefore just think a little that even I am not utterly away from the hearth! And afterwards—journalism or no journalism (these are mighty considerations) do, I emphatically beg you, write me the letters and send me Books & pay me the visits; & above all keep as tight hold as you can of the temper & the faith of your almost unbearably enviable youth! I am a hundred years old—it's my one merit— but the breath of your enviability (that name says all for it,) quickens again, after all, yours with every good wish

Henry James

ALS: Walpole Collection (Recipient)
Harry Ransom Humanities Research Center, University of Texas at Austin

LAMB HOUSE, RYE, SUSSEX.

ANUARY 8*th 1909.*

My dear young Hugh! It greatly interests & amuses & cheers me to hear from you—especially now that your plot seems to "thicken;" but don't measure my sympathy by the size of these restricted tablets.[23] I have been writing letters for a hundred years—while you bleat & jump like a white lambkin on the vast epistolary green which stretches before you coextensive with life. This means that I positively invite you & applaud your gambols. I find it "splendid" that you should think so many things so, & beg you to keep it up for me so long as you candidly can. You won't find anything "splendid" here, *pace* A[rthur]. C[hristopher]. B[enson].; I don't want to scare you, but I've never made Letters particularly or even very conveniently "pay"—& indeed I hate to talk about that side of them. It's an excellent side in itself, but any view of it should be kept in a totally

---

21. See the biographical register for Arthur Christopher Benson.
22. Tremans has not been identified.
23. HJ is writing on 4 × 5 card stock, imprinted with his Rye address.

distinct compartment of the mind from the view of the loved objects in themselves. The complicated "firm" abashes me a little, but the Chelsea studio[24] strongly attracts—& I'm especially drawn to that piece of ⟨soap?⟩ by reason of its large proportionate value in the picture. I have before me here a very busy & scribbly stretch of time (till May, I should think,) but then I come up to town to stay a bit—other dashes uncertain & breathless; or perhaps I may even get hold of you for a few hours down here in the interval. I have spilled over on another card but only—almost—to have space to ring out to you cheerily the very most auspicious goodnight of your all well-wishing

Henry James

ALS: Walpole Collection (Recipient)
Harry Ransom Humanities Research Center, University of Texas at Austin

LAMB HOUSE, RYE, SUSSEX.

My dear Hugh. [28 March 1909]

I have had so bad a conscience on your score, ever since last writing to you with that as yet unredeemed promise of my poor image or effigy, that the benignity of your expression has but touched me the more. On coming to look up some decent photograph among the few odds & ends of such matters to be here brought out of hiding, I found nothing that it wasn't hateful to me to put into circulation. I have been very little & very ill (*always* very ill) represented—& not at all for a long time, & shall never be again; & of two or three disinherited illustrations of that truth that I have put away for you to choose between you must come here & *make* selection, yourself carrying them off. My reluctant hand can't bring itself to "send" them. Heaven forbid such sendings!——————Can you come some day—some Saturday—in April?—I mean after Easter. Bethink yourself, & let it be the 17th or the 24th if possible. (I expect to go up to town for four or five weeks the 1st May.) You are keeping clearly such a glorious holiday now that I fear you may hate to begin again; but you'll have with me in every way much shorter commons, much sterner fare, much less purple & fine linen, & in short a much more constant reminder of your mortality than while you loll in A[rthur]. C. B[enson].'s chariot of fire.[25] Therefore, as I say, come grimly down. Loll none the less, however, meanwhile, to your utmost—such opportunities, I recognise, are to be fondly

---

24. Walpole moved into a room at 20 Glebe Street, Chelsea on 1 February (Hart-Davis, *Hugh Walpole*, 66).

25. I.e., his motor car.

cherished. If you give A. C. B. this news of me, please assure him with my love that I am infinitely, that I am yearningly aware of *that*. He'd see soon enough if he were some day to let *me* loll. However I am going to Cambridge for some as yet undetermined 48 hours in May, & if he will let me loll for one of those hours at Magdalene it will do almost as well—I mean of course he being there.[26] However, even if he does flee at my approach—& the possession of a fleeing-machine *must* enormously prompt that sort of thing—I rejoice immensely meanwhile that you have the kindness of him—I am magnanimous enough for that. Likewise I am tenderhearted enough to be capable of shedding tears of pity & sympathy over young Hugh on the threshold of fictive art—& with the long & awful vista of large productions in a largely producing world before him.[27] Ah dear young Hugh it will be very grim for you with your faithful & dismal friend

Henry James
March 28th 1909.

ALS: Walpole Collection (Recipient)
Harry Ransom Humanities Research Center, University of Texas at Austin

LAMB HOUSE, RYE, SUSSEX.

My dear, dear Hugh. *April 27th* 1909.

Not in many vain words, yet without dull (& vainer) delay do I assure you of my exceeding great pleasure in your delightful, your admirable & beautiful letter. Your confidence & trust & affection are infinitely touching & precious to me, & I all responsibly accept them & give you all my own in return. Yes, all "responsibly", my dear boy—large as the question of "living up" to our splendid terms can't but appear to loom to me. Living up to them—for *me*—takes the form of wanting to be more sovereignly & sublimely—& ah so tenderly withal!—good for you & helpful to you than words can well say. This is, in vulgar phrase, a large order but I'm not afraid of it—& in short it's inspiring to think how magnificently we shall pull together, all round & in every way. See therefore how we're at one, & believe in the comfort I take in you. It goes very deep—deep, deep, deep;

---

26. HJ traveled to Cambridge on 10 June for a weekend visit with a "dear Triumvir" of admirers—Geoffrey Keynes, Charles Sayle, and Theodore Bartholomew—with whom previously he had only corresponded. See Geoffrey Keynes, *Henry James in Cambridge* (Cambridge: W. Heffer and Sons, 1967). In "The Cult of Homosexuality in England, 1850–1950," *Biography* 13 (1990), Lord Noel Annan lists "Charles Sayle and his playmate A. T. Bartholomew" among those who "moved in uranian circles" (191).

27. Walpole was on the "threshold of fictive art" after 13 February 1909, when Smith Elder accepted for publication his first novel, *The Wooden Horse*.

so infinitely do you touch & move me, dear Hugh. So for the moment enough said—even though so much less said than felt. It won't be long, no—before we shall meet again:[28] I *don't* come up on Saturday, but I do as early as possible next week—& my days go, & I suppose yours do. Hold me in your heart, even as I hold you in my arms—though verily I think *no* gallant youth less of a Baby. Say "*Très*-cher Maitre",[29] or "my very dear Master" (for the present,) & believe how faithfully I am yours always & ever

Henry James

ALS: Walpole Collection (Recipient)

Harry Ransom Humanities Research Center, University of Texas at Austin

REFORM CLUB, PALL MALL.S.W.

Dearest Hugh! June *3d 1909.*

"Think of you"—? I think of you constantly, affectionately, tenderly—& even, if that were possible, to the inconvenience of other thoughts. It isn't *really* possible though—for you "work in" beautifully everywhere. You worked in even while lately (from directly after last seeing you,) I had to tumble into bed with an attack of gout—a quite beastly one—in my poor old right & hitherto "immune" foot. I walked home that day—on parting with you after our Lovelace-Lascelles tea[30]—all along the Embankment, thinking I had conjured away certain premonitory twinges I had been feeling for 2 or 3 days. But not so, & that night I was seized & the next day & for 75, long & dreary hours following, stupidly supine. I thought a little of making you a signal to come & see me for a half hour—then dashed it away with the sense that I *couldn't*—wouldn't for the world—exhibit to you my sordid infirmity. We will do without that—especially as I hadn't had such a visitation (from the gout-devil,) for 8 years—& reckon now

---

28. HJ writes immediately after Walpole's weekend visit at Lamb House. See Walpole's diary entry for Monday, 26 April 1909: "Spent a wonderful week-end with Henry James. Much more wonderful than I had expected. I am very lucky in my friends. The house and garden are exactly suited to him. He is beyond words. I cannot speak about him" (Walpole, H. Works—Diaries, 1908–1909, HRC). Walpole subsequently wrote about HJ in the portrait of the novelist Henry Galleon in *Fortitude* (1913), in the story "Mr. Oddy" in *All Souls' Night* (1925), in *The Apple Trees* (1932), and again in "Henry James: A Reminiscence," *Horizon* (London) 1 (1940): 74–80.

29. Joseph Conrad (1857–1924) addressed HJ similarly in his letters, according to Edel, *Henry James, 1901–1916: The Master*, 56.

30. Countess Mary Caroline Wortley (Mrs. Ralph Gordon Noel King) (1848–1941) was the second wife of the second earl of Lovelace, the grandson of Lord Byron. See the biographical register for Helen Lascelles (Mrs. Eric) Maclagan.

never to have another. And I at last got away into the country on Sunday *p.m.*—& returned yesterday—hobbling in a sorry substitute for a shoe— but now almost without pain. I can't walk much—but can drive; & only tell you these things to show you how, for a good bit, I have "thought" of you all at my own expense, as it were, & not a bit at yours—or with the disposition to sacrifice you. Thus you too were nobly employed—by which I mean athletically, which is noble except for Idiots, in whom it isn't interesting. So much the better therefore. The thing that *isn't* the better, however, is that London & Life so complicate themselves that I can't at this moment propose to you an occasion—for our reunion; for which, yet, I am earnestly looking out. Do you the same—& we shall find it & pounce. Feel meanwhile how little we are *dis*united, & believe me, dearest Hugh, your faithfullest & fondest old

Henry James

ALS: Walpole Collection (Recipient)

Harry Ransom Humanities Research Center, University of Texas at Austin

LAMB HOUSE, RYE, SUSSEX.

*"So sorry!"[31]   *July 24*th* 1909.

Dearest Hugh.

Your little word has come, & I participate in your fatigue & your collapse—inevitable (& even interesting) consequences, as well as not at all fatal ones, of the wonderful rate at which you live: I participate, as I say, just as I do in everything that happens to you or concerns you. And this is a word only to soothe & sustain & reassure & at the same time ease you off—not a bit to further stir you up—to lash or to goad, to prod or to worry you: only to *give,* in fine, & never a scrap to ask. Of course I shall deeply rejoice in any sign of affectionate remembrance from you— "affectionate remembrance"!—forgive the deadly conventional phrase, but you know what I mean! On the other hand I only want to be *in* your mind, & not a whit grossly "on" it; which you can always believe & know that you're in mine quite as entirely. I am yours, yours, yours, dearest Hugh, *yours!*

H.J.

ALS: Walpole Collection (Recipient)

Harry Ransom Humanities Research Center, University of Texas at Austin

---

31. HJ apologizes for smearing the date.

Dearest Hugh. [16 August 1909]

Your words are few & feverish, but I make the most of them: they give me a sort of a kind of a dim ghost of a scrap of a sense of being with you & of your feeling yourself, even in the fury of your perspiration, with me.[32] You *are* that, goodness knows, whether you write or not—though when the little outward & visible sign arrives you put on for the hour a comparative & a charming (though an all too meagre) palpability. Right you are, through the thick or the thin of it, to lead your multitudinous life & keep bounding through the hoops of your apparently perpetual circus. Great must be your glories & triumphs & rounds of applause, & I break into solitary clapping here, late in the sultry night, when I hear of your lawn tennis greatness. It all sounds awfully hot & brave & unmorbid & objective—keep it up, to my fond vision, therefore, as long as you can stand it. I can do my own alembications—*you* must do my gymnastics. That admonition, however, is clearly unnecessary. I am spending here very still & canicular[33]—but very fruitful &, I think & trust, artistically felicitous, days. This is the summer most exempt from social agitations & complications that I have been blest with for several years—though I fear it may change a little next month. Edmund Gosse,[34] who came on Saturday, went away this a.m., & *he* is slightly agitating—but the bump of the portmanteau has been, since I came back from town, unprecedentedly infrequent on my stair. (Gosse goes next Saturday to Arthur Benson at Harrogate, & afterwards with him to Settle in Yorkshire,[35] for a fortnight, I believe. He tells me that A.B. still describes himself as in the depths. I *can't*, dearest Hugh, send you the photograph, for I have ⟨been?⟩ & gone & had it *framed,* for Glebe Place,[36] & with its black & gilt & glass &c it is too clumsy & brittle for you to carry about with you. Have a gentle patience, I shall have it packed & addressed to No. 20. But I beseech you to let me have yours. That was exactly a prayer I meant to utter to you on next

---

32. Walpole spent early August 1909 at several country houses, including that of the Darwins at Dryburn and Ashley Combe, the Somerset home of Lady Lovelace (Hart-Davis, *Hugh Walpole,* 71).

33. Canicular: of or relating to the dog days.

34. See the biographical register for Edmund Gosse.

35. Harrogate is approximately eighteen miles north of Leeds; Settle, in North Yorkshire, is approximately twelve miles NNW of Haworth.

36. Walpole lived at No. 20 Glebe Place, Chelsea from 1 February 1909 until May 1911, when he moved to 16 Hallam Street.

writing—so your mention of it is telepathic. I want you too much here before me—too much not to rightfully have you. Good-night, dearest boy. Heaven send our reunion. I haven't heard from Seaman,[37] but it's all right of course; & I am all affectionately your devotissimo

H.J.

Aug: 16: 1909.

P.S. Your envelope arrived this a.m. *unglued*—not having evidently received, on its gum, the lick of your silver tongue. Your gentle text wd. have been accessible—but there was no harm done. Do, however, always apply the lingual caress.

ALS: Walpole Collection (Recipient)
Harry Ransom Humanities Research Center, University of Texas at Austin

LAMB HOUSE, RYE, SUSSEX.
Dearest Hugh.
August 24*th 1909.*

It is not so much, in hearing from you, by your literary or epistolary compositions that I am dazzled & charmed as by the reflection given me of the magnificence of your life & the splendour & prowess of your youth. Of what a deluge of society you breast the waves, in what an ocean of contacts & conquests, clearly, you shiningly swim! I expect you, fondly (kindly remember,) to bring me, like a peerless pearl-diver (when you rise again to the surface—*my* sequestered surface,) other priceless particles than those contained in your letters—by which I evidently mean all those that are *not* so contained! What I *most* evidently mean, at any rate, dearest Hugh, is that I take no end of affectionate pleasure (forgive my *banal* terms!) in this impression of your blooming, bursting, bounding vitality! I only long for the day when we can talk it all over—so meanwhile let it continue to accumulate, & believe, meanwhile, also, that I tend to yearn over you & your rich young experience, much more than less. I sit sedately on the bank while you plash in the stream—but I am content with my part, which suits much better my age & my figure, likewise what I am pleased to call, for the occasion, my genius; & so long as I don't lose sight of you all is well. The little snapshot picture contributes its small amount to my not doing that; though I am sorry you are relegated to the remoter distance with the

<hr>

37. HJ's pocket diary entry for 30 September 1909 reads "Owen Seaman 1:30 Savile, 'taking' H.W." (*The Complete Notebooks of Henry James,* ed. Leon Edel and Lyall Powers [New York: Oxford UP, 1987], 309). Sir Owen Seaman (1861–1936) was a prolific British poet and, from 1906 to 1927, editor of the London illustrated magazine *Punch.*

anonymous strangers, to whom I decidedly prefer you, standing in the forefront. Happy anonymous stranger, however, to be seated beside you! My blessing will go with you to Porlock,[38] since it's thither you push your merciless ravage. (I had it stupidly in my head that you were going to Lady L[ovelace]. at Ockham[39]—which accounts for my vain, in the sense of vague, remark, though you may have forgotten it, that I might possibly be able to look in there during your stay. Looking in at Porlock won't, decidedly, be in the cards for me.) I leave this [place] none the less for a few days next week—even ten days or so perhaps—& shall be a few scraps of that time in London. If you go *straight* to Somersetshire there's no chance of any coincidence for us there (in town,) I fear—& much straightness now apparently marks your every proceeding. We must make it up later here—when you begin to be out of breath. Then I invite you to flop on me—but meantime rejoice, as I say, in your age & your constitution. I'm delighted to hear that your work hasn't utterly suffered—in fact rather (since the haughty Muse has succumbed to you too, between trains, or "events", or whatever you all-round men most *generally* call them,) brilliantly gained, oh wonder-working Hugh! I have only to-day an answer from Owen Seaman in Cornwall—kindly about the Savile, but telling me he is no longer on the Committee &c.[40] He suggests however that for him to speak for you to such others as from personal knowledge, I should bring you there to see him (he speaks of luncheon) toward the end of September. As I shall have again to be in town for a day or two about that time we must try to arrange this. I daresay it's important for you. But goodnight, dearest Hugh. For goodness sake do let that photograph, the other, swim into my ken. This has been an infamous day here—of utterly unceasing downpour for 24 hours & the end is not yet. I write you in the dead unhappy night when the rain is on the roof—but you see how interminably I am yours

Henry James

ALS: Walpole Collection (Recipient)
Harry Ransom Humanities Research Center, University of Texas at Austin

---

38. Walpole's diary indicates that he was at Ashley Combe, Porlock—the Somerset home of the widowed Lady Lovelace—from 4 until at least 12 September.
39. Lady Lovelace's principal residence was at Ockham Park, Surrey.
40. See note 37.

Dearest Hugh.   [8 September 1909]

I too, even poor ponderous & superannuated I, am leading the Life for a little, in my clumsy way & with a vocation & a genius so inferior to yours; whereby I but snatch a moment, with everything about me awkward for it, to make you this poor small sign of gratitude & affection. However, I am more or less under the fond illusion of your presence—I have set you up before me, & while you look out at me from your little browny desert as with really a quite beautiful direct recognition & intelligence, I can tell you to your handsome young face that it gives me infinite pleasure thus to possess you. You direct upon me a consideration that has quite the air of being rather *intended* for me—share as I may the small fallacy with a hundred others; & in responding to which, while our eyes meet, I seem almost to do something (in the way of guarding it & getting hold of it tighter,) for our admirable, our incomparable relation. So there you are— by which I mean *here,* so intimately, you are; & here *we* are—if it isn't "there," rather. I should say I am myself—by which I mean, again, (pardon these alembications,) at 20 Glebe Place, in a neat little box & frame, unless I be smashed to pieces;[42] & turning my nose away from you a little more than I could wish, though not in the faintest degree, I need scarcely say, turning it "up!" This photographic intercourse is but a hollow stopgap at the best, but, as photographic intercourse goes, it will serve; & in short, dearest Hugh, it does help me to live with you a little more. Thus am I leading the Life, as I say, with greater intensity. The people of this house are very old & comfortable friends (of mine & of many persons—some of whom are gathered in here) but my general privilege of the occasion is one you would do much more honour to—with your immeasurably finer musical vibration. I have promised to stay, incredibly, till Friday a.m., but the Festival, in the ⟨serried?⟩ Cathedral, already a little palls on me, though I listened to Elgar's "Apostles" last night with a dim approach to intelli- gence. And I pay another visit—in Gloucestershire—next week, & an- other, in Norfolk directly thereafter—a strange & unnatural riot for me, at the prospect of which I begin already to be appalled. But after it I shall rest forever. I don't come back from Overstrand, I fear, till the 20th, but expect

---

41. From 6–11 September HJ was the guest of the daughter of Fanny Kemble and her husband, James Wentworth Leigh, the dean of Hereford, at the 1909 Three Choirs Festival (see *Complete Notebooks,* 308).

42. See HJ's 16 August 1909 letter for his plans to send Walpole a framed photograph.

to be in town after that till about the end of the month.[43] Thereby we shall meet, a poor piecemeal & impracticable sort of business as meeting in town at the best seems to insist on being. Meet we will, nevertheless, & I will arrange the Seaman interview,[44] & then, as early as possible next month we will get some calmer hours down chez moi [Fr.: at my home]. I rejoice in the benefits that accrue to you from Lady Lovelace (to whom I send no message, lest she should by a concatenation accordingly *invite* me—& I can't oh I can't come;) but she does appear to have at her command a choice collection of the children of darkness—whom it isn't fair to ask a child of light to meet. And you don't mention Miss Lascelles,[45] the *one* other child of light. If she *is* there give her my blessing, please—it really means my love! Even in this case there is no end left, dearest Hugh, for you in the deepest old heart of your

H.J.

Sept. 8*th* 1909.

ALS: Walpole Collection (Recipient)

Harry Ransom Humanities Research Center, University of Texas at Austin

LAMB HOUSE, RYE, SUSSEX.

Dearest Hugh.   [14 October 1909]

Just a fond word to speed you on your way tomorrow by the 4.25,[46] & as a hint of how wide I open my arms—to say nothing of how tight I shall thereafter close them. We are doing our best for you in advance—so that at a pinch there is almost nothing you need positively bring *with* you—save your "personality" pure & simple & your genius. The striped grey "suiting" if you insist, but I can always lend you "suitings." I hope the "shop" people or [*sic*] question haven't been making your life a burden—& of this I shall be keen to hear.——On Fridays, by the way (for the convenience of the efflux of golfers the thing appears to be done at such week-ends) the 4.25 usually doesn't—or didn't last year—make you change for this place at Ashford, the Rye carriages running straight through—after only a little *wait* at A. Make sure at any rate—for it saves the Ashford bother very

43. HJ's country house visits—to Edward and Gertrude Abbey in Fairford, Gloucestershire and to the Frederick Macmillans at Overstrand—are summarized in the *Complete Notebooks*, 308.

44. See note 37.

45. See the biographical register for Helen Lascelles.

46. Walpole's diary entry for Monday, 15 October 1909 reads: "I go down to Henry James to-day" (Walpole, H., Works—Diaries, 1908 [1909], HRC). HJ's own pocket diary records Walpole's arrival on 15 and his departure on 21 October (*Complete Notebooks*, 309).

advantageously. And leap promptly, at 6.30, (though not prematurely) at your waiting & watching old *friend*

H.J.

October 14*th 1909*.

ALS: Walpole Collection (Recipient)
Harry Ransom Humanities Research Center, University of Texas at Austin

Dearest Hugh. [23 October 1909][47]

I find your brave little letter as I come down to breakfast—lonely & unuplifted—this roaring & more or less ⟨pouring?⟩ (or poaring) morning (no, it's a lie: there's a wondrous sudden sun-burst!)—& of course its effect is to draw straight out of me with one irresistible little pull, the tenderest little response. Beautiful & admirable of you to have threshed through the tropic jungle of your 30 waiting letters to get at *this* elephant—who accordingly winds round you, in a stricture of gratitude & affection all *but* fatal, his well-meaning old trunk. I abominably miss you—having so extravagantly enjoyed you; but it's a great enrichment of consciousness, all the while, that we are in such beautiful, such exquisite relation; & to lead my life, each day, from one thing to another, is to find that I'm following fondly, but at a respectful distance, the imagination, the so gallantly darting & dashing & soaring & plunging *figure* of yours. The pluck & the cheer & the generosity & all the gifts of you are magnificent & I yearn over you with the sense of these things. I am decently at work & decently better, & your tribute to the dismal drama, (I shall never do the dismal again) is like the breath of morning in a floppy sail—under which, as it swells, I dream of the golden islands—with you there, along with me, for my man Friday.[48] *Such* a run, now, on *the* Friday here! The Elephant paws you oh so benevolently—which his name is your all devoted old

H.J.

Oct. 23, 09.

ALS: Walpole Collection (Recipient)
Harry Ransom Humanities Research Center, University of Texas at Austin

---

47. HJ writes two days after Walpole's 15–21 October visit to Lamb House. See Walpole's diary entry for Saturday, 23 October 1909: "Been down to H.J. for a week and of course my depression is completely gone. . . . Most blissful time with H.J. Every day with him is better than the last. The house and place are so beautiful. They all belong so absolutely to him" (Walpole, H., Works—Diaries, 1908 [1909], HRC).

48. HJ alludes to Daniel Defoe's *Robinson Crusoe* (1719).

Dearest Hugh.   [26 October 1909]
    I am so glad you are following that pleasant little clue. Mrs. Clifford[49]
lives at *7 Chilworth St., Paddington,* & the Praed St. Station is at 3 minutes'
walk from her door—up the st. that skirts the station (the departure side;)
the first st. out of that over to the left, & & the [*sic*] the 5th house or so on
the left *in* said street, which runs on to Westbourne Terrace. There you are!
Go on Sunday afternoon about 5—& I will write her a word to tell her I've
told you to. She will be very kind to you—for my sweet sake, & your own!
How you must be *living!*—I can almost *hear* you here, & feel the air
vibrate with your intense vital performance. But go on—I live a good deal
in you. So feel *me* there (in your vivid young guts!)—after the same
fashion. So, across the Chelsea jungle does the faithful old Elephant (with
the *empty* howdah on his back) make a long proboscis to nose ever so
gently the very idea & absent image of you—till he lifts you up into the
howdah again. He is a steady old beast—and *so* gentle!—which his name
is *your*

                              H.J.
                              Oct: 26: 1909.

ALS: Walpole Collection (Recipient)
Harry Ransom Humanities Research Center, University of Texas at Austin

Dearest Hugh.   November 10*th 1909.*
    The breath of your life, the glory of your youth, the charm of your spirit,
rise from your ingenuous page & send your old Elephant careering, under
their fine influences, though in wide & respectful circles, round & round
the Jungle. It does indeed all sound very glorious & great, & I'm delighted
you're enjoying it (with the becoming reserve you signify.) I want every
detail, however, & grate my teeth, not to say tusks, at having so to wait. Of
course you'll come down in January, if you can brave that rigour, & I
fortunately pass 4 or 5 days in town (after Ockham!)[50] till the Saturday of
that week. There we can briefly re-unite—I say briefly because I'm already
appalled at the number of things I find myself pledged to do at that

---

49. See the biographical register for Lucy Lane Clifford.

50. HJ went to Ockham on 27 November (with Jocelyn Persse) to examine with John
Buchan (1875–1940) Byron papers in Lady Lovelace's possession in order to render their
opinion on Byron's affair with his half-sister (*Complete Notebooks,* 310, 110n).

moment (you see the drawback of loving, if I may be allowed the expression, a Person with an Awful Past!) & we shall be able possibly to meet but once. A reason the more, however, for meeting bravely there. I am deeply disconcerted meanwhile at hearing you are not yet bidden to that sane seat & gathering, if gathering it is to be—but don't quite know what to do about it if Helen Lascelles, delicately prodded (very, very delicately though!) by your finest finger, can't work the oracle. It is quite most probable, I should *think,* that the oracle will still speak—but if she doesn't—not "Sir", but Lady—I shall be full of woe, for your presence there (I thought you had been *"secured"?*) had figured from the first, to me, as the basis & bribe of the whole thing, & I shall feel* the victim of false pretenses. A herd of mere children of darkness—I flinch at the prospect! However, you will miss nothing—with the rest of your Devil's Dance, & the next Novel will perhaps leap more headlong on its course if you're lolling a week-end the less on the social sofa. (Not that that will make a difference, I hear you indeed pityingly retort; you will loll but the more loosely & wildly, you give me to understand, in some other corner of the large lap of your fortune.) The way the very publishers dandle you on their bloated knee, each wishing to make the rosy Babe crow & kick for *him,* is a phenomenon indeed uncanny in its sort. (Don't attempt too precipitately to feed on the arid bosom of *Heinemann,*[51] let me interpose—with whom I've had an experience—a very long one—beggaring belief;[52] but don't either, please, quote me as the source of that warning.) With Max B[eerbohm].,[53] at the Savile, you are clearly on the road. But goodnight—the minster-bell has just struck two, & the owl, your elephant-owl, for all his feathers, is a-cold.[54] Have you got, àpropos of feathers, an *eider-down* in Glebe Place? & if not what is your Mother thinking of? *I* shall have to be

51. William Heinemann (1863–1920) was a British publisher and writer who commissioned translations of foreign authors for his international library.

52. HJ's letter of 24 January 1900 to Lucy Lane Clifford mentions "A lively row (temporarily calmed) with Heinemann—over Pinker!" (*"Bravest of Women and Finest of Friends: Henry James's Letters to Lucy Clifford,* ed. Marysa Demoor and Monty Chisholm, English Literary Studies Monograph Series 80 [Victoria: University of Victoria Press, 1999], 33). See note 106 on James Brand Pinker, HJ's literary agent.

53. See the biographical register for Max Beerbohm.

54. Cf. John Keats, "The Eve of St. Agnes" (1819), l. 2: *"The owl, for all his feathers, was a-cold."*

your mother. I will arrange with you for after the 29th. Ever, dearest Hugh, your devotissimo

H.J.

*I blush—ink-black—for my foul smudge.

ALS: Walpole Collection (Recipient)

Harry Ransom Humanities Research Center, University of Texas at Austin

LAMB HOUSE, RYE, SUSSEX.

My dear, dear Hugh.   [21 November 1909]

It has been impossible to me to reply till this late hour of this Sunday night to your touching little note—as tiny as touching—of a few days ago. Yes, dearest Hugh, I *did* go up to town for three intensely crowded & complicated days—& I even remained for a fourth, under the same pressure of complications. But it was impossible to me to arrange either in advance or on the spot to see you; for these brief snatches of London, after longish absences,—with heavy accumulations of things to be done & difficulties to be dealt with, in a very short & hurried time, make a very stiff problem to handle at the best. Remember that your poor old ponderous Elephant has his awful Past always on his back—his heavy heritage of old relations & involvements—& that in 3 or 4 days an Elephant can scarce turn round. I shall be at the Reform Club, however, for several days after the preposterous Ockham (preposterous without you, who mooted to me, weeks ago, the whole thing!)—and hope you can dine with me either on that Tuesday, that Wednesday or Thursday or Friday. There you are—let me hear which. I keep these all free till I do hear: I can't, dearest Hugh, say fairer. (*Tuesday* would, I just remember, not be very convenient; the others, on the other hand all right.[)] And I could even, at a pinch, do Saturday (4th Dec.). I hope you are in heart & hope; I greatly desire the sight & sound of you, & am always, dearest Hugh, your faithfully fondest old

H.J.

Nov. 21*st* 1909.

ALS: Walpole Collection (Recipient)

Harry Ransom Humanities Research Center, University of Texas at Austin

LAMB HOUSE, RYE, SUSSEX.

Dearest Hugh.   December 23*d 1909.*

It's no figure of speech, but a plain unvarnished truth, that even if your delightful letter hadn't just come in I should still at this moment be all affectionately & all faithfully writing to you. I have only waited till my poor missive could have something of the quality of coming in on the Day its very self; but now I daresay it will come in on the Eve. I too, dearest Hugh, have wanted, with the last particularity, to "give" you some small tangible token of my unspeakable sentiments—but have had to struggle with the troublesome fact that tokens don't grow, in any form worth speaking or thinking of, in the rude soil of our poor little tawdrified High Street,[55] & that other resources or expedients (of purchase & research) are just now perversely closed to me. So I am just crudely sticking a very modest little cheque for Five Pounds into this—as my only way of getting you to help me to help you—to some small convenient object (no matter what!) that you wouldn't have got perhaps otherwise. *So* let it be, then, with my tenderest benediction! Your gentle offering to *me* will be that of your personal presence when you come down here next month—than which no gift from you could be more delectable or valuable. The case with me about *that* happy prospect is as follows: that there comes down to me this afternoon a lone & stranded old friend who isn't of the last degree of the thrilling, but unfortunate & disconsolate, & who has in the 1st place proposed himself a day sooner than I asked him, & *may* linger a day or two later than the limit I proposed.[56] He will make rather a hole in my time at a crisis of some intensity & I shall have to *make up* after his departure the many hours that he will have mildly dissipated. My calculation is that I shall have made them up, about, by *Wednesday Jan. 12th*—on which day I fondly invoke your advent. (It isn't only a question of *him*—but of the huge cavity that a mountain of present & urgent correspondence shall have operated to punch a gaping hole in my dear diligence withal.) Let me count on you for the 12th;[57] I shall do so with an exceeding great desire. So much for your hopeful hypothesis of my "liking to have you with me." I am deeply moved by your word to the effect that you will "love me till you die"; it gives me so beautiful a guarantee of a certain measurable resistance

---

55. High Street passed through Rye below Lamb House.

56. The old friend was T. Bailey Saunders (1860–1928), the British journalist and translator (see *Complete Notebooks*, 311).

57. The 12 January invitation was soon withdrawn because of HJ's worsening depression, early signs of which had appeared in 1909. For an account of HJ's debility in the first half of 1910, and his gradual recovery through the second half of the year, see Edel's *Henry James, 1901–1916: The Master*, 434–45.

to pure earthly extinction. Yes, I want that to happen, & the thought penetrates me: that your affection will hold out to the end—the far, far end. But this is all your mere beginning—& I pray your parental Christmastide may glow and overflow, abound & resound. But we shall have matter for a great jaw, which will richly accumulate, & I am yours, dearest Hugh, ever so faithfully

Henry James

P.S. Oh I can imagine that Ockham with the ghosts, mainly, of what might have been was a bit stodgy. But if you had been there "my" Sunday we should have been kept furiously apart by the task urgently laid upon me & which took all day.

ALS: Walpole Collection (Recipient)

Harry Ransom Humanities Research Center, University of Texas at Austin

LAMB HOUSE, RYE, SUSSEX.

Dearest Hugh.   [28 December 1909]

This is just a little word—on receipt of your own so charming ones—to say: *Don't*, please, proceed to the acquisition of a writingtable on that so poor and inadequate Five-Pound basis; but *keep* the sum in question, (if you *can*,) for a portion of that purchasing power, till that I greatly hope not distant moment when I shall be able to help you further about it. The year's end & beginning overwhelm & deplete me financially—& rather formidably so this year; but there are probabilities of such early relief as will enable me to supplement the scant fund above-named—in a sufficient degree to bring about, at any rate, some fairly decent form of the result we desire. Therefore, I repeat, hang on a little, & we will discuss it fondly & further. It has been a devil of a year—but there is hope. Sit tight, singly—I accordingly reiterate—till we can do so collectively. I long with intensity for your advent on the 12th; when we will treat of far other things, however, than even *such* amusing little importances. I have had a very minor-key Xmas, but should have hated a blatant and bouncing one. *You* will have bounced a good deal, I gather; but I hope you won't have had occasion to "blate"—or at least, lamb-like in the parental pasture, to bleat. I wish I might have gone with you to the "Standard" Pantomime—at which rate what treasures you will have to tell your faithfullest old

H.J.

Dec: 28th 1909.

ALS: Walpole Collection (Recipient)

Harry Ransom Humanities Research Center, University of Texas at Austin

Most dear, dear Hugh.   *L[amb] H[ouse] Feb. 6th 1910*

I thank you as gratefully for your tender little letter of just now as I do for all your discreet & blessed staying of your hand from appeals for news for so many considerate days. For really, I have been having a most beastly little time & couldn't then have done anything decent in the way of response. Now I *can,* distinctly more—for within a couple of days I have taken a *much* better turn, rather a sudden one, & feel that I shall probably go straight. (I kept falling back, before, after illusive—illusory?—flickers-up.) I am doing today a *long* sitting up—since 11 a.m.; it's now 8.30 & I'm not yet in bed. I *eat* at last, in a manner, & that means recovery—for the obstinately sick inability to do so was all that was the matter with me. Bear with me a little longer—& I will make you some sign for a short visitation. I can't *plan* yet—& my Nurse is still to be in possession, it seems, for this coming week. We'll make everything up, dearest boy—we'll rejoice to-gether again yet. I'm glad you see Lucy Clifford—best of women. I wrote her quite copiously yesterday. How much you'll have to tell me, & how I yearn over you & stick to you through all my limpness! Believe in our better days & how your beautiful & generous note has touched—has deeply moved—your faithfullest fondest old

H.J.

ALS: Walpole Collection (Recipient)
Harry Ransom Humanities Research Center, University of Texas at Austin

LAMB HOUSE, RYE, SUSSEX.

Dearest, Dearest Hugh.   May 13*th 1910*

I have been utterly, but necessarily silent—so much of the time lately quite too ill to write. Deeply your note touches me, as I needn't tell you— & I would give anything to be able to have the free use of your "visible" & tangible affection—no touch of its tangibility but would be dear & helpful to me. But, alas, I am utterly unfit for visits—with the black devils of Nervousness, direct, damnedest demons, that ride me so cruelly & that I have perpetually to reckon with. I am mustering a colossal courage to try— even to-morrow—in my blest sister-in-law's company (without whom & my brother, just now in Paris, I couldn't have struggled on at all) to get away for some days by going to see a kind friend in the country—in Epping Forest.[58] I feel it a most precarious & dangerous undertaking—

---

58. HJ went with his sister-in-law Alice to Hill Hall, the Essex estate of Charles and Mary Smyth Hunter.

but my desire & need for change of air, scene & circumstances after so fearfully overmuch of these imprisoning objects, is so fiercely intense that I am making the push—as to save my life—at any cost. It *may* help me—ever much, & the doctor intensely urges it—& if I am able, afterwards (that is if the experiment isn't disastrous,) I shall *try* to go to 105 Pall Mall[59] for a little instead of coming abjectly back here. Then I shall be able to see you—but all this is fearfully contingent. Meanwhile the sense of your personal tenderness to me, dearest Hugh, is far from not doing much for me. I adore it.——I "read", in a manner Maradick[60]—but there's too much to say about it, & even my weakness doesn't alter me from the grim & battered old *critical* critic—no *other* such creature among all the "reviewers" do I meanwhile behold.[61] Your book has a great sense & love of life—but seems to me very nearly as irreflectively juvenile as the Trojans,[62] & to have the prime defect of your having gone into a subject—i.e. the marital, sexual, bedroom relations of M. & his wife & the literary man & his wife—since these *are* the key to the whole situation—which have to be tackled & faced to mean anything. You don't tackle & face them—you *can't*. Also the whole thing is a monument to the abuse of voluminous dialogue, the absence of a plan of composition, alternation, distribution[,] structure, & other phases of presentation than the dialogue—so that *line* (the only thing *I* value in a fiction &c,) is replaced by a vast formless featherbediness—billows on which one sinks & is lost. And yet it's all so loveable—though not so *written*. It isn't written *at all,* darling Hugh—by which I mean you have—or, truly, only in a few places, as in Maradick's *dive*—never got expressions *tight* & in close quarters (of discrimination, of specification) with its subject. It remains loose & far. And you have never made out, recognised, nor stuck to, the *centre of your subject.* But can you forgive all this to your fondest old reaching-out-his-arms-to you

H.J.?

ALS: Walpole Collection (Recipient)

Harry Ransom Humanities Research Center, University of Texas at Austin

---

59. HJ gives the address of the "lodging department" of the Reform Club where beginning in December 1900 he maintained a bed-sitting room for use during London visits.

60. Walpole's novel *Maradick at Forty* was published in April 1910.

61. HJ would have seen the unfavorable review of *Maradick* in the 28 April 1910 *Times Literary Supplement.*

62. A reference to Walpole's first novel, *The Wooden Horse* (1909).

Dearest, dearest Hugh! July 20*th 1910*.

Yes, it has all been hideous & horrible, our long separation—but it has been tragically inevitable; & if your letter hadn't just come I shld. still have been writing to you at this moment, for I infinitely yearn to see you. Things are very complicated with me, for not only am I still the victim of a deplorable nervous condition which demands a battle of every hour— every minute, but I am exceedingly anxious & tormented over my brother's precarious state (of renewed heart-trouble,)[63] & many material & personal questions. We sail for America on Aug. 12th, but go down to Rye either tomorrow p.m. or Saturday. Can't you come & see me *here* tomorrow (Thursday) *a.m.* at 11.30—coming straight up to my room, for which I will leave orders, where we can talk in freedom?[64] I can't make any plan or arrangement, ahead, more complex or hospitable than this—I am too much at the mercy of many things. I know your mornings are precious, but this [is] a rare & high case, & I have taken for so long so little of your time. And oh for a close talk with you! It's the deeply affectionate desire of your poor old much-troubled

Henry James

P.S. My brother & sister's being with me at Rye demands all my room.

ALS: Walpole Collection (Recipient)

Harry Ransom Humanities Research Center, University of Texas at Austin

[95 Irving Street, Cambridge, Mass.]

My dearest, dearest Hugh. [27 October 1910]

How shall I tell you the woeful long story of my hateful & hideous silence since your beautiful & best letter (from Arthur Benson's) came to me, & then, just after, your so gentle & tender & faithful note on hearing of my beloved Brother's deplorable death? The difficulty of such situations & embarrassments is that one *can't* remount the stream of time or recover the lost threads of the dire tangle. I shall therefore attempt no story, but only tell you again, as I have told you before, that I have again had a succession of miserable & scarce bearable weeks, & that writing to you

---

63. William James suffered from increasingly severe heart disease from 1899 until his death on 26 August 1910.

64. Walpole did indeed visit HJ at his Reform Club room the following day: "a long morning with Henry James. H. better and more cheerful. Talked of 'Helen—not quite of Troy'—which message I shall not give her. As affectionate and delightful as ever" (Walpole, H., Works—Diaries, 21 July 1910, HRC).

miserably has been an odious thought to me—so odious that I have waited for better light & a less stricken state to come. At *first,* after my brother's death, I thought it *had* come—I bore up, under the stress of absolute necessity & a measure of responsibility & a sort of dismal tension & excitement, better than I could have believed. But there came a wretched time again—with a deluge of letters from far & wide (at the prospect & need of answering which I could only howl in desperation;[)] thereafter came more black weeks & more (even like a complete relapse & reaction into my condition of last spring;) during which I stayed my infinitely worried & worthless hand from forming for you characters of woe. *And,* my beloved Hugh, I did well, for I have gained by waiting, & it looks as if, during the last fortnight, a really & truly better day & a positively firmer faith & strength, had at last descended upon me. I can believe in it, for certain reasons, more stoutly this time than I have ever been able to in any hitherto mocking & treacherous gleam during the past horrible year; so now I lay my oh so tenderly fraternal, so pacified & pacifying hand on you, & draw you all beseechingly back to me from the distance to which you may so well have strayed. (I say this with a clumsy awkwardness, as if I didn't know that, the most angelic & magnanimous of all earthly, or even heavenly, Hughs, you are incapable of straying an inch. I *really* have my poor old arm over your gallant young shoulder all the time—& you really feel me there, dearly affectionate, as I feel *you,* divinely ditto; which gives us a power to stick out together almost anything of the mere basely accidental & superficial interfering kind.) I lately came back from their summer refuge in the New Hampshire mountains with my admirable sister-in-law & my so delightful & interesting nephews & niece—back to this their winter home, just 3 miles from Boston, & practically all continuous with the same, as you may vaguely know; where Harvard University, the scene of my wonderful brother's long & illustrious activity, bristles & "composes" rather effectively, though not by a long shot as it would in "Europe", as our immediate background.[65] We cleave closely together now, these my only remaining near relatives in the world & I, & I shall keep on here for some months not to be far from them & then, when I return to England, shall hope not to have ever to recross the sea again, as they will be much more in a position (as they have been in the past) to come out to see me in England than I shall be freshly to take up my pilgrim's staff. Have patience

---

65. The Cambridge home of William and Alice James at 95 Irving Street adjoined the Harvard campus.

with me therefore, and, returning as I absolutely hope to do late in the spring,[66] we shall meet with the fondest concussion imaginable & be able to talk with a high & noble lucidity. Not that it will be meanwhile, however, that my thoughts won't hang ever so insistently, so clingingly, so embracingly, about you. Write me again—with a forgiving generosity,—give me something to take hold of & love you the more for—if that be fantastically possible. I won't badger you with questions, but I thirst for dear, for intimate, for attaching, for glorifying & uplifting facts about you. Of course you are sinking with genial work & of course you are swimming in social whirlpools. Swim, swim, but don't sink, for though I would take *any* header to save you I am far off & occupied at present with my own salvation; to which, yes, I believe I am each day more & more on the way. You *must* be seeing dear Lucy Clifford, for I fondly & fatuously believe that you each occasionally feel that you must talk of me to the other. I have been as damnably dumb to *her,* blest woman, as to you, blest youth, but now that the dark spell is broken, yes really broken, as I insist on believing, a letter to her will follow on the heels of this. I like to think of you, the handful of the few I can still number betwixt Chelsea & Paddington or wherever, gathering in again to the autumn afternoon fires & the renewals of the friendly teapot. I send a very cordial remembrance to Lady Lovelace, & make a more familiar sign to Helen not quite, no, but all *but,* of Troy.[67] I rejoice (Helen *quite* would forgive the juxtaposition) in your rich image of our least "sensuous" friend morally (even letting physically aside) profiting by finding himself in the closest possible quarters with a large, loose, genial lady! But goodbye, belovedest Hugh. I have directed my small red book of the other day[68] to be a bit belatedly sent you (& Lucy C.) from your all faithfully affectionate

Henry James
95 Irving St. Cambridge Mass.
Oct. 27*th* 1910

ALS: Walpole Collection (Recipient)
Harry Ransom Humanities Research Center, University of Texas at Austin

---

66. The 14 June departure date was later changed to 2 August (see letter of [May 1911]), although HJ eventually sailed aboard the *Mauretania* on 30 June.

67. See the biographical register for Helen Lascelles.

68. The "small red book of the other day" was the first English edition of *The Finer Grain,* published in "rust-brown" covers by Methuen on 13 October 1910. See Leon Edel, Dan Laurence, and James Rambeau, *A Bibliography of Henry James,* 3d ed. (Oxford: Clarendon, 1982), 144–46.

Belovedest little Hugh! [15 April 1911]

Your dearest little convalescent letter—the Lord be praised—bring[s] tears to my aged eyes. It is moreover no fond figure of speech, but the very stiffest stretch of veracity, that even if it hadn't come I should have absolutely been writing to you—as of late intensely & yearningly intended & again & again foully frustrated—either today or tomorrow. What a hell of a black, or rather fiery red, little time you must have been having, & what a dismal hour for my irrepressible Hugh when he found himself gloomily conveyed by cowled ministrants from Glebe Place, or wherever ("as I say",) to grey & sinister suburbs.[70] I take heart, however, from your evidence of the way it has clearly answered—I hug the sweet thought that if you have in the course of a fortnight got more or less out of the wood the great jolly highway along which the sight of your leaps & bounds has hitherto endeared you to so many hearts (for who the devil is the Dedication-wretch of "Mr. Perrin",[71] who has—the brute!—"more understanding & sympathy than *any one you have ever* met?") will already have opened to your view. I'll forgive you all—by which I mean all of that most insidious & most invidious of digs—straight into my soft & aching substance—if you'll now only go softly & smoothly. Feel me, dearest boy, seated, discreetly, even on your hospital cot (my finger in Mr. Perrin—but stuck fast, so pointingly, at the so objectionable preliminary page;) feel me hang over you, & hover about you, feel me lay my faithful hand on you with the tenderest, let us say frankly divinest, healing & soothing influence. By the time this reaches you your attendant dragons & gorgons, all the cowled ministrants, will doubtless have opened your door a little to profaner presences, & I feel that were I by that date in London nothing would prevent my getting at you. Let me then get at you a little this way—I mean

---

69. HJ is writing from the New York home of Mary Cadwalader Jones (see biographical register).

70. Walpole had contracted scarlet fever. Beginning with the 17 March 1911 entry, his diary reads simply "SF" for every day until April 15. Walpole finally left the North London hospital on 7 May 1911.

71. Walpole's third novel, *Mr. Perrin and Mr. Traill* (1911), was dedicated "To Punch—because you have more understanding and sympathy than anyone I have ever met." Punch was Percy Anderson (b. 1851), an artist and stage designer whose 1895 work on *Guy Domville* HJ had commended. Walpole's diary indicates that he first met Anderson in February 1909, when Anderson was fifty-nine. The men became intimate companions, with Anderson moving into Walpole's Cornwall cottage, The Cobbles, in March 1913.

all *but* as intimately as if I were bringing you jelly or grapes or the Strand Magazine or even Arnold Bennett's last up to that hour.[72] Make me another sign, I beseech you, as soon as they begin to let you loose. I hope your mother has been to see you—even if she has had to come up from Edinburgh for the fond purpose. But that may be none of my business, & I write you, you see, in almost thick darkness, relieved only by the blest shimmer of your own fair—or at least fairly quite normal—hand. I have of course your previous little letter—written from the H[ouse]. of L[ord].'s & telling me you were leaving Chelsea & making other inscrutable arrangements.[73] That communication & the precious Mr. Perrin I have had it much at heart to acknowledge—while in a personal state still, however, that represents a sad & constant leak in my powers of execution—as distinguished from my inward yearnings & dreams. I am immensely better from the condition in which I left England, but the ground I have gained only seems to tell me more & more from how very, very far away I have had, & shall still have, slowly to struggle back; witness the frequent breaks & arrests & interruptions, direfully sickening & depressing, into which I am still liable to sink up to my neck. I don't know where I find courage, but I do more or less continue to find it—& I bore you with these dark references only that you shall be easy with your poor shipwrecked & but just barely saved old friend, dearest Hugh; be easy always & ever. I rejoice with you heartily over your rich disposal of Mr. Perrin, as I understand you, in these strange parts. Strange they are ineffably, & huge & incommensurable & indescribable the monstrous Public & its mighty maw. There is nothing in England like this latter—& the fodder of the gigantic beast is mixed & tossed & pitchforked on a scale that takes millions of miles square for the process. If you enter—as Mr. Perrin—into the mixture, may you indeed have brave news of it all! I congratulate you ever so gladly on Mr. Perrin—I think the book represents a very marked advance on its predecessors. I am an atrocious reader, as you know—with a mania for appreciation, or in other words for criticism, since the latter is the one sole gate to the former. To appreciate is to appropriate, & it is only by

---

72. A reference perhaps to *Hilda Lessways* (1911), by the English novelist Arnold Bennett (1867–1931), a novel that HJ later disparaged as "the slow wringing out of a dirty sponge" (Walpole, H., Works—Diaries, 1912–1915, HRC; see the entry for 1 March 1912). More generally, HJ's remark is perhaps a glancing reference to the productivity of a writer who, besides criticism and plays, published thirty novels between 1898 and 1931.

73. In May 1911 Walpole gave up his Chelsea flat for rooms at 16 Hallam Street, in the more fashionable West End of London.

criticism that I can make a thing in which I find myself interested at all *my own*. But nobody that I have encountered for a long time seems to have any use for any such process—or, much rather, does almost every one (& exactly the more they "read") resent the application of it. All of which is more or less irrelevant, however, for my telling you that I really & very charmedly made your book very *much* my own. It has life & beauty & reality & is more closely *done* than the others, with its immense advantage, clearly, of resting on the known & felt thing; in other words on depths, as it were, of experience. If I weren't afraid of seeming to you to avail myself foully of your supine state to batter & bruise you at my ease (as that appears to have been for you, alas, the main result of my previous perusal of your works) I should venture, just on tiptoe & holding my breath, to say that—well, I should *like* to make, seated by your pallet and with your wrist in my good grasp & my faithful finger—or thumb—on your young pulse, one or two affectionately discriminative little remarks. One of these is to the effect that, still, I don't quite recognise here the *centre of your subject,* that absolutely & indispensably fixed & constituted point from which one's ground must be surveyed & one's material wrought. If you say it's (that centre) in Mr. P.'s exasperated consciousness I can only reply that if it *might* be, it yet isn't treated as such. And, further, that I don't quite understand why, positing the situation as also a part of the experience of Mr. Traill, you yet take such pains to demonstrate that Mr. Traill was, as a vessel of experience, absolutely *nil*—recognising, feeling, knowing, understanding, appreciating, that is, absolutely nothing that happened to him. Experience—reported—is interesting, is *recorded* to us, according to some vessel (the capacity & quality of such,) that contains it, & I don't make out Mr. Traill's capacity at all. And I note this—*shall* you feel, hideously?— because the subject, your subject, *with* an operative, a felt centre, would have still more harmoniously & effectively expressed itself. Admirable, clearly, the subjects that you had before you & which when all is said, dearest, dearest Hugh, has moved you to write a book that will give a great push to your situation. So (as that recognition is so great a point,) don't feel that your infatuated old friend discriminates only to destroy—destroy, that is, the attachment to him that it is his very fondest dream all perpetually & intensely to feel in you!————————I have been spending some weeks in New York—which is a very extraordinary & terrific & yet amiable place, as to which my sentiment is a compound of an hourly impression of its violent impossibility & of a sneaking kindness for its pride & power (it's so clearly destined to be the great agglomeration of the world!) born of early associations & familiarities—of the ancient natal order. I return to Boston & its neighbourhood (very different affairs,) presently, & my plan still holds for sailing for England on June 14th—whereby, I ought, if all goes well, to reach "town" by the 20th. I send you herewith a small photograph of a life-sized head of me lately done by my very able & promising painter-nephew.[74] The thing is pronounced a miracle of re-semblance, & is excellently painted, but has suffered much from the reduction to smallness. Try to fancy, at any rate that my grave but kind eyes are fixed on *you,* dearest Hugh, & believe me your faithfully fond old

Henry James
New York
April 15*th* 1911.[75]

ALS: Walpole Collection (Recipient)
Harry Ransom Humanities Research Center, University of Texas at Austin

95 IRVING STREET CAMBRIDGE MASSACHUSETTS

Belovedest little Hugh.   [May 1911][76]

I am rather distressed to see by your letter (very tender & touching to me,) that you were still in Hospital——April 26*th;* however, as you don't tell me of any set-back I take it you have simply followed the normal course of recovery & that your confinement is the inevitable one. Only I do pray the powers that you be by this time blessedly at large—& with every kind of personal & intimate largeness & re-expansion attending you. You will indeed shrink a little when I tell you that I have just had to shift my sailing back to England from June 14th to six weeks later——August 2d. This has become overwhelmingly necessary—for urgent & intimate family & per-sonal reasons;[77] but alas it means that we must *wait*—even while we most distractedly yearn. It is wretched, it is well nigh intolerable to us, yes, to wait;

---

74. For a summary of the artistic career of Alexander James (1890–1946), son of William and Alice James, see R. W. B. Lewis, *The Jameses: A Family Narrative* (New York: Farrar, Straus and Giroux, 1991), 625–30.

75. James does not mention that the letter is written on his sixty-eighth birthday.

76. This undated letter follows that of 15 April 1911, in which HJ makes a "qualificatory glance" at *Mr. Perrin and Mr. Traill.* In his letter of 12 May 1911 to Dr. J. William White, HJ announces in similar language that he will postpone his return to England until August 2 (see *Letters of Henry James,* 2:185).

77. The "urgent & intimate family" reasons, cited in several May 1911 letters, are unclear, but the "personal" reasons are more certain: HJ was still seeing doctors in New York and in Boston following a late April relapse (see *Letters of Henry James,* 2:188; Kaplan, *Henry James,* 535).

but the case *might* be worse, & I beg you to hug, as I do, the assurance that when I do return it will be not again, for the rest of my days, D[eo]. V[olente]. [Lt.: God permitting], to perpetrate a similar absence. And meanwhile the weeks will ebb—I find that in spite of everything, & above all, in spite of my dire impatience, they simply melt away here now. Your release from confinement, will be affectionately acclaimed on every side; your path will be strewn with roses & your brow crowned with laurel— you'll be so deliciously dealt with, in short, that the few extra weeks of my delay will pass without your having had time to miss me. Won't the very most intelligent & sympathetic of your Dedicatees (Mr. P.,) moreover, have rejoined you by that time?—in whose company many of your requirements will be amply met. (Forgive this harmless & imbecile pleasantry—a weak & innocent experiment in tantalization; your mention of Mr. P.'s great spiritual services to you on some occasion of trouble filling *me* even with the liveliest grateful appreciation, for your sake, of Mr. P.) Well, dearest Hugh, this is all for the moment; save that I do beg you to make me some sign of your liberation & your finding your feet—(—feet—not fat!) what do I say? your renewing your mighty youth—again. I am touched by your sweet patience under my qualificatory glance at the slightly constitutional infirmity of "Mr. Perrin". I didn't in the least mean that fools & duffers shan't figure, or be of interest, in fiction; I only meant that *their experience* can only in a very minor degree. They may be rare & rich as the experience of others of the sentient & the perceiving—like Shakespeare's[,] Thackeray's & even Miss Austen's. So, ⟨it?⟩ no experience of T.'s—only T. of P.'s (comparatively.) I don't think your *girl* was really an experience of anybody's. You must work that sort of thing—kind of relation—closer. But we will talk of these things & I will convince you afresh of the tender affection & fond fidelity of yours, dearest Hugh, always, always &c

Henry James

HILL THEYDON MOUNT EPPING.[78]
TELEPHONE: 21 EPPING.

Dearest, dearest Hugh.   Aug: 22*d 1911.*

I have been back a whole fortnight, & the trying conditions I have encountered (after 3 months of dreadfully oppressive & blighting climatic

---

78. HJ writes again from Hill Hall, the Essex estate of Charles and Mary Smyth Hunter.

& atmospheric ones in America) have made the time seem even longer—I allude of course to the awful heat & the scorched blackened land, convulsed with such dire political & economic strife. One had got really to the end of one's tether "on the other side"—& to find even aggravation here has given badly on my poor old nerves. But to hear from you, even from afar, is a joy & a charm, & to know we shall soon meet is really, beloved boy, something to hold on to, & by. We must have that sacred half-hour "all to ourselves" as soon after you touch English soil as possible[79]—since it's to be so long before you are in town for more than that moment; only I can't quite yet be sure—by reason of impending complications—where I shall be the very 1st days of next month, & the hitherto so torrid & dusty London won't very *naturally* just then hold me. I will make every effort that our meeting shall be possible, but we *may* have to wait till you can really come down to Rye—in which case we shall immensely make up for our long separation. This meanwhile is the merest sketchiest stopgap—a fond, free, too futile gesture of affection. What adventures, what experiences, what initiations & acquisitions you must be having & making. You'll see how I shall see—or at least how I shall want to—into the rich picture. I came down here 3 days ago—bolted away from the hot glare of the South Coast to these hospitable shades—& I may stay on some days. But signal me always at Rye & believe me all & always your

H. J.

ALS: Walpole Collection (Recipient)
Harry Ransom Humanities Research Center, University of Texas at Austin

THE REFORM CLUB

Darling, darling little Hugh!   October 13*th* *1911*.

First, the enclosed has come to my care from one of your admirers & I pass it on.

Second, I have just been reading the Standard[80] at breakfast, & I am touched, I am *melted* by the charming gallantry & magnanimity of it—my

---

79. Walpole spent August 1911 travelling with Percy Anderson to Berlin, Stockholm, Munich, and Bayreuth. He returned at the end of the month and saw HJ on 6 September: "Exceedingly wonderful day. In the morning to Henry James at the Reform. Was there all the morning and he was quite splendid—his old self well again and able to work" (Walpole, H., Works—Diaries, 6 September 1911, HRC).

80. The 13 October *Standard* published Walpole's laudatory review of James's *The Outcry* (1913).

notices of *your* compositions having been so comparatively tepid. Tit *not* for Tat! Well, D.D.L.H., (it looks like "d—d" little H.", but isn't meant for that,) you do the thing handsomely when you do do it—& I seem to myself to swim in a blaze of glory—I shall wear my thrifty old hat when I next go out like a wreath of the bay imitated in fine gold. Had I known you meant to crown me I shld[.] have liked to say a thing or two for your guidance—however incorrect such a proceeding would have been as from author to reviewer. It wouldn't have been—between *us*—however from A. to R., but from Friend (putting it mildly) to Friend & Maître to Elève. Never mind,—you will sell the edition for me—& no edition of mine has ever sold yet! But I shall thank you better more face to face, more cheek by jowl—which will perhaps be on the occasion of our Gotterdämmerung [Ger.: "twilight of the gods"; a collapse of a regime or society marked by catastrophic violence and disorder.]—which (I am zealously watching it,) isn't announced yet. *Now* you can tell Mrs. Y[ates]. T[hompson].[81] that I adore her—& you can also add if you like that I adore *you*—which won't, I hope, diminish the value for her. Yours, my damndest little Hugh, in that posture,

Henry James

ALS: Walpole Collection (Recipient)
Harry Ransom Humanities Research Center, The University of Texas at Austin

105, PALL MALL, S.W.[82]

Dearest Hugh.   April 18*th* *1912.*

I kind of sniff it in the air that you draw near me again—you diffuse such a scent of the balmy South,[83] & eke of its rankest localities—& I send this small word to meet & greet you. Let me hear that your return is, or is about to be, a fact, & I will reach out to you & get hold of you. I very faithfully & affectionately welcome you—the old grizzled & blear-eyed house dog looks up, that is, & grunts & wags his tail at the damaged but still detectable Prodigal Son. Dim of vision though he be, he has mastered the Prelude[84]—he began it a day or two after you left & then couldn't, of

---

81. Elizabeth (Mrs. Henry Yates) Thompson was the daughter of the publisher George Murray Smith and wife of the former owner of the *Pall Mall Gazette.*

82. See note 59.

83. Hart-Davis notes, "At the beginning of April Hugh spent a fortnight with Percy Anderson in the South of France" (*Hugh Walpole*, 89).

84. HJ refers to Walpole's fourth novel, *The Prelude to Adventure* (1912).

course put it down, & wants you to know that he found lots of good—that is of charm—in it. It is as much of an advance on Mr. Perrin, I think, as Mr. Perrin was on *his* predecessor, & is exceedingly interesting, genial & promising besides being so very performing. I should have more to say of it (I mean many things,) were we really to go into the matter—in fact I shall if you will let me. I only want to let you have it from me now that I feel you to have written a very attaching & engaging, a very coercing & rewarding thing, which will infallibly get itself greatly read, & that this gives no end of joy to yours, dearest Hugh, all devotedly

H.J.

LAMB HOUSE, RYE, SUSSEX.

Darlingest Hugh.   [27 September 1912]

A deep little joy to me your so tender & true little letter. I give you of that joy again on your being with your gentle mother, to whom I send my best regards & respects, congratulating her on having gathered in such a companion! You had luck in crossing without death the bristling Lucas lines—& must have wondered from that vantage & amid that scramble at the small expense to which your friend appeared to have gone to entertain you here, & at the monstrous monotony of his life. That indeed is my little joke; for I know, dearest boy, that we never yet have had better hours together than those 2 deep evenings in particular made us. You are verily right—we were nearer together (we *are* so) than ever before; we were beautifully, exquisitely, nobly so. And even that is nothing (comparatively;) for we shall be more so still, infallibly; than which, again, nothing will have been, or can possibly be, more interesting & admirable—more sublime! Let us have all the beauty & the truth & the greatness of it. And meanwhile may your Cornwall be kind to you! You make me long for a sight of the glory, or whatever it is, that surrounds you. Poor dear old Walt![85]—what would *he* make of The Sacred Fount![86] Yet that strange author makes

---

85. "Walt" has not been identified.

86. The central theme of HJ's *The Sacred Fount* (1901)—an "exchange" or "conversion" of vitality between dissimilarly aged partners, whether in a marriage or in a secret liaison— is relevant in light of HJ's obsession with Walpole's vitality. See the 1894 and 1899 entries in the *Complete Notebooks*, 88, 176.

much of *him*. And makes everything of you, dearest Hugh, & is ever so tenderly & constantly yours

Henry James

Sept: 27*th* 1912.

ALS: Walpole Collection (Recipient)

Harry Ransom Humanities Research Center, University of Texas at Austin

Dictated[87]

Garlant's Hotel Suffolk Street Pall Mall S.W.

My dear Hugh.   25th. December, 1912.

Let the mere sight of these rude characters (yet so much more polished than my own) give you a hint, to begin with, of my still sorry physical state. I can't sit down to penmanship for more than a minute or two at a time without aggravation of what remains to me of the "beastly disease" you only too mildly qualify; but I shall none the less add with my own hand a few more emphatic words to this. On the present muggy, dusky Christmas morning here I am, as happens, rather peculiarly unfit; yet I want without an hour's delay to express to you a little of the interest, and all the other sentiments, your so disconcerting, so touching, yet all so courageous and admirable letter has caused to work in me; making me above all wish to see you and rejoice that I can tell you that you will to all appearance find me here (by which I mean at 21 Carlyle Mansions, Cheyne Walk, S.W.)[88] as soon as you again, with all the force of your genius and your pluck, launch yourself upon London. *How* you will find me (apart from the question of motor-busses and things) is another matter; for my beastly disease, thanks to another internal complication grafted upon it to its unspeakable aggravation, has dragged itself out in a manner of which I considerately withhold from you at present the dire[89] particulars. I came up to town, under the violent prodding of my (local) Doctor some ten days ago—he but too desirous to get rid of me and promising miracles from "change"; also to see a London specialist of authority,[90] and to have, not least, the benefit of this very aid to composition (which had ceased for me at Lamb

---

87. HJ dictated the letter to his typist, Theodora Bosanquet.

88. In the late fall of 1912 HJ leased a Chelsea apartment—21 Carlyle Mansions, Cheyne Walk—and moved there in January 1913. Thereafter he returned to Lamb House only during the summers.

89. "Dire" is added in James's hand.

90. Suffering from shingles since early September 1912, HJ came up to London in the second week of December 1912 to consult the neurologist Henry Head.

House,) in my inability to help myself. I have been too unwell to occupy my little perch in Pall Mall,[91] a very poor place in illness; and so am huddling at this little hotel, where you came to see me in April 1910, till I can get into my small flat, as I hope to do during the first week in January. Meanwhile I am a very lame duck, though absolutely determined again to spread my wings in spite of everything: ducks' wings being now all that I shall aspire to. So much, for the moment, and at this great disadvantage of communication, about my poor old self. We shall have everything out better the first hour I can offer you some sort of mild hospitality; materially mild, I mean—but affectionately *wild*,[92] let me not omit to add. Then shall I tell you more properly how deeply I participate in the horrid inconvenience you must be temporarily suffering at the hands of the foredoomed Standard:[93] foredoomed, I mean, to descend to depths to which, even should they have tried to drag you, you couldn't have consented to sink with it. But don't take it, the beastly little fortune of war, harder, a mite, than you can help: *it's one of those things that happens,* simply—I mean in the common work-a-day way, at your stage of young efflorescence; and the efflorescence itself, by another stroke of fortune and before you can turn round, will smother the base incident in flowers. By which I mean that you have too many intrinsic advantages, and are too ready and present and appreciated, are in fine too unmistakeable a young actuality, for the whirligig of time not to pounce on you and pick you up and toss you quite aloft again. Your intricate resources, in short, are precious, and from the quarter in which they will presently be desired for annexation, some happy proposition will issue. This is but to say, however, I repeat, that we will thresh these things well and bravely out. It's a pang to me to hear that you've been blighted with influenza, for your moment, into the bargain; but that will have been but a matter of the harsh breath of Edinburgh,[94] and I feel how London awaits you with more liberal and embracing arms. This is all this way—and Xmas morning here has dumped on me a load of appeals. Yesterday p.m. brought your letter on from Rye.

---

91. See note 59.

92. "Wild" is underlined in ink by HJ.

93. Walpole records in his diary for December 1912 that he "all in a second got the chuck from the Standard. Four years' work and not a word of thanks" (qtd. in Hart-Davis, *Hugh Walpole*, 95).

94. Walpole spent Christmas 1912 with his parents in Edinburgh.

[*The remainder of the letter is in James's hand.*] Let the above, dearest, dearest Hugh, serve as a poor expressional stopgap till we do meet. Only addressing you by that impersonal mechanism is scarce better than making love to you through the telephone would be. I enter with the tenderest affection into everything that concerns you—& quite hellishly incommoded as I continue myself to be (for making any demonstration yet awhile quite *active,*) I forecast, with this same passion, all your revenges, your *revanches* [Fr.: revenges, returns], & hunger & thirst to contribute any ounce of my own weight to them. The bravery of it all shall be inspiring & crowning, & I am always & ever your all-fond old

Henry James

TL/ALS: Walpole Collection (Recipient)

Harry Ransom Humanities Research Center, University of Texas at Austin

Dictated.

21 CARLYLE MANSIONS CHEYNE WALK, S.W.

My dear Hugh.   January 30th., 1913.

I respond with all my heart: but the luncheon-hour, from the moment we make it 2 o'clock, which gives both of us a margin, is the time that will suit me best. My evenings are still too apt to come to an end in pain and bed much too early for any other use of them; and in the afternoon I must absolutely get out for air and for such circulation as I can manage, in order to sleep at night and in other ways to work off troubles for which some modicum of "exercise" and ventilation are directly remedial, or at any rate mitigating. Come therefore on *Tuesday* p.m. of next week, 4th, at *two,* and partake of some simple food. We will go into things more then. By which I mean that I have received a massive Volume,[95] and am taking it (as, more or less impenetrable and utterly critical brute that I am, I can only take contemporary fiction—which I can't take *at all* save when it's a favoured, or favouring, young friend's) in successive gustatory sups, or experimental go's, of a certain number of pages each. So when the pages foot up *very* high, you see, it takes me some time to work along. But I have absorbed and accumulated some 150 of you, and shall have assimilated perhaps fifty more by the time we meet. "Then we'll talk"—or rather perhaps won't so much as try to, according to the light in which my fatal necessity to

---

95. The "massive Volume" was *Fortitude,* Walpole's fifth novel, published one week earlier. Walpole's diary entry for 4 February 1913 reads, "Most of the day with Henry J. Wonderful to hear him on 'Fortitude'. Abuses the first part but praised the second" (Walpole, H., Works—Diaries, 1912–1915, HRC).

appreciate (that is, I mean, *estimate*) what I read may strike you as most blandly or most portentously showing. The great thing is that I do work you down—which I can't for the life of me do anyone else—save, that is, Wells and Arnold B[ennett].[96] So you make with them my trio. And you are not, my dear Hugh, the least "spirited" of the three, or the least sincere, or the least formed to conciliate the most anxious attention of your all-affectionate old

Henry James,

[*This final remark is in James's hand.*] who entertains sentiments for you which he can't flaunt, you see, in the bewildered face of Remington.

TL/ALS: Walpole Collection (Recipient)
Harry Ransom Humanities Research Center, University of Texas at Austin

21, CARLYLE MANSIONS, CHEYNE WALK.S.W.

2417 KENSINGTON.

Darling Hugh! March 18*th 1913.*

(Excuse my warmth!) I have promptly wired to Jarvis to despatch the bureau-desk, carefully packed, to the bower of your muse & the retreat of your modesty, with every charge utterly prepaid. I hope it will start, by the G[reat]. W[estern]. at the very 1st hour, & if any further pence are demanded of you for "delivery" or whatever let me immediately know & I will passionately remit. I hope the thing will seem to you of an adequate shape & aspect, & that when you lean your inspired elbows on its extended table you will feel a little as if resting them on your poor old friend's still sufficiently broad & sturdy & all-patient back.[97] I vociferously applaud in advance the leaping & bounding volume that you are already astride of for riding to glory.[98] May the glory be great—&, incidentally, even the work. You shall have *my* lump of twaddle as soon as it appears—I don't think it's due till the end of the month.[99] *The* blunder of the brilliant Pugh (his

---

96. Herbert George Wells (1866–1946) was a prolific English writer, historian, and sociologist who HJ met in 1898. Their friendship eroded after Wells satirized HJ in *Boon* (1915) and HJ subsequently criticized Wells. See notes 72 and 134 on Arnold Bennett.

97. Walpole is less than ebullient in his 24 March 1913 diary entry about the arrival of the desk on Easter Monday: "Rather a mis-spent day, because Henry's desk arrived and that was rather disturbing as the windows had to be taken out" (Walpole, H., Works—Diaries, 1912–1915, HRC).

98. Walpole was at work on *The Duchess of Wrexe,* published in 1914.

99. HJ's *A Small Boy and Others,* the first of three autobiographical volumes, was published by Charles Scribner's Sons on 29 March 1913, and by Macmillan and Company on 1 April 1913.

book)[100] is surely in the stupidity [of] its cheap & humbugging auto-biographic *form,* of which the consequence (one of 'em) is that he inconceivably & hideously "gives away" his old vulgar Mother—to an impossibility—& violates in other helpless ways his own consciousness. Had he made the picture truly objective he cld. have done so much more. The only point of a situation like that with Rocky is that its interest is in its being a *relation;* which involves above all (especially an autobiography) 'Arry's hungering view of Rocky's view of *him*—the grounds, motive-force &c, of R.'s side of the matter. This isn't so much as dreamed of. Otherwise, his own vision of Rocky *is,* I think, rather given. Only one doesn't really know which *kind* of a Rocky he wd. have us suppose it to be.——But what a pity we can't jaw! How little your 'Arry does have of *you, dear* Rocky Hugh—though I *have* been to tea with you & your Mother. I hope you aren't too desolately sole. An Easter party you will at least have. The landscape of P[olperro]. I grasp, but not the figures. You are of course *the* figure—but all alone on the slate? Let me know when the mild offering reaches port. Yours, dearest Hugh, so exceedingly

Henry James

ALS: Walpole Collection (Recipient)

Harry Ransom Humanities Research Center, University of Texas at Austin

21, CARLYLE MANSIONS, CHEYNE WALK.S.W.

2417 KENSINGTON.

Dearest Hugh.   [29 April 1913]

Your letter of April 20th gave & continues to give me, as it lies here before me & again & again engages my fondest attention, the greatest joy. But these last ten days have been bad ones, the very worst, for writing. My prodigious Birthday[101] (prodigious by the measure of *my* sequestered vale of life) has taken a vast deal of acknowledgment—under the vain effort of which push of the pen I have languished, stumbled, almost quite collapsed. Which doesn't mean however that so generous & gracious a demonstration hasn't deeply touched & uplifted me—it has been really a most charming & reviving experience to know. Be tenderly thanked, beloved boy, for your gentle & faithful share in it. I think of your noble detachment from the

---

100. HJ refers to *Harry the Cockney* (1912), by Edwin William Pugh (1874–1930).

101. On his seventieth birthday (15 April 1913), 270 of HJ's friends—organized by Percy Lubbock, Hugh Walpole, Edmund Gosse, and others—presented him with a silver-gilt porringer and commissioned John Singer Sargent to paint his portrait. See Edel, *Henry James, 1901–1916: The Master,* 483–89.

scene about me here meanwhile with infinite sympathy, envy, applause, & believe you are having, if the work marches, days & weeks that you may count hereafter as among the happiest of your life. You will find—must already have found, your liberal sacrifice on the Great Altar a great help to the knowledge of your own powers. May that garden bloom & rustle & draw you on into more luxuriant bowers in proportion as you trustfully explore it. I thank you ever so for your patience with the fatuous & presumptuous Small Boy;[102] an extraordinarily impudent attempt surely, that of regaling the world with the picture of my rare consciousness from the age of 6 months to that of my earlier teens—& aggravated by the fact that when I began to tap the fount I found it come, the crystal stream—& *liked* the way of its coming. It's full at any rate of an ancient piety & a brave intention. You disconcert me a little—or call it much—by saying that some passages "defeat" you—that is if I know what you mean. I take you to mean that you found them difficult, obscure or *entortillés* [Fr.: involved, using circumlocutions]—& that is the pang & the proof that I am truly an uncommunicating communicator—a beastly bad thing to be. Here at least I said to myself is a thing at every inch of its way on the [*missing text*][103] the meanest intelligence! [*missing text*] would seem, I don't get flat *enough* down on my belly—there's a cherished ideal of platitude that, to make "success," I shall never be able to achieve. Don't try for it *you*, dearest Hugh, for God's sake—if that's what your remark would imply; & when you come to town again *do* let me read you over the said baffling or bewildering morsels. I don't think I ought to so despair of driving them through your skull. But "thou hast great allies", as Wordsworth says to the captive Toussaint[104]—since the acute Pinker[105] told me a day or two ago that Arnold Bennett had said to him of the thing: "Not ea[*missing text*] but how beautiful [*missing text*] obliged for the beautiful but I lose myself in wonder at such a restriction on the part of an *expert* dabbler in the mystery, like A[rnold]. B[ennett]. It makes me indeed ask myself about the others; & indeed if you ask me in *what* "mystery" the aforesaid *is* a dabbler I shan't say in that of style. But don't think, dearest boy, that you have set me off—

---

102. HJ sent Walpole a copy of *A Small Boy and Others* (1913).

103. An approximately 2″ × 1″ piece of the upper left corner of the final sheet of this three-sheet letter is missing, taking with it the opening words of the first two lines on both pages 5 and 6.

104. HJ quotes from Wordsworth's sonnet "To Toussaint L'Overture" (1802).

105. James Brand Pinker (1863–1922) was HJ's literary and dramatic agent from 1898 onward; in 1912 he became Walpole's agent as well (Hart-Davis, *Hugh Walpole*, 93).

even though if you had called my complacent infant a prattler & a twaddler I should have found *that* quite in the line of the higher criticism & felt justly exposed. I think with a great elation of the possibility of seeing you here a month hence—if I understand you. I hope myself to hang on through June—that is if you'll sometimes put your legs under my poor mahogany. Goodnight for now. My dear & delightful von Glehns,[106] neighbours & quasi-cousins, tell me they are starting for Cornwall & the hope of some small grab of you. See them if you (conscientiously) can, that they may tell me of you. I shall love you all three the better for it. I lately had a Sunday p.m. hour or two with our lady of Ockham,[107] who snuffled & yawned as socially as ever. (Burn me at the stake *always*.) But she was very nice & believes entirely in Helen's marriage.[108] Let *us* therefore. Your faithfully fondest old

H.J.

April 29*th* '13.

ALS: Walpole Collection (Recipient)
Harry Ransom Humanities Research Center, University of Texas at Austin

LAMB HOUSE RYE SUSSEX

TELEPHONE 51 RYE

Belovedest Hugh.   *Aug: 21: '13*

It's proof of your poor old infatuated friend's general & particular difficulties that a couple of days, rather than a couple of hours, have elapsed, & that he has had to let them do so, since your dear letter came to bless him. But here he is with you now, though too late at night—he has had to sink to slumber awhile since dinner; & he hardly knows how to put it strongly enough that he rejoices even across this dire gulf in space in your company & conversation. You give him, it would seem, a jolly good account of yourself, & he fairly gloats over the picture. Beautiful must be your Cornish land & your Cornish sea, idyllic your Cornish setting, this flattering, this wonderful summer, & ours here doubtless may claim but a modest place beside it all. Yet as you have with you your Mother & Sister,

---

106. The British painter Wilfred von Glehn (1870–1951) married the painter Jane Emmet (1873–1961), cousin to HJ. One of HJ's address books records his address as "73 Cheyne Walk, Chelsea S.W." (*Complete Notebooks*, 614).

107. See note 30 on Lady Lovelace.

108. See the biographical register on Helen Lascelles. Walpole's diary entry 8 July 1913, her wedding day, records that he attended, sitting next to HJ "who kept making ribald remarks" (Walpole, H., Works—Diaries, 1912–1915, HRC).

which I am delighted to hear & whom I gratefully bless, so I can match them with my nephew & niece (the former with me alas indeed but for these 10 or 12 days,)[109] who are an extreme benediction to me. My niece, a charming & interesting young person & *most* conversable, stays, I hope, through the greater part of September, & I even curse that necessary limit—when she returns to America. Cultivate with me, darlingest Hugh, the natural affections, so far as you are lucky enough to have matter for them. I meant don't wait till you are 80 to do so—though indeed *I* haven't waited, but have made the most of them from far back. I like exceedingly to hear that your work has got so bravely on, & envy you that sovereign consciousness. When it's finished—well, when it's finished let some of those sweet young people the *bons amis* [Fr.: good friends] (yours) come to me for the small change of remark that I gathered from you the other day (you were adorable about it,) they have more than once chinked in your ear as from my poor old pocket, & they will see, *you* will, in what coin I shall have paid them. I too am working with a certain shrunken regularity— when not made to lapse & stumble by circumstances (damnably physical,) beyond my control. These circumstances tend to come, on the whole (thanks to a great power of patience in my ancient organism,) rather *more* within my management than for a good while back; but to live with a bad & chronic anginal demon preying on one['s] vitals takes a great deal of doing. However, I didn't mean to write you of that side of the picture (save that it's a large part of that same,) & only glance that way to make sure of your tenderness even when I may seem to you backward & blank. It isn't to exploit your compassion—it's only to be able to feel that I am not without your fond understanding: so far as your blooming youth (*there's* the crack in the fiddle-case!) *can* fondly understand my so otherwise-conditioned age. However, there's always understanding enough when there's affection enough, & you touch me almost to tears when you tell me how I touched the springs of yours that last time in London. I remember immensely wanting to. I gather that that planned & promised visit of dear Jocelyn P[ersse].'s[110] hasn't taken place for you (from your not naming it:) it's a

<hr />

109. Margaret Mary "Peggy" James (1887–1950) and Alexander Robertson "Aleck" James (1890–1946), children of William and Alice James, were staying with HJ at Lamb House. See HJ's letter of 15 April 1911 to Walpole about Aleck's portrait of his uncle.

110. Walpole's 2 February 1911 diary entry characterizes Jocelyn Persse as "eager to be liked, easily pleased." When Persse visited The Cobbles, the diary entries are progressively less charitable: "Then Jocelyn arrived—amiable and kind and placid" (23 September 1913); "Did a good deal of work in spite of Jocelyn" (25 September 1913); "Walked with J.P. and

Jocelyn P. so whirlable into space at any incalculable moment that no want of correspondence between the bright sketch & the vague sequel is ever of a nature to surprise. And the bright sketches are so truly genial, & even the dim vaguenesses without the invidious sting: "We'll see him again, we'll see him again!" as the old Jacobite song says of bonny Prince Charlie. Perhaps I shall achieve seeing him here in the course of the autumn—& perhaps, oh beloved Hugh, *you* will achieve, for my benefit, a like—or a more likely—snatch of pilgrimage. My desire is to stay on here as late into the autumn as may consort with my condition—I dream of sticking on through November even if possible: Cheyne Walk & the black-barged yellow river will be the more agreeable to me when I get back to them. I make out that you will then be in London again—I mean *by* November, though such a black gulf of time intervenes; & then of course I may look to you to come down to me for a couple of days. It will be the lowest kind of "jinks"—so halting is my pace; yet we shall somehow make it serve. Don't say to me, by the way, à propos of jinks—the "high" kind that you speak of having so wallowed in previous to leaving town—that I ever challenge you as to *why* you wallow, or splash or plunge, or dizzily & sublimely soar (into the jinks element,) or whatever you may call it: as if I ever remarked on anything but the absolute inevitability of it for you at your age & with your natural curiosities, as it were, & passions. It's good healthy exercise, when it comes but in bouts & brief convulsions, & it's always a kind of thing that it's good, & considerably final, to *have* done. We must know, as much as possible, in our beautiful art, yours & mine, what we are talking about—& the only way to know it is to have lived & loved & cursed & floundered & enjoyed & suffered—I think I don't regret a single "excess" of my responsive youth—I only regret, in my chilled age, certain occasions & possibilities I didn't *embrace*. Bad doctrine to impart to a young idiot or a duffer; but in place for a young friend (pressed to my heart,) with a fund of nobler passion, the preserving, the defying, the dedicating, & which always has the last word; the young friend who can dip & shake off & go his straight way again when it's time. But we'll talk of all this—it's abominably late. Who is D. H. Lawrence,[111] who, you think, would interest me? Send him & his book

---

answered his stupid questions" (27 September 1913); "Practically no work done. Jocelyn so amiable that it seems wicked to be bored but oh! I *am*—and it will be a relief when he goes tomorrow" (28 September 1913); "Jocelyn departed 11 o'clock. Oh! I *was* glad and danced all the way home. But he *is* the kindest nicest of creatures" (29 September 1913). See Walpole, H., Works—Diaries, 1911 and 1912–1915, HRC.

111. *Sons and Lovers,* by D. H. Lawrence (1885–1930), appeared in 1913.

along—by which I simply mean Inoculate me, at your convenience (don't address me the volume;) so far as I can *be* inoculated. I always *try* to let anything of the kind "take". Last year, you remember, a couple of improbabilities (as to "taking") did worm a little into the fortress. (Gilbert Cannan was one.[112]) I have been reading over Tolstoi's interminable *Peace & War* & am struck with the fact that[113] I now protest as much as I admire.[114] He doesn't *do* to read over, & that exactly is the answer to those who idiotically proclaim the impunity of such formless shape, such flopping looseness & such a denial of composition, selection & style. He has a mighty fund of life, but the *waste,* & the ugliness & vice of waste, the vice of a not finer *doing,* are sickening. For me he but makes "composition" throne, by contrast, in effulgent lustre! Ever your fondest of the fond,

H.J.

ALS: Walpole Collection (Recipient)
Harry Ransom Humanities Research Center, University of Texas at Austin

LAMB HOUSE RYE SUSSEX
TELEPHONE 51 RYE
October 14th 1913.

Dearest little Hugh: (vide the Russians in general—I have just been re-reading over Tolstoi—for the tender force of the diminutive.) It is the sweetest kind of comfort to be able to think of you as at all impending: impend therefore, impend as hard as you can, impend for all you are worth. Keep 3 or 4 early days after your return to town for coming down to me. On casting about a bit, verily—I have to *consider* so much, in my condition, in these days, as to the disposal of my times & the conservation of my so shrunken powers—I make out that something of about November 10th would be the favourable date for me—it allows for my very final finishing of a Book,[115] which I am, under disadvantages, struggling toward; & nothing better than your so sympathetic society could accrue to me in celebration of that relief. I shall be twice as much yours, for the

---

112. In 1913 the English novelist, dramatist, critic, and translator Gilbert Cannan (1884–1955) published *Round the Corner: Being the Life and Death of Francis Christopher Folyat, Bachelor of Divinity and Father of a Large Family.*

113. Omitted here is HJ's parenthetical remark "(see p. 7)" as he moves from the margin of page 1 to the margin of page 7 to complete the letter.

114. In his letter to Walpole of 19 May 1912 HJ discusses Tolstoy further.

115. *Notes of a Son and Brother* (1914) was the second of HJ's three autobiographical volumes.

fleeting interval, & capable of at least trying twice as much to make you mine, when that carking care is off my mind. And I shall feel all the deeper harmony in that you too will have then a finish to commemorate.[116] We will drink deep together—great flowing bowls from the pump—to each other's triumphs. And you will tell me much of all the elements that shall make for yours. Well can I conceive that you have found the deep peace of your refuge a benefit & a balm—though able (*I* am) to figure not less that the joy of battle in London will in due course inflate your young nostril even almost to bursting. Such is the strange rotation of our fate—that is of yours; for mine, thank God, has long since ceased to rotate, & if I accomplish an in the least safe immobility I am but too devoutly grateful. I have no fear at all but that Jocelyn found his bright account in your kind company—though when you come to the question of "subjects in common", heaven save the mark!—or of the absence of them—I have nothing to say to you but that I know (none better) what you mean. One gets on with him in a way without them, however, & says to one's self, I think, that if *he* doesn't mind, well, why should one either? At any rate I am glad you were gentle with him. I am infinitely & gladly so—but the basis shrinks, & I haven't seen him these 4 months or so, though with a hope of getting him down before long for 24 hours. (My physical disabilities utterly undermine, alas, all my social initiative.) I too have read my Wells & even written him 8 pages about the matter[117]—which left him extravagantly apologetic & profoundly indifferent. Artistically, expressively of any subject but *himself,* he has gone to the dogs. But that self remains to me demonic—for life & force, cheek & impudence & a wondrous kind of vividness *quand même* [Fr.: all the same]. He *inveterately* goes to pieces about the middle—in this last thing the 1st half promised & then the collapse was gross. And he will never do anything else, & will never dream of so much as wanting to. They all seem to me money-grubbers pure & simple, naked & unashamed; & Arnold Bennett now with an indecency, verily an obscenity, of nudity—! But goodnight—the hour is, as usual, absurd. Yours, dearest Hugh, all affectionately,

Henry James

ALS: Walpole Collection (Recipient)

Harry Ransom Humanities Research Center, University of Texas at Austin

---

116. HJ refers to the imminent completion of Walpole's *The Duchess of Wrexe* (1914).

117. HJ's letter of 21 September 1913 to Wells is published in *Henry James Letters,* 4:686–88.

LAMB HOUSE RYE SUSSEX
TELEPHONE 51 RYE
Darlingest Hugh!   November *3d 1913*.

I am wondering & yearning over you, & one of the forms it takes is to
ask myself which *day* it was for which I some little time back suggested
your gently coming down here. Wasn't it *Saturday next 8th* & if so couldn't
you, won't you, kindly confirm it to me & let me absolutely expect you
then? I find I have made no note of it, tending as I ever do with you to
swim in a *general* beatific confidence. I greatly long to see you, even if I feel
what a devil of a dreary old hash my increasing limitations of ease &
dilapidations of state must condemn me to appear to you. We communicate across the gulf of Time, awful Time, while I grow relentlessly older &
you shamelessly younger; but let us never the less do it as we can & under
whatever disadvantages—let us keep the possibility just enough *ahead* of
the difficulty. To this end, for one thing, I shall within the few days
practically have cleared my decks of that interminable piece of work of
which I spoke to you[118]—& I shall receive you on a virtually disencum-
bered scene. I take it that you are meanwhile leading in London the great,
the greatest, life, & I shall insist on the benefit of every storied inch of it.
Let me know that on Saturday at 6.30 you do arrive, & you shall then have
another word from me before you start. I seem ever to write you a yard for
any (written) inch I ever get from you; but what does ⟨this⟩ make me—
show me for—but exactly more & more your all-affectionate old
Henry James

ALS: Walpole Collection (Recipient)
Harry Ransom Humanities Research Center, University of Texas at Austin

---

21 CARLYLE MANSIONS CHEYNE WALK S.W.
TELEPHONE 2417 KENSINGTON.
Belovedest Hugh.   January *29th* 1914.

I do my best that this should "meet" you at Mrs. Alhusen's,[119] for that is
what would have for me too the supreme beauty. But I have lost a little
time through my having a painful congested throat, from a beastly bad
cold, that has been making social, & all literary, graces impossible to me, &

---

118. See Walpole's diary entry for 7 April 1914: "Finished H.J.'s 'Notes of a Son and
Brother' and the last chapter on Mary [*sic*] Temple is one of the most beautiful things in our
language. God bless him!" (Walpole, H., Works—Diaries, 1912–1915, HRC).

119. Walpole's hostess may have been the English novelist Beatrice May Butt (c. 1856–
1918), identified in the *Wellesley Index to Periodicals* as "Beatrice M. Allhusen."

your arrival there may anticipate it. But even so let your being the cynosure of every eye not divert your own bright orb from my fond page. Your letter from the Châlet gave me great joy,[120] even though almost intolerably flinging across my grey old pate the cold glitter of youth & sport & the awful winter-breath of the Alps—her having immersed herself in which presents little Elizabeth to me too, on her frozen height, like some small shining quartz-crystal set in the rock to which she is kindred, & yet hard enough to break by her firm edge the most geological hammer. Which means of course that if envy, aged impotent envy, of your *joie de vivre* [Fr.: joy of life] could kill, you would already be stretched lifeless at my feet. You will have particular anecdotes to inflict that I shall do my best to bear without smiting you, & that I should still deeply desire from you even if that danger were greater. In the matter of dangers I draw a long breath at having you—as I think you are by this time—well off the fell toboggan.[121] Lord, what things you'll have to tell me! I shall have scant & mean coin to repay you withal. I lead my narrow precautionary life & only complain when the precautions don't sufficiently avail or closely enough shut me in. (A note from the little black burden of a Colefax interrupts me[122]—by the way, it was *you* let her loose on me!—but I flick her aside & proceed.) Trying to turn back on you a little the sense of privation, I bethink myself that I am dining tomorrow night with Jocelyn Persse at the Garrick Club, your own native heath—ha-ha!—"to meet" (only) Max Beerbohm:[123] so that wouldn't you give the little finger you *didn't* break in the ice-world to assist at that symposium, compared to which nothing Mrs. Alhusen can serve you will be "in" it! Oh yes, and I've had a letter from Compton Mackenzie ("Monty Compton," as I call him!!) & have answered it at the

---

120. Gräfin Mary Annette ("Elizabeth") Beauchamp Von Arnim (1866–1941) was the author of numerous books, including *Elizabeth and Her German Garden* (1898), *The Adventures of Elizabeth in Rugen* (1904), *The Pastor's Wife* (1914), *In The Mountains* (1920), and *Enchanted April* (1923). Walpole's acquaintance with her, begun in 1907 when he tutored her children, is characterized by Hart-Davis as "the longest-enduring and one of the firmest of all his friendships with women" (*Hugh Walpole*, 52). Walpole had recently stayed at her new home in southwestern Switzerland, the Châlet Soleil, Randogne-sur-Sierre.

121. For HJ's apprehensions about "the fell toboggan," see Walpole's diary entry for 22 January 1914: "Then terrific 'luge' down the hill. Elizabeth hurt herself pretty badly" (Walpole, H., Works—Diaries, 1912–1915, HRC).

122. Sibyl (Mrs. Arthur) Colefax (1874–1950) was a London hostess and friend of Edith Wharton.

123. See the biographical register for Max Beerbohm.

most beautiful length,[124] & have been to see his mother about him (an old friend & a very nice woman,) & talked with her an *hour*—yes, *all* about Monty; & am to have his very interesting photograph from her, & am generally, by what I have heard, much worked up: though to tenderness of compassion largely, as the poor chap, banished to Capri by a painful (excruciating) malady—spinal neuritis—suffers much & is greatly handicapped & compromised; the real prescription & remedy for him being to knock off work utterly for 2 years. This he doesn't see his way to be able to, apparently—with resources very limited; his father has just had a heavy loss of money through the black business villainy of a trusted associate or agent, & has never been less able to help him: so, with the 2d vol. of Sinister Street wholly uncommenced, he is trying at Capri to write short tales "to order" (for America of course;) which his mother says "he knows he doesn't do well" & is therefore unhappy about. Fortunately his wife is excellent for him & *to* him, Mrs. C. tells me; devoted, protective, able, & 5 years older than himself; all of which will interest your generous heart, as it does mine—more susceptible to nothing than to the union of youth, genius & misfortune. You have seen for yourself how the 2 former elements even under the happiest star transport & bedevil me when combined in a noble form—& the appeal of such a case as Monty's is a touch even beyond that! Don't, however, to qualify yourself for this competition, go back to the Chalet to break a leg for me, or even linger on at ⟨Stake Page's?⟩ to break a heart:[125] restore yourself to me in unblushing felicity & I will make the best of you as you are. Take it easy: the voluminous Duchess will clearly be upon me before[126]—by all presumability, as I gather from Mrs. C.—a rejoinder comes from Capri (to the letter, mine, above-mentioned;) & once caught in that spell I shall be held fast till you are able to renew again the more personal attention to my case. Gently wriggle—but don't too distressfully squirm, therefore!——Less figuratively, the sharpest impression I have recently had is one that will probably come up for yourself as soon as you get back & will be as dreadful to you as I have just felt it— that of the tragically demoralized state of poor Bobby Ross[127] under the

---

124. See *Henry James Letters*, 4:696–98 for HJ's letter of 21 January 1914 to Compton Mackenzie.

125. Stake Page has not been identified.

126. *The Duchess of Wrexe* was published on 5 February 1914.

127. Robert Baldwin Ross (1869–1918) was entrusted by Oscar Wilde with the manuscript of *De Profundis*, Wilde's prison "letter" to Alfred Douglas. He published an abridged

hellish machinations of his arch-enemy, whose toils are apparently closing round him, or *have* closed, in a manner that it is extremely stupefying to hear that such a personage as that has been able to achieve credit for. (For God's sake don't leave this about in the Alhusen whispering gallery!) Poor Ross is in a pitiful condition, too distressful to behold, & throws himself on all he can borrow an ear from—he told me all a short time since at the Reform Club, & you must brace yourself for his probably doing the same by you. The thing is to try to help him to keep his head & stiffen his heart—which one *can* by kindness & intelligence; & I find it impossible not to believe that the other man, for all his black impudence, will be overwhelmed by the last discomfiture. Ross's friends can contribute to that by standing close to him. He told me that Edmund Gosse is being extraordinarily kind & helpful—in particular about bringing home to the "authorities" the scandal of their *listening* to a man with A[lfred]. D[ouglas].'s history.————————————Well, dearest Hugh, I must draw off; you are vague about the duration of your stay in the gilded halls where I trust this will await you, but the first sign of your drawing nearer will be greatly blessed by your fondly faithful & faithfully fond old

Henry James

ALS: Walpole Collection (Recipient)

Harry Ransom Humanities Research Center, University of Texas at Austin

LAMB HOUSE RYE SUSSEX

TELEPHONE 51 RYE

Dearest, dearest Hugh.   September 9*th* *1914*

I am deeply moved by your news, & only a bit heartbroken at the thought you will have left London, I gather, by the time this gets there— though I write it but an hour after receipt of your note; so that the best I can do is to send it to the Garrick[128] to be "forwarded". You will probably be so much forwarder than my poor pursuing missive always, that I feel the

---

version in 1905, omitting all references to Douglas, but subsequently read the excised passages in court in 1913 when Douglas sued Arthur Ransome for allegedly libelous statements in *Oscar Wilde: A Critical Study* (1912). After the failure of his suit against Ransome, Douglas attacked Ross to his friends "until the pressure became so great that Ross . . . had to sue for libel. On the witness stand Douglas proved too much for him, and though Ross escaped prosecution, he felt harried until his death in 1918." See Richard Ellmann's *Oscar Wilde* (New York: Knopf, 1988), 587.

128. Walpole belonged to the Garrick Club, founded in 1831 as a place where "actors and men of education might meet on equal terms."

dark void shutting me out from you for a long time to come—save as I shall see your far-off light play so bravely over the public page.[129] Your adventure is of the last magnificence of pluck, the finest strain of resolution, & I bless & cheer & honour it for all I am worth. It will be of the intensest interest & of every sort of profit & glory to you—which doesn't prevent however my as intensely yearning over you, my thinking of you with all the ache of privation. But of such yearnings & such aches, such privations & such prides, is all our present consciousness made up; & I wait for you again with a confidence & courage which I try to make not too basely unworthy of your own. Feel yourself at any rate, dearest boy, wrapped round in all the affection & imagination of your devotedest old
Henry James

ALS: Walpole Collection (Recipient)
Harry Ransom Humanities Research Center, University of Texas at Austin

21, CARLYLE MANSIONS, CHEYNE WALK.S.W.

2417 KENSINGTON.

My very dear Hugh. October 29*th*. 1914.

This little letter—but oh so little and so void!—has at least and at last come, and by no such long stretch, inasmuch as it's only of Oct. 14th. Forgive my using this comparatively impersonal form to thank you for it; the form is after all, under the conditions we are living in, the most personal, that is the promptest, clearest, and most possible to the writer— which remark sustains me in being, as I am, altogether reduced to it now. I greatly grieve at the loss of whatever else you may have addressed me,[130] for I have ever so wonderingly and hopingly waited and watched. The one definite word I have had of you was from the good Pinker,[131] the excellent, never more excellent than he has been showing himself of late; who spoke to me three weeks ago of a wee word from you, which gave me more or less of a longed-for assurance. However, if my heart leaped up this morning at sight of your hand, it scuttled down again fairly fast under the inexorable blankness, so to call it, of your page. This page of mine may suffer, on its way to you, perhaps, by not being blank enough: still, I risk a few merely

---

129. When his efforts to enlist in August 1914 failed because of weak eyesight, Walpole traveled to Russia as a correspondent, leaving England on 12 September (Hart-Davis, *Hugh Walpole*, 117–19).

130. The letter from Walpole was apparently censored.

131. See note 106 on James Brand Pinker.

personal assurances, asking myself why, between such devoted Allies, we should be condemned to mere bareness. What I should have blessed from you would have been some word about your learning of Russian for instance (for I hope you are quite mastering it, for the resource it will be to you in the future) and the interest of that, and the interest of the character of Moscow, or *some* fond little formulation of a good Russian impression. I seem to make out that your impressions are of the happiest—Pinker tells me you wrote him of much friendship and hospitality; but let me not seem to overhaul you, or to wish to, for any short-coming! I hope with all my heart indeed you *may* be allowed to get to Warsaw, for the more you see and can bring home of the treasure of observation the more fortunate and the more interesting to us will you be. Here I am, you will recognise, under absolute preference at present; I returned to town almost immediately after receiving your note of farewell—the country with its want of contacts and informations and satisfactions to all one's anxieties, became quite impossible to me. London is in the highest degree interesting and uplifting—but much too distracting for any concentration of interest on work. I can't write, except letters, and only this way, and I curse the time of life and the state of health which keep me from what is *the* enviable condition, that of straightforward action and performance, the doing of some daily, constantly helpful job of the sort that fixes and rewards the devoted attention. Blest are those who have *that* portion—like the magnificent young, however engaged, in general. I hope your innumerable friends write to you—though don't much suppose it unless you write to *them:* for of your more special circle (if so multitudinous a one as yours has anything so mean as a specialty!) I fear I've not seen much: people are so steeped in the active occupations of the time that we of course meet much less in a general way than we did in the days that seem now so far off. It happens, however, oddly enough, that I go by appointment this afternoon to tea with the dear old Colvins[132]—and it happens with a rare perversity that Compton Mackenzie comes to lunch with me an hour hence. Let me extenuate so far as immediately to add that this is our first encounter of the sort! He has but lately returned, I believe, from his long absence abroad—and I see him today practically for the first time. I believe he has just finished the second part of Sinister Street and that it is almost immediately to come forth.[133]

---

132. In 1903 the British socialite Frances Sitwell (1839–1924) married Sidney Colvin (1845–1927), director of the Fitzwilliam Museum and later keeper of prints and drawings at the British Museum.

133. The second volume of *Sinister Street* appeared in 1914.

Arnold Bennett has just published an intensely, I find even a rather mechanically, Five Towns thing, *not* of the Clayhanger series, and Wells very much such another—I mean of the thorough-going industrial order.[134] It must have been one of those he was turning off, as you told me, last summer at the Châlet, the mistress thereof, by the by, has just been delivered of a member of her own series, the Anglo-German—meaning by series her literary family.[135] Books accordingly are being published a bit, and Pinker is optimistic—in spite of which my own Muse remains heavy-headed, heavy-handed and heavy-footed as never in all her days before. But let me not draw this out if it's liable to misadventure. I pray with all my heart, however, that it shall reach you with all the sentiments of your affectionate old

Henry James

P.S. I hope you were reached in time by a letter I wrote you the moment I got that last word from you at the Garrick; I mean that it overtook you before your start. It expressed so many benedictions![136]

TLS: Walpole Collection (Recipient)
Harry Ransom Humanities Research Center, University of Texas at Austin

21 CARLYLE MANSIONS CHEYNE WALK S.W.
TELEPHONE 2417 KENSINGTON.

Dearest Hugh. November *21st 1914.*

This is a great joy—your letter of November 12th has just come, to my extreme delight, & I answer it, you see, within a very few hours.[137] It is by far the best letter you have ever written me, & I am touched & interested by it more than I can say. Let me tell you at once that I sent you that last thing in typecopy because of an anxious calculation that such a form would help to secure its safe arrival. Your own scrap was a signal of the probable

---

134. Apparently a reference to Arnold Bennett's story collection *The Matador of the Five Towns* (1912), which followed the novel *Anna of the Five Towns* (1902) and the story collection *The Grim Smile of the Five Towns* (1907). Which work of 1914 by Wells—*The World Set Free, When the Sleeper Wakes, The Wheels of Change, The Wife of Sir Isaac Harman*—HJ has in mind is unclear, although HJ refers to the last-mentioned novel in his letter of 21 November 1914.

135. HJ apparently refers to Elizabeth von Arnim's *The Pastor's Wife* (1914).

136. Walpole's 11 November 1914 diary entry is a tepid response to HJ's letter: "Long not very interesting letter from Henry James" (Walpole, H., Works—Diaries, 1912–1915, HRC).

137. Walpole's letter of 12 November 1914 is reprinted in Hart-Davis, *Hugh Walpole,* 125–27.

non-arrival of anything that seemed in the least to defy legibility; therefore I said to myself that what was flagrantly & blatantly legible *would* presumably reach you. At the same time the extreme spareness of your own note appeared to give me the pattern of the very little I should do well to attempt to say. It was all wretched enough—as have been the 2 postcards I have addressed you since, being advised that *they* would be probably the most likely-to-come-to-hand things, beggarly as they could only be. But this full free letter from you is a blissful reassurance; it has come straight speedily (for the distance & the other conditions,) & makes me feel that anything is possible. Therefore may the present be no less successful. For I want you to know that the vision of your homesickness & loneliness & the "family" within your gates wrings tears of the tenderest pity from my aged eyes. You must indeed have had a regular hell of a time, & the strain on your nerves & resolutions have been of the direst. I hope the worst in that way is over—over above all with your started acquisition of the tongue, which must indeed be magnificent, & also that you have some other friends than the regular companions of your board, if not of your bed. I had better make use of this chance, however, to give you an inkling of *our* affairs, such as they are, rather than indulge in mere surmises & desires, fond & faithful though these be, about your own eventualities. London is of course under all our stress very interesting, to me deeply & infinitely moving, but on a basis & in ways that make the life we have known here fade into grey mists of insignificance. People "meet" a little, but very little, every social habit & convention has broken down, save with a few vulgarians & utter mistakers (mistakers, I mean, about the decency of things;) & for myself, I confess, I find there are very few persons I care to see—only those to whom & to whose state of feeling I am really attached. Promiscuous chatter on the public situation & the gossip thereanent of more or less wailing women in particular give unspeakably on my nerves. Depths of sacred silence seem to me to prescribe themselves in presence of the sanctities of action of those who, in unthinkable conditions almost, are magnificently *doing* the thing. Then right & left are all the figures of mourning—though such proud erect ones—over the blow that has come to them. *There* the women are admirable—the mothers & wives & sisters; the mothers in particular, since it's so much the younger lives, the fine seed of the future, that are offered & taken. The rate at which they are taken is appalling—but then I think of France & Russia & even of Germany herself, & the vision simply overwhelms & breaks the heart. "The German dead, the German dead!" I above all say to myself—in such hecatombs have *they* been ruthlessly piled up by those who have driven them, from behind, to their fate; & it for the moment almost makes me forget Belgium—though when I *remember* that disembowelled country my heart is at once hardened to *every* son of a Hun. Belgium we have hugely & portentously with us; if never in the world was a nation so driven forth, so on the other hand was one never so taken to another's arms. And the Dutch have been nobly hospitable! I have been going to a great hospital (St. Barts',)[138] at the request of a medical friend there, to help to give the solace of free talk to a lot of Belgian wounded & sick (so few people appear to be able to converse in the least intimately with them,) & have thereby almost discovered my vocation in life to be the beguiling & drawing-out of the suffering soldier. The Belgians get worked off, convalesce & are sent away &c; but the British influx is steady, & I have lately been seeing more (always at Barts') of *that* prostrate warrior, with whom I seem to get even better into relation. At his best he is admirable—*so* much may be made of him; of a freshness & brightness of soldier-stuff that I think must be unsurpassable. We only want more & more & more & more, of him; & I judge that we shall in due course get it. Immensely interesting what you say of the sublime newness of spirit of the great Russian people—of whom we are thinking here with the most confident admiration. I met a striking specimen the other day who was oddly enough in the Canadian contingent (he had been living 2 or 3 years in Canada & had volunteered there;) & who was of a stature, complexion, expression, & above all of a shining candour, which made him a kind of army-corps in himself. But about individuals more immediately touching us what shall I tell you? The difficulty is that my contacts are so few & so *picked,* & that innumerable of the younger men are bearing arms. Jocelyn P[ersse]. (I think I *have* told you,) has joined the Royal Fusiliers (in camp as yet in Essex;) Wilfred von G[lehn].[139] exercises & drills the day long in the Artists' corps; Desmond McCarthy[140] is at the front in the Red Cross, Rupert Brooke[141] was at the

---

138. For a summary account of HJ's Belgian Relief work, and his ministrations to the wounded in St. Bartholomew's Hospital, see Edel, *Henry James, 1901–1916: The Master,* 515–19. For HJ's own account, see "The Long Wards," in *The Book of the Homeless (Le livre des sans-foyer),* ed. Edith Wharton (London: Macmillan, 1916).

139. See note 106 on Wilfred von Glehn.

140. Sir Charles Otto Desmond MacCarthy (1877–1952), was a literary and dramatic critic, biographer, editor, and weekly columnist for the *New Statesman.*

141. Rupert Brooke (1887–1915) published *Poems* (1911) and the sonnet sequence *1914 and Other Poems* (1915) before dying of blood poisoning while serving in the British navy.

seige (& surrender, alas) of Antwerp; Philippe Gosse[142] has got a commission (his father has ceased to be in the H[ouse]. of L[ords].'s;) in short almost everyone of anything less than my age is, or is preparing to be, in the imminent deadly breach. Little Marie Belloc[143] lunched with me the other day & bristled with the fruits of ubiquity & omniscience in a manner remarkable even for her. She struck me as being really much in the "know" (her husband & her brother minister to that;) & was most interesting, was charmingly conversible. She *works* gallantly in spite of the stricken state of the worker's mind—mine is utterly blighted; book-makes & keeps the pot boiling, at the same time that she is all over the place, in a manner the most defiant of comprehension. She's the Whole Thing in petticoats. And books are being published—*some;* about as many as ought ever to be. You *shall* have my poor old "Notes"[144]—superannuated quite now, bless you; they shall be addressed to you registered. I feel as if I were always pushing Compton M[ackenzie]. into your ken—but he's to lunch with me tomorrow, Sunday, again, though it makes but the 2d time of my seeing him. He goes into sanitary exile (to Capri,) on Monday, I believe; so he reassured. His huge II of Sinister Street[145] is 1/2 a deadly failure & 1/2 an extraordinary exhibition of talent. The Oxford moiety (I like that elegant word) is of a strange platitude; but the London sequel, all about prostitutes *(exclusively,)* offers a collection of these, studied *sur le vif* [Fr.: from life], which is far beyond anything done, ever, in English (naturally,) & yet is not in the least an emulation of anything French—is really an original & striking performance. But I don't know what it *means*—beyond the 2 facts of his opportunities of observation & his ability. However, the thing affects me on the whole as a mere wide waste. Wells has published a mere flat tiresomeness ("Sir Isaac Harman's Wife";) at least I had, for the 1st time with anything of Wells's, simply to let it slide.[146] The Gräfin has produced "The Pastor's Wife" (the daughter of an English Bishop married in Germany to a Pfarrer & condemned to bear 9 children;) which I am told is

---

142. The physician Philip Gosse (1879–1959), son of Ellen Epps and Edmund Gosse, traveled from London to Rye in autumn 1912 to examine HJ during his affliction with shingles.

143. Marie Adelaide (Mrs. Frederic S. Lowndes) Belloc-Lowndes (1868–1947) was the sister of Hilaire Belloc and a writer of historical works, novels, and mysteries.

144. *Notes of a Son and Brother* (1914) was the second volume of HJ's autobiography.

145. The first volume of Compton Mackenzie's *Sinister Street* appeared in 1913, the second in 1914.

146. Wells's *The Wife of Sir Isaac Harman* appeared in 1914.

mere crude obstetrics.[147] That lady & Wells don't seem to have brought each other luck. She came to England directly the war broke out to be naturalized—but I believe she is back at the Chalet now, where I suppose her name (which she keeps) is less awkward for her. Poor Bobby Ross is again in hapless litigation, against the atrocious Alfred D[ouglas]. himself this time—but it's a deplorable squalid note in the midst of *big* bloody things. (The hearing, or whatever it's called, has but just begun; no result yet—& it *may* again be against the ravaged Ross—it's capable of being!)[148] But goodnight, dearest Hugh. I sit here writing late, in the now extraordinary London blackness of darkness & (almost) tension of stillness. The alarms we have had have as yet come to nothing. Please believe in the fond fidelity with which I think of you. Oh for the day of reparation & reunion! I hope for you that you *may* have the great & terrible experience of Ambulance service at the front. Ah how I pray you also *may* receive this benediction from your affectionate old

H.J.

ALS: Walpole Collection (Recipient)
Harry Ransom Humanities Research Center, University of Texas at Austin

21 CARLYLE MANSIONS CHEYNE WALK S.W.
TELEPHONE 2417 KENSINGTON.

Dearest Hugh.   [7 January 1915]

I lose not a moment in thanking & blessing you for the relief of your quite holy little letter from Moscow (Dec. 23d) on your return from your wondrous adventure at the Front—it came but an hour ago.[149] Not the least of my grounds of rejoicing in it is the proof it gives me that we *do* now effectively correspond—that my last (in answer to your beautiful previous one) did get to you & that this shining little one of today gets to *me* to tell me so. Extraordinary visions & sensations have clearly been your portion, a rich & strong & prodigious experience *as* experience (bless it!) & Lord how pale any poor old prattle that *I* can treat you to will sound in the desperate echoes you'll set rolling. Too pale in fact would any information I might at this actual moment offer you—if [I] *had* any to take such a liberty with, appear to your ensanguined spirit. Your mere hints of your exposures &

---

147. HJ refers to Elizabeth von Arnim's *The Pastor's Wife* (1914).

148. See HJ's letter of 29 January 1914, and note 127, on Robert Baldwin Ross.

149. Walpole's letter to HJ of 23 December 1914 survives in the Houghton and is partly reprinted in Hart-Davis, *Hugh Walpole*, 128–29.

escapes reduce me to a sense [of] my own restriction to twaddle which fairly makes me sick. Well, the sense of *that* in turn is that here I am, & here *we* are, & that all things go on—even to the point of so minimised a little Martin Secker's coming the other day to luncheon with me.[150] Misfortune—i.e. the War—makes strange bedfellows! I don't mean that he stayed all night—but I name him for local colour. Jocelyn P[ersse]., ill with pneumonia after a few deluvian weeks in camp, has been restored to the friend who most naturally must have missed him. We are having in Western Europe the most deplorably drenching winter ever recorded, & my riverside windows here seem to look out upon the inpenetrable water-wall of that quarter of the earth. You probably are in glorious shining snows & gorgeous princely furs (or such as wd. pass for such in sloppy London.) I throw up my hat in jubilation over (1) your admirable acquisition of Russian—let it be *consummate,* simply; & (2) over its being calculable that we shall meet again in April, glorious thought.[151] *Do* be careful, however, of where you take your walks when you return to the Front. If I could lend you even *my* poor old eyes (as people lend their ears) you would thread the labyrinth in such a manner as to restore you absolutely without a flaw to your affectionate old

H.J.

January *7th 1915*

P.S. I see very very few people. We all do, but I *almost* work again.

ALS: Walpole Collection (Recipient)

Harry Ransom Humanities Research Center, University of Texas at Austin

21, CARLYLE MANSIONS, CHEYNE WALK.S.W.

2417 KENSINGTON.

Dearest Hugh. February *14th* 1915

"When you write," you say; & when *do* I write but just exactly an hour after your letter of this evening, that of February 1st, a fortnight ago to a day, has come to hand?[152] I delight in having got it, & find it no less

---

150. Martin Secker (1882–1978) was the English publisher who, beginning in 1915, issued the fourteen-volume *Uniform Tales of Henry James.*

151. Walpole's 23 December 1914 letter to HJ anticipated his return to England in early April 1915; his letter of 1 February 1915 moved the date to September; not until October 1915 did he finally reach England (Hart-Davis, *Hugh Walpole,* 129, 130, 145).

152. Walpole's letter to HJ of 1 February 15 survives in the Houghton and is published in Hart-Davis, *Hugh Walpole,* 130–31.

interesting than genial—bristling with fine realities. Much as it tells me, indeed, I could have done with still more; but that is of course always the case at such a time as this, & amid such wonderments & yearnings; & I make gratefully the most of what there is. The basis, the connection, the mode of employment on, & in, & under, which you "go off," for instance, are matters that leave me scratching my head & exhaling long & sad sighs—but as those 2 things are what I am at in these days most of my time I don't bring them home *most* criminally to you. Only I am moved to beseech you this time not to throw yourself into the thick of military operations amid which your want of even the minimum of proper eyesight apparently may devote you to destruction, more or less—after the manner of the blind mauvais quart d'heure [Fr.: unlucky quarter of an hour] described to me in your letter previous to this one.[153] I am sorry the black homesickness so feeds upon you amid your terrific paradoxical friends, the sport alike of their bodies & their souls, of whom your account is admirably vivid;[154] but I well conceive your state, which has my tenderest sympathy—that nostalgic ache at its worst being the invention of the very devil of devils. Don't let it break the spell of your purpose of learning Russian, of really mastering it—though even while I say this I rather wince at your telling me that you incline not to return to England till September next. I don't put that regret on the score of my loss of the sight of you till then—that gives the sort of personal turn to the matter that we are all ashamed together of giving to any matter now. But the being & the having been in England—or in France, which is now so much the same thing—during at least a part of this unspeakable year affects me as something you are not unlikely to be sorry to have missed—there attaches to it—to the being here—something so sovereign & so initiatory in the way of a British experience. I mean that it's as if you wouldn't have had the full general British experience without it, & that this may be a pity for you as a painter of British phenomena—for I don't suppose you think of reproducing *only* Russian for the rest of your shining days. However, I hasten to add that I feel the very greatest aversion to intermeddlingly advising you—your completing your year in Russia all depends on what you *do* with the precious

---

153. In his letter of 23 December 1914, Walpole recounted how "I was caught under two German aeroplanes and the whole Russian army began to fire on either side of me" (qtd. in Hart-Davis, *Hugh Walpole*, 128).

154. In his letter of 1 February 1915, Walpole offered a long list of the perceived paradoxes of the Russian character. See Hart-Davis, *Hugh Walpole*, 131.

time. You may bring home fruits by which you will wholly be justified. Address yourself indeed to doing that & putting it absolutely through—& I will, for my part, back you up unlimitedly. Only, bring your sheaves with you, & gather in a golden bundle of the same. I detest, myself, the fine old British horror—as it has flourished at least up to now, when in respect to the great matter that's upon us, the fashion has so much changed—of doing anything consistently & seriously. So if you *should* draw out your absence I shall believe in your reasons. Meanwhile I am myself of the most flaming British complexion—the whole thing is to me an unspeakably intimate experience—if it isn't abject to apply such a term when one hasn't had one's precious *person* straight upon against the facts. I have only had my poor old mind & imagination—but no one *can* have them here; & I live partly in dark abysses & partly in high &, I think, noble elations. But how, at my age & in my conditions I could have beautifully done without it! I resist more or less—since you ask me to tell you how I "am"; I resist & go on from day to day because I want to & the horrible interest is too great not to. But that same is adding the years in great shovel-fulls to our poor old lives (those at least of my generation:) so don't be too long away after all if you want ever to see me again. I have in a manner got back to work— after a black interregnum; & find it a refuge & a prop—but the conditions make it difficult, exceedingly, almost insuperably, *I* find, in a sense far other than the mere distracting & depressing. The subject-matter of one's effort has become *itself* utterly treacherous & false—its relation to reality utterly given away & smashed. Reality is a world that was to be capable of *this*—& how represent that horrific capability, *historically* latent, historically ahead of it? How on the other hand *not* represent it either—without putting into play mere fiddlesticks?————————————————I had to break off my letter last night from excess of lateness, & now I see I misdated it. *Tonight* is the 15th,[155] the p.m. of a cold grey Sunday such as we find wintry here, in our innocence of your ferocities of climate; to which in your place I should speedily succumb. That buried beneath the polar blizzard and the howling homesick snowdrift you *don't* utterly give way is, I think, a proof [of] very superior resources & of your being reserved for a big future. We have been having weeks & weeks of most unholy wet, defying description

---

155. HJ was confused about the weekend dates, for 14 February was a Sunday. He apparently began this letter on Saturday the thirteenth and concluded it on Sunday the fourteenth.

at the front, but all with an affect, for myself, of the quick passage of time, through all the nightmare, the anomaly of which I can't account for. Here we are in the 7th month of the terrible business, & though every individual anxiety & oppressions seems, God knows, long enough, the rush of the whole is extraordinary & February is melting away in one's hands. I see a few people, & *need* to see those I can bear at all—the chatter of many is intolerable to me (I could mention names, & you would know them well, if I would.) I shall stay in London late—I can't face in these conditions the solitude & confinement of the country, & I have lent Lamb House to the unfortunate for some months to come,[156] but I hope to be back there, for the summer, from July 1st on. I happen to have seen little Marie B[elloc].-L[owndes]. several times lately—she has in fact lunched with me twice; always in a great omniscient little bustle over the public situation—as to which she produces in fact a good many interesting lights. She has innumerable contacts, & her brother, as the great, much the most able & expert, War-reporter, in the weekly *Land & Water*,[157] puts her in the way of knowing things. And she continues a heroine withal of industry & domesticity—I mean maternity. A heroine of maternity is also the married maid of Ockham who now wears enormous tortoise-shell spectacles,[158] with whom I had tea other day, & whom domesticity, connubiality & fecundity have completely flattened out. The baby & its papa joined us, I had the former in my lap for 30 minutes (I missed my career, which should have been that of a nursemaid,) & the affair was a great success. But the capacity of lively young women to become banalised, or quite extinguished, by marriage is not to be expressed. I shouldn't be able to do it again, often! Poor dear J[ocelyn]. P[ersse]. volunteered for a rainy month, but couldn't stand it—he is after all 42 years old; & is now again, I apprehend, more or less in residence with his best friend. In general, however, everyone is doing something, & the behaviour of the country, on the whole, to my sense, magnificent. That of "Society" simply sublime—in the matter of the men, the mothers & the wives; & that of the "People" scarcely less so. There are certain greyish middle strata that might, I

---

156. HJ had made Lamb House available to various tenants from October 1914 until October 1915.

157. Joseph-Pierre Hilaire Belloc (1870–1953), the brother of Marie Belloc-Lowndes and a naturalized English citizen, was a French-born poet, essayist, historian, journalist, and MP (1906–10).

158. See note 30 on Lady Lovelace.

apprehend, do more—but they will come to it, will *have* to. Goodnight, however, now really, dearest Hugh. I follow your adventure with all the affectionate solicitude of your all-faithful old

H.J.

ALS: Walpole Collection (Recipient)

Harry Ransom Humanities Research Center, University of Texas at Austin

Index

James, Henry (HJ) (*continued*)
76n, 77–78; first meeting, 15; HJ
as brother, 21, 38; HJ as confidant, 20; HJ as dove, 40; HJ as
father, 21, 23; HJ as lover, 38; HJ
as old friend, 65; meeting and
visiting, 15, 19, 21, 25, 25n, 27,
29, 30, 32, 34, 35, 36, 36n. 47, 38,
38n, 40–41, 44, 45, 47, 48, 51,
52n. 64, 53, 56, 56n. 69, 57, 59,
61, 63, 63n. 77, 68, 69, 71, 75,
79, 88, 88n. 16, 129; on his
"megalomania," 18, 49, 71–72,
76–77, 78; youthfulness, 29, 31,
75

and relationship with Dudley
Jocelyn Persse: correspondence,
84; dining with, 85, 93, 94, 96,
107, 108; first meeting, 84, 84n.
5; gifts, 95, 113; meetings and
visits at Lamb House, 85, 93, 101,
103, 107, 152, 152n. 87; meetings
and visits at Ockham, 86, 104,
104n. 49, 106, 108, 108n. 57;
meetings and visits in London,
88, 89, 92, 94, 105, 107, 110, 224;
music halls, 85, 85n. 9, 96; sociability, 87, 92, 93; sponsorship
for Athenaeum Club, 85; theatre-
going, 85, 86, 92, 93, 94, 96,
101–2, 102n. 46, 108

and relationship with Howard O.
Sturgis: collaboration, 134; criticism of *Belchamber,* 8, 119, 131–
32, 131n. 46, 132n. 47, 133, 134,
135, 136, 141; exchange of gifts,
118, 126; HJ as boa constrictor,
120; HJ as dog, 118; HJ as
puppy, 125; living with, 115, 124,
126, 133; meeting and visiting,
120, 123, 124, 125, 128, 129–30,
134, 136, 137–38, 138, 142, 144,
147, 149, 151, 152, 153, 156, 157,
160, 160–61, 163, 170

and relationship with Hugh Walpole: bewilderment with, 179;
gifts to, 197, 198, 215, 215n. 97;
HJ as elephant, 178, 178n. 11,

193, 194, 195, 196; HJ as house
dog, 210; HJ as Master, 186,
186n. 29; HJ as owl, 195; meeting and visiting, 176, 177, 179,
183, 184, 186, 186n. 28, 189, 190,
192, 192–93, 192n. 46, 193n. 47,
194–95, 196, 197, 198, 199, 200,
201, 201n. 64, 202–3, 203, 209,
209n. 79, 213, 214, 218, 219, 220,
221, 223, 234n. 151, 236; photograph of, 189, 191; purpose of letters, 177; sentimental and
melodramatic language, 179–80

and travel and travel commentary:
(France): Amiens, 149; Brittany,
149; Normandy, 149; Paris, 21,
41, 47, 69, 69n. 85, 97, 98, 143,
144, 145–46, 145n. 70, 146n. 71,
147, 149; southern France, 98;
(Germany): Nauheim, 155, 155nn.
94–95; (Italy): 19, 21, 24, 28, 30,
37, 41, 42, 55–56, 63n. 77, 67,
95, 122, 144; Rome, 33, 37, 60,
63, 96–97, 146, 147, 148; Sicily,
145; Turin, 146, 147; Venice, 63;
(Spain): Madrid, 144; (Switzerland): 155; (U.K.): Ashley
Combe, Porlock, 190, 190n. 38;
Cambridge, 185, 185n. 26;
Cliveden, 164; Dover, 150, 151;
Folkestone, 152; Forfarshire, 100,
100n, 101, 159, 159n;
Gloucestershire, 191, 192n. 43;
Hereford, 191, 191n. 41; Hill
Hall, Epping, 70, 70n. 88, 155,
155n. 93, 199, 199n, 209; London:
brief visits in, 24, 30, 31, 54, 62,
67, 90, 96, 99, 104, 107, 128, 133,
135, 136, 137, 149, 150, 151, 156,
157, 184, 190, 192, 194, 196, 209;
extended winter stays in, 28, 34,
38, 39, 42, 46, 47, 69, 91, 128; illness in, 39, 127, 167, 186; impossibility of summer in, 138;
preference for, 161; refuge from
Rye in, 160, 237; therapeutic
value of, 167, 200, 200n. 59;
wartime conditions in, 81; Nor-

244

folk, 191; Ockham, 86, 104, 104n. 49, 106, 108, 108n. 57, 194, 194n. 50, 196, 198; Overstrand, 191, 192n. 43; Queen's Acre, Windsor, 116, 133, 141, 142, 157, 161, 169; Torquay, 40; Wancote, Guildford, 162, 162n. 104; (U.S.): 26, 27, 31, 47, 49, 50, 70, 137n, 138, 139, 140, 141, 156, 156n. 96, 157, 208–9; Biltmore, NC, 140–41, 140n. 61; Boston, 21, 49, 50, 51, 52, 53, 56, 69, 141, 207; California, 141; Cambridge, 105–7, 138, 139, 144, 202, 202n; Chicago, 141; Chocorua, NH, 156n. 96, 157, 202; Cotuit, MA, 139, 139n, 144; Florida, 106, 139–40; Georgia, 106; Lenox, MA, 138, 141, 157; Louisiana, 106; Nahant, MA, 53, 69, 69n. 86, 157; New England, 51, 157; Newport, 21, 53, 56, 69, 69n. 86, 79, 122n. 23; New York, 27, 51, 106, 137, 141, 156, 156n. 97, 206–7; Palm Beach, 139–40; St. Augustine, 140; St. Louis, 141; Salisbury, CT, 157; W. Barnstable, MA, 139

Works: *The Ambassadors,* 4, 8, 87, 87n, 129, 129n. 41, 136, 136n. 55; *The American Scene,* 66, 66n. 83, 145; *The Awkward Age,* 122, 122n. 24; "The Beast in the Jungle," 4; "Covering End," 102n. 46; *The Finer Grain,* 203, 203n. 68; "Gabriele D'Annunzio," 54, 54n. 66; *The Golden Bowl,* 8, 88, 88n. 15; *Guy Domville,* 204n. 71; *The High Bid,* 102, 102n. 46, 149–50, 150n. 82; *Italian Hours,* 63, 63n. 77, 147, 147n. 77; "The Jolly Corner," 4; *New York Edition,* 146; *Notes of a Son and Brother,* 122n. 23, 169, 169n. 117, 221, 221n. 115, 223, 223n. 118, 232, 232n. 144; *The Outcry,* 108, 108n. 55, 209n. 80; *The Portrait of a Lady,* 171n. 122; *The Princess*

Casamassima, 146, 146n. 74; *Roderick Hudson,* 171n. 122; *The Sacred Fount,* 211, 211n. 86; *The Sense of the Past,* 127, 127n. 38; *A Small Boy and Others,* 85, 169, 215, 215n. 99, 217, 217n. 102; *Uniform Tales of Henry James,* 234n. 150; *William Wetmore Story and His Friends,* 129, 129n. 42, 130–31, 131n. 45; *The Wings of the Dove,* 8, 43, 43n

James, Henry, II, "Harry" (nephew), 105, 105n. 52, 153–54n. 89

James, Louisa Cushing (Mrs. Edward Holton), 145, 145n. 68

James, Margaret Mary, "Peggy" (niece), 28n. 31, 105, 105n. 52, 110, 110n. 60, 219, 219n. 109

James, Mary Holton (Mrs. Robertson), 145n. 68

James, Robertson (brother), 52n. 63, 145n. 68

James, William (brother): at Bad Nauheim, 155, 155nn. 94–95; at Cambridge with Henry James, 138–39; at Chocorua with Henry James, 138; death of, 105, 105n. 51, 156n. 96, 201–2, 201n. 63; and Harvard University, 10, 10n. 36, 107, 202, 202n; and health, 28, 28n. 31, 32, 156n. 96, 201, 201n. 63; and Hendrik Andersen, 16n. 4, 34, 34n. 42; at Lamb House with Henry James, 28, 28n. 31, 32, 35, 99, 99n. 43, 101, 153–54n. 89, 156; in London, 156; in Paris, 199; and photograph with Henry James, 33

James, William, II, "Billy" (nephew), 105, 105n. 52, 144, 144n, 162, 162n. 105

Jekylls, 125, 125n. 31

Jenkinson, Francis, 117, 117n. 4, 119

Johnston, John, 2n. 2

Jones, Mary Cadwalader Rawle (Mrs. Frederick), 49n, 100, 100n. 141, 156n. 97, 159, 159n, 171, 204n. 69

Julien atelier, 144, 144n. 67